Constitution

and

Canons

Together with

The Rules of Order

For the governance of the Protestant Episcopal Church in the United States of America, otherwise known as

The Episcopal Church

Adopted and Revised in General Conventions 1785–2022

Table of contents

Constitution of the General Convention

Preamble

Articles

Canons of the General Convention

Title I: Organization and Administration

Canons

Title II: Worship

Canons

Title III: Ministry

Canons

Title IV: Ecclesiastical Discipline

Canons

Title V: General Provisions

Canons

Rules of Order

House of Bishops

House of Deputies

Joint Rules – House of Bishops and House of Deputies

Indices

CONSTITUTION

Preamble

The Protestant Episcopal Church in the United States of America, otherwise known as The Episcopal Church (which name is hereby recognized as also designating the Church), is a constituent member of the Anglican Communion, a Fellowship within the One, Holy, Catholic, and Apostolic Church, of those duly constituted Dioceses, Provinces, and regional Churches in communion with the See of Canterbury, upholding and propagating the historic Faith and Order as set forth in the Book of Common Prayer. This Constitution, adopted in General Convention in Philadelphia in October, 1789, as amended in subsequent General Conventions, sets forth the basic Articles for the government of this Church, and of its overseas missionary jurisdictions.

Name of Church. Anglican Communion.

Article I: Of the General Convention

Sec. 1. There shall be a General Convention of this Church, consisting of the House of Bishops and the House of Deputies, which Houses shall sit and deliberate separately; and in all deliberations freedom of debate shall be allowed. Either House may originate and propose legislation, and all acts of the Convention shall be adopted and be authenticated by both Houses.

General Convention.

Sec. 2. Each Bishop of this Church having jurisdiction, every Bishop Coadjutor, every Bishop Suffragan, every Assistant Bishop, and every Bishop who by reason of advanced age or bodily infirmity, or who, under an election to an office created by the General Convention, or for reasons of mission strategy determined by action of the General Convention or the House of Bishops, has resigned a jurisdiction, shall have a seat and a vote in the House of Bishops. A majority of all Bishops entitled to vote, exclusive of Bishops who have resigned their jurisdiction or positions, shall be necessary to constitute a quorum for the transaction of business.

House of Bishops.

Quorum.

*Election of
Presiding
Bishop.*

Sec. 3. At the General Convention next before the expiration of the term of office of the Presiding Bishop, it shall elect the Presiding Bishop of the Church. The House of Bishops shall choose one of the Bishops of this Church to be the Presiding Bishop of the Church by a vote of a majority of all Bishops, excluding retired Bishops not present, except that whenever two-thirds of the House of Bishops are present a majority vote shall suffice, such choice to be subject to confirmation by the House of Deputies. The term and tenure of office and duties and particulars of the election not inconsistent with the preceding provisions shall be prescribed by the Canons of the General Convention.

Succession.

But if the Presiding Bishop of the Church shall resign the office as such, or if by reason of infirmity shall become disabled, or in case of death, the Bishop who, according to the Rules of the House of Bishops, becomes its Presiding Officer, shall (unless the date of the next General Convention is within three months) immediately call a special meeting of the House of Bishops, to elect a member thereof to be the Presiding Bishop. The certificate of election on the part of the House of Bishops shall be sent by the Presiding Officer to the Standing Committees of the several Dioceses, and if a majority of the Standing Committees of the Dioceses shall concur in the election, the Bishop elected shall become the Presiding Bishop of the Church.

*House of
Deputies.*

Sec. 4. The Church in each Diocese which has been admitted to union with the General Convention, each area Mission established as provided by Article VI, and the Convocation of Episcopal Churches in Europe, shall be entitled to representation in the House of Deputies by not more than four ordained persons, Presbyters or Deacons, canonically resident in the Diocese and not more than four Lay Persons, confirmed adult communicants of this Church, in good standing in the Diocese but not necessarily domiciled in the Diocese; but the General Convention by Canon may reduce the representation to not fewer than two Deputies in each order. Each Diocese, and the Convocation of Episcopal Churches in Europe, shall prescribe the manner in which its Deputies shall be chosen.

To constitute a quorum for the transaction of business, the Clerical order shall be represented by at least one Deputy in each of a majority of the Dioceses entitled to representation, and the Lay order shall likewise be represented by at least one Deputy in each of a majority of the Dioceses entitled to representation.

Quorum.

Sec. 5. The vote on all questions which come before the House of Deputies shall be governed by the following provisions, supplemented by such procedural provisions as the House of Deputies may adopt in its Rules of Order:

Majority vote.

Unless a greater vote on any question is required by this Constitution or by the Canons in cases not specifically dealt with by this Constitution or unless a vote by orders on a question is required, the affirmative vote of a majority of all of the Deputies present and voting shall suffice to carry any question. A vote by orders on any question shall be taken if required for that question by this Constitution or by the Canons or if the Clerical or Lay representation from three or more separate Dioceses shall so request at the time of the call for the vote on that question. In all cases of a vote by orders, the vote of each order, Clerical and Lay, shall be counted separately, each order in each Diocese shall have one vote, and a vote in the affirmative by an order in a Diocese shall require the affirmative vote of a majority of the Deputies present in that order in that Diocese. To carry in the affirmative any question being voted on by orders requires concurrence in the affirmative by both orders and, unless a greater vote is required by this Constitution or by the Canons in cases not specifically dealt with by this Constitution, concurrence in the affirmative by an order requires the affirmative vote in that order by a majority of the Dioceses present in that order.

Vote by Orders.

Sec. 6. In either House any number less than a quorum may adjourn from day to day. Neither House, without the consent of the other, shall adjourn for more than three days, or to any place other than that in which the Convention shall be sitting.

Adjournment.

Sec. 7. The General Convention shall meet not less than once in each three years, at a time and place determined in

Time and place of meeting.

accordance with the Canons. Special meetings may be held as provided for by Canon.

Article II: Of Bishops

Election of Bishops.

Sec. 1. In every Diocese the Bishop or the Bishop Coadjutor shall be chosen agreeably to rules prescribed by the Convention of that Diocese, *provided* that the retirement date of the Bishop Diocesan shall not be more than thirty-six months after the consecration of the Bishop Coadjutor. Bishops of Missionary Dioceses shall be chosen in accordance with the Canons of the General Convention.

Ordination of Bishops.

Sec. 2. No one shall be ordained and consecrated Bishop until the attainment of thirty years of age; nor without the consent of a majority of the Standing Committees of all the Dioceses, and the consent of a majority of the Bishops of this Church exercising jurisdiction. No one shall be ordained and consecrated Bishop by fewer than three Bishops.

Jurisdiction of Bishops.

Sec. 3. A Bishop shall confine the exercise of such office to the Diocese in which elected, unless requested to perform episcopal acts in another Diocese by the Ecclesiastical Authority thereof, or unless authorized by the House of Bishops, or by the Presiding Bishop by its direction, to act temporarily in case of need within any territory not yet organized into Dioceses of this Church.

Bishops Suffragan.

Sec. 4. It shall be lawful for a Diocese, at the request of the Bishop of that Diocese, to elect not more than two Bishops Suffragan, without right of succession, and with seat and vote in the House of Bishops. A Bishop Suffragan shall be consecrated and hold office under such conditions and limitations other than those provided in this Article as may be provided by Canons of the General Convention. A Bishop Suffragan shall be eligible for election as Bishop Diocesan or Bishop Coadjutor of a Diocese, or as a Bishop Suffragan in another Diocese.

May become Ecclesiastical Authority.

Sec. 5. It shall be lawful for a Diocese to prescribe by the Constitution and Canons of such Diocese that upon the death, removal or deposition of the Bishop or if the Bishop resigns, a Bishop Suffragan of that Diocese may become temporarily the Ecclesiastical Authority thereof until such time as a new Bishop shall be chosen and consecrated; or that during the disability or absence of the Bishop, a Bishop Suffragan of that Diocese may be placed in charge of such diocese and become temporarily the Ecclesiastical Authority thereof.

Sec. 6. A Bishop may not resign jurisdiction without the consent of the House of Bishops.

Resignation.

Sec. 7. It shall be lawful for the House of Bishops to elect a Bishop Suffragan who, under the direction of the Presiding Bishop, shall be in charge of the work of those chaplains in the Armed Forces of the United States, Veterans' Administration Medical Centers, and Federal Correctional Institutions who are ordained Ministers of this Church. The Bishop Suffragan so elected shall be consecrated and hold office under such conditions and limitations other than those provided in this Article as may be provided by Canons of the General Convention. The Bishop Suffragan shall be eligible for election as Bishop Diocesan, Bishop Coadjutor or Bishop Suffragan of a Diocese.

Bishop Suffragan for Armed Forces.

Sec. 8. A Bishop Diocesan or Coadjutor who has served as the Bishop Diocesan or as the Bishop Coadjutor of a Diocese for any period of time, may be elected as Bishop Diocesan, Bishop Coadjutor, or Bishop Suffragan of another Diocese only if five or more years have passed since the Bishop first served as Bishop Diocesan or Bishop Coadjutor of the Diocese in which the Bishop is currently or last served as Bishop Diocesan or Bishop Coadjutor. Before acceptance of such election a resignation of jurisdiction in the Diocese in which the Bishop is then serving, conditioned on the required consents of the Bishops and Standing Committees of the Church to such election, shall be submitted to the House of Bishops, and also, if the Bishop be a Bishop Coadjutor, a renunciation of the right of succession. Such resignation, and renunciation of the right of succession in the case of a Bishop Coadjutor, shall require the consent of the House of Bishops.

Election of Bishops to other jurisdictions.

Sec. 9. Upon attaining the age of seventy-two years a Bishop shall resign from all jurisdiction.

Compulsory retirement age.

Article III: Of Bishops Consecrated for Foreign Lands

Bishops consecrated for foreign lands.

Bishops may be consecrated for foreign lands upon due application therefrom, with the approbation of a majority of the Bishops of this Church entitled to vote in the House of Bishops, certified to the Presiding Bishop; under such conditions as may be prescribed by Canons of the General Convention. Bishops so consecrated shall not be eligible to the office of Diocesan or of Bishop Coadjutor of any Diocese in the United States or be entitled to vote in the House of Bishops, nor shall they perform any act of the episcopal office in any Diocese or Missionary Diocese of this Church, unless requested so to do by the Ecclesiastical Authority thereof. If a Bishop so consecrated shall be subsequently duly elected as a Bishop of a Missionary Diocese of this Church, such election shall then confer all the rights and privileges given in the Canons to such Bishops.

Article IV: Of the Standing Committees

Standing Committees.

In every Diocese a Standing Committee shall be elected by the Convention thereof, except that provision for filling vacancies between meetings of the Convention may be prescribed by the Canons of the respective Dioceses. When there is a Bishop in charge of the Diocese, the Standing Committee shall be the Bishop's Council of Advice. If there be no Bishop or Bishop Coadjutor or Bishop Suffragan canonically authorized to act, the Standing Committee shall be the Ecclesiastical Authority of the Diocese for all purposes declared by the General Convention. The rights and duties of the Standing Committee, except as provided in the Constitution and Canons of the General Convention, may be prescribed by the Canons of the respective Dioceses.

Article V: Of Admission of New Dioceses

Sec. 1. A new Diocese may be formed, with the consent of the General Convention and under such conditions as the General Convention shall prescribe by General Canon or Canons, (1) by the division of an existing Diocese; (2) by the junction of two or more Dioceses or of parts of two or more Dioceses; or (3) by the erection into a Diocese of an unorganized area evangelized as provided in Article VI. The proceedings shall originate in a Convocation of the Clergy and Laity of the unorganized area called by the Bishop for that purpose; or, with the approval of the Ecclesiastical Authority, in the Convention of the Diocese to be divided; or (when it is proposed to form a new Diocese by the junction of two or more existing Dioceses or of parts of two or more Dioceses) by mutual agreement of the Conventions of the Dioceses concerned, with the approval of the Ecclesiastical Authority of each Diocese. After consent of the General Convention, when a certified copy of the duly adopted Constitution of the new Diocese, including an unqualified accession to the Constitution and Canons of this Church, shall have been filed with the Secretary of the General Convention and approved by the Executive Council of this Church, such new Diocese shall thereupon be in union with the General Convention.

Admission of new Dioceses.

Sec. 2. In case one Diocese shall be divided into two or more Dioceses, the Bishop of the Diocese divided, at least thirty days before such division, shall select the Diocese in which the Bishop will continue in jurisdiction. The Bishop Coadjutor, if there be one, subsequently and before the effective date of the division shall select the Diocese in which the Bishop Coadjutor shall continue in jurisdiction, and if it not be the Diocese selected by the Bishop shall become the Bishop thereof.

Rights of Bishops when Diocese divides.

Sec. 3. In case a Diocese shall be formed out of parts of two or more Dioceses, each of the Bishops and Bishops Coadjutor of the several Dioceses out of which the new Diocese has been formed shall be entitled, in order of seniority of

Diocese formed from other Dioceses.

consecration, to the choice between the Bishop's Diocese and the new Diocese so formed. In the case the new Diocese shall not be so chosen, it shall have the right to choose its own Bishop.

Constitution and Canons of new Dioceses.

Sec. 4. Whenever a new Diocese is formed and erected out of an existing Diocese, it shall be subject to the Constitution and Canons of the Diocese out of which it was formed, except as local circumstances may prevent, until the same be altered in accordance with such Constitution and Canons by the Convention of the new Diocese.

Whenever a Diocese is formed out of two or more existing Dioceses, it shall be subject to the Constitution and Canons of that one of the said existing Dioceses to which the greater number of Members of the Clergy shall have belonged prior to the erection of such new Diocese, except as local circumstances may prevent, until the same be altered in accordance with such Constitution and Canons by the Convention of the new Diocese.

Number of Presbyters and Parishes.

Sec. 5. No new Diocese shall be formed unless it shall contain at least six Parishes and at least six Presbyters who have been for at least one year canonically resident within the bounds of such new Diocese, regularly settled in a Parish or Congregation and qualified to vote for a Bishop. Nor shall such new Diocese be formed if thereby any existing Diocese shall be so reduced as to contain fewer than twelve Parishes and twelve Presbyters who have been residing therein and settled and qualified as above provided.

Cession of diocesan territory.

General Convention to approve.

Sec. 6. By mutual agreement between the Conventions of two adjoining Dioceses, consented to by the Ecclesiastical Authority of each Diocese, a portion of the territory of one of said Dioceses may be ceded to the other Diocese, such cession to be considered complete upon approval thereof by the General Convention or by a majority of Bishops having jurisdiction in the United States, and of the Standing Committees of the Dioceses, in accordance with the Canons of this Church. Thereupon the part of the territory so ceded shall become a part of the Diocese accepting the same. The provisions of Section 3 of this Article V shall not apply in such case, and the Bishop and Bishop Coadjutor, if any, of the Diocese ceding such territory shall continue in their jurisdiction over the remainder of such Diocese, and the Bishop and Bishop Coadjutor, if any, of the Diocese accepting cession of such territory shall continue in jurisdiction over such Diocese and shall have jurisdiction in that part of the territory of the other Diocese that has been so ceded and accepted.

Rights of Bishops.

Article VI: Of Missionary Dioceses

Sec. 1. The House of Bishops may establish a Mission in any area not included within the boundaries of any Diocese of this Church or of any Church in full communion with this Church, and elect or appoint a Bishop therefor.

Area Missions.

Sec. 2. The General Convention may accept a cession of the territorial jurisdiction of a part of a Diocese when such cession shall have been proposed by the Bishop and the Convention of such Diocese, and consent thereto shall have been given by three-fourths of the Parishes in the ceded territory, and also by the same ratio of the Parishes within the remaining territory.

Cession of jurisdiction.

Any territorial jurisdiction or any part of the same, which may have been ceded by a Diocese under the foregoing provision, may be retroceded to the said Diocese by such joint action of all the several parties as is herein required for its cession, save that in the case of retrocession of territory the consent of Parishes within the territory retroceded shall not be necessary; *provided* that such action of the General Convention, whether of cession or retrocession, shall be by a vote of two-thirds of all the Bishops present and voting and by a vote by orders in the House of Deputies in accordance with Article I, Sec. 5, except that concurrence by the orders shall require the affirmative vote in each order by two-thirds of the Dioceses.

Retrocession of such jurisdiction.

Sec. 3. Missionary Dioceses shall be organized as may be prescribed by Canon of the General Convention.

Missionary Dioceses.

Article VII: Of Provinces

Provinces.

Dioceses may be united into Provinces in such manner, under such conditions, and with such powers, as shall be provided by Canon of the General Convention; *provided, however*, that no Diocese shall be included in a Province without its own consent.

Article VIII: Of Requisites for Ordination

Requisites for ordination.

No person shall be ordered Priest or Deacon to minister in this Church until the person shall have been examined by the Bishop and two Priests and shall have exhibited such testimonials and other requisites as the Canons in that case provided may direct. No person shall be ordained and consecrated Bishop, or ordered Priest or Deacon to minister in this Church, unless at the time, in the presence of the ordaining Bishop or Bishops, the person shall subscribe and make the following declaration:

Declaration.

I do believe the Holy Scriptures of the Old and New Testaments to be the Word of God, and to contain all things necessary to salvation; and I do solemnly engage to conform to the Doctrine, Discipline, and Worship of The Episcopal Church.

Proviso.

Provided, however, that any person consecrated a Bishop to minister in any Diocese of an autonomous Church or Province of a Church in full communion with this Church may, instead of the foregoing declaration, make the promises of Conformity required by the Church in which the Bishop is to minister.

If any Bishop ordains a Priest or Deacon to minister elsewhere than in this Church, or confers ordination as Priest or Deacon upon a Christian minister who has not received Episcopal ordination, the Bishop shall do so only in accordance with such provisions as shall be set forth in the Canons of this Church.

No person ordained by a foreign Bishop, or by a Bishop not in full communion with this Church, shall be permitted to officiate as a Minister of this Church until the person shall have complied with the Canon or Canons in that case provided and also shall have subscribed the aforesaid declaration.

Admission of foreign clergy.

A Bishop may permit an ordained minister in good standing in a church with which this church is in full communion as specified by the Canons who has made the foregoing declaration, or a minister ordained in the Evangelical Lutheran Church in America or its predecessor bodies who has made the promise of conformity required by that Church in place of the foregoing declaration to officiate on a temporary basis as an ordained minister of this church. No minister of such a Church ordained by other than a Bishop, apart from any such ministers designated as part of the Covenant or Instrument by which full communion was established, shall be eligible to officiate under this Article.

Clergy of Churches in full communion.

Article IX: Of Courts

The General Convention may, by Canon, establish one or more Courts for the Trial of Bishops.

Court for trial of Bishops.

Presbyters and Deacons shall be tried by a Court instituted by the General Convention by Canon.

For trial of Presbyters and Deacons.

The General Convention, in like manner, may establish or may provide for the establishment of Courts of Review of the determination of diocesan or other trial Courts.

Courts of Review.

The Court for the review of the determination of the trial Court, on the trial of a Bishop, shall be composed of Bishops only.

The General Convention, in like manner, may establish an ultimate Court of Appeal, solely for the review of the determination of any Court of Review on questions of Doctrine, Faith, or Worship.

Court of Appeal.

Bishop to pronounce sentence.

None but a Bishop shall pronounce sentence of admonition, or suspension, or deposition from the Ministry, on any Bishop, Presbyter, or Deacon; and none but a Bishop shall admonish any Bishop, Presbyter, or Deacon.

Suspension.

A sentence of suspension shall specify on what terms or conditions and at what time the suspension shall cease. A sentence of suspension may be remitted in such manner as may be provided by Canon.

Article X: Of The Book of Common Prayer

The Book of Common Prayer.

Alterations or additions.

The Book of Common Prayer, as now established or hereafter amended by the authority of this Church, shall be in use in all the Dioceses of this Church. No alteration thereof or addition thereto shall be made unless the same shall be first proposed in one regular meeting of the General Convention and by a resolve thereof be sent within six months to the Secretary of the Convention of every Diocese, to be made known to the Diocesan Convention at its next meeting, and be adopted by the General Convention at its next succeeding regular meeting by a majority of all Bishops, excluding retired Bishops not present, of the whole number of Bishops entitled to vote in the House of Bishops, and by a vote by orders in the House of Deputies in accordance with Article I, Sec. 5, except that concurrence by the orders shall require the affirmative vote in each order by a majority of the Dioceses entitled to representation in the House of Deputies.

Exceptions.

But notwithstanding anything herein above contained, the General Convention may at any one meeting, by a majority of the whole number of the Bishops entitled to vote in the House of Bishops, and by a majority of the Clerical and Lay Deputies of all the Dioceses entitled to representation in the House of Deputies, voting by orders as previously set forth in this Article:

Lectionary.

a. Amend the Table of Lessons and all Tables and Rubrics relating to the Psalms.

Trial use.

b. Authorize for trial use throughout this Church, as an

alternative at any time or times to the established Book of Common Prayer or to any section or Office thereof, a proposed revision of the whole Book or of any portion thereof, duly undertaken by the General Convention.

c. Authorize for use throughout this Church, as provided by Canon, alternative and additional liturgies to supplement those provided in the Book of Common Prayer. *additional Liturgies.*

And *provided* that nothing in this Article shall be construed as restricting the authority of the Bishops of this Church to take such order as may be permitted by the Rubrics of the Book of Common Prayer or by the Canons of the General Convention for the use of special forms of worship. *Special forms of worship.*

Article XI: Of Dioceses and Missionary Dioceses

Whenever the term "Diocese" is used without qualification in this Constitution, it shall be understood to refer both to Dioceses and to Missionary Dioceses and also, wherever applicable, to all other jurisdictions entitled to representation in the House of Deputies of the General Convention. *Interpretation of "Diocese."*

Article XII: Of Amendments to the Constitution

No alteration or amendment of this Constitution shall be made unless the same shall be first proposed at one regular meeting of the General Convention and be sent to the Secretary of the Convention of every Diocese, to be made known to the Diocesan Convention at its next meeting, and be adopted by the General Convention at its next succeeding regular meeting by a majority of all Bishops, excluding retired Bishops not present, of the whole number of Bishops entitled to vote in the House of Bishops, and by an affirmative vote by orders in the House of Deputies in accordance with Article I, Sec. 5, except that concurrence by the orders shall require the affirmative vote in each order by *Alterations or amendments to Constitution.*

a majority of the Dioceses entitled to representation in the House of Deputies.

Notwithstanding the provisions of the foregoing paragraph, the adoption of any alteration or amendment of this Constitution which inserts or repeals an Article, or a Section or Clause of an Article, shall effect the necessary change in numbers or letters of Articles or Sections or Clauses of an Article, that follow, and in references made in this Constitution to any other part, without the necessity of specific provision therefore in the alteration or amendment.

Effective date. Each duly adopted alteration or amendment to this Constitution, unless otherwise expressly stated therein, shall take effect on the first day of January following the adjournment of the General Convention at which it is finally adopted.

CANONS OF THE GENERAL CONVENTION

Title I: Organization and Administration

Canon 1: Of the General Convention

Sec. 1

a. At the time and place appointed for the meeting of the General Convention, the President of the House of Deputies, or, if absent, the Vice-President of the House, or, if there be neither, a presiding officer *pro tempore* appointed by the members of the House of Deputies on the Joint Committee of Arrangements for the General Convention, shall call to order the members present. The Secretary of the House of Deputies, or, if absent, a Secretary *pro tempore* of the House of Deputies appointed by the presiding officer, shall record the names of those whose testimonials, in due form, shall have been presented, which record shall be *prima facie* evidence that the persons whose names are therein recorded are entitled to seats. In the event that testimonials are presented by or on behalf of persons from jurisdictions which have not previously been represented in a General Convention, then the Secretary of the House of Deputies, or one appointed instead as provided herein, shall proceed as provided in Clause c. If there be a quorum present, the Secretary of the House of Deputies shall so certify, and the House shall proceed to organize by the election, by ballot, of a Secretary of the House of Deputies, and a majority of the votes cast shall be necessary to such election. Upon such election, the presiding officer shall declare the House organized. If there be a vacancy in the office of President or Vice-President, the vacancy or vacancies shall then be filled by election, by ballot, the term of any officer so elected to continue until the adjournment of the General

Organizing the House of Deputies.

Convention. As soon as such vacancies are filled, the President shall appoint a committee to wait upon the House of Bishops and inform it of the organization of the House of Deputies, and of its readiness to proceed to business.

Election of President and Vice-President.

b. There shall be a President and a Vice-President of the House of Deputies, who shall perform the duties normally appropriate to their respective offices or specified in these Canons. They shall be elected not later than the seventh day of each regular meeting of the General Convention in the manner herein set forth. The House of Deputies shall elect from its membership, by a majority of separate ballots, a President and a Vice-President, who shall be of different orders. Such officers shall take office at the adjournment of the regular meeting at which they are elected, and shall continue in office until the adjournment of the following regular meeting of the General Convention. They shall be and remain *ex officio* members of the House during their term of office. No person elected President or Vice-President shall be eligible for more than three consecutive full terms in each respective office. In case of resignation, death, absence, or inability, of the President, the Vice-President shall perform the duties of the office until the adjournment of the next meeting of the General Convention. In case of resignation, death, absence, or inability of the Vice-President, the President shall appoint a Deputy of the opposite order, upon the advice and consent of the lay persons, presbyters and deacons of the Executive Council, who shall serve until the adjournment of the next meeting of the General

Appointment of Advisory Council and Chancellor.

Convention. The President shall be authorized to appoint an Advisory Council for consultation and advice in the performance of the duties of office. The President may also appoint a Chancellor to the President, a confirmed adult communicant of the Church in good standing who is learned in both ecclesiastical and secular law, to serve so long as the President may desire, as counselor in matters relating to the discharge of the responsibilities of that office.

c. In order to aid the Secretary of the House of Deputies in preparing the record specified in Clause .a, it shall be the duty of the Secretary of the Convention of every Diocese to forward to the Secretary of the House of Deputies, as soon as may be practicable, a copy of the latest Journal of the Diocesan Convention, together with a certified copy of the testimonials of members aforesaid, and a duplicate copy of such testimonials. Where testimonials are received for persons from jurisdictions which have not previously been represented in General Convention, the Secretary of the House of Deputies shall ascertain that the applicable provisions of Article V, Section 1, of the Constitution have been complied with prior to such persons being permitted to take their seats in the House.

Diocesan Journals to be forwarded.

Testimonials required.

d. The Secretary shall keep full minutes of the proceedings of the House; record them, with all reports, in a book provided for that purpose; preserve the Journals and Records of the House; deliver them to the Registrar, as hereinafter provided; and perform such other duties as may be directed by the House. The Secretary may, with the approval of the House, appoint Assistant Secretaries, and the Secretary and Assistant Secretaries shall continue in office until the organization of the next General Convention, and until their successors be chosen.

Secretary to keep minutes and records.

e. It shall be the duty of the Secretary of the House of Deputies, whenever any alteration of the Book of Common Prayer or of the Constitution is proposed, or any other subject submitted to the consideration of the several Diocesan Conventions, to give notice thereof to the Ecclesiastical Authority of the Church in every Diocese, as well as to the Secretary of the Convention of every Diocese, and written evidence that the foregoing requirement has been complied with shall be presented by the Secretary to the General Convention at its next session. All such notices shall be sent by electronic means, with the Secretary's certificates to be returned. The Secretary shall notify all diocesan Secretaries that it is their duty to make known such proposed alterations of the Book of Common Prayer, and of the Constitution, and

Amendments to Constitution and Prayer Book.

such other subjects, to the Conventions of their respective Dioceses at their next meeting, and to certify to the Secretary of the House of Deputies that such action has been taken.

Secretary and Treasurer to have seat and voice.

f. The Secretary of the House of Deputies and the Treasurer of the General Convention shall be entitled to seats upon the floor of the House, and, with the consent of the President, they may speak on the subjects of their respective offices.

Rules of the House of Deputies.

g. At the meetings of the House of Deputies the Rules and Orders of the previous meeting shall be in force until they are amended or repealed by the House.

h. In case of the resignation, death, or total disability of the President and Vice-President during the recess of the General Convention, the Secretary of the House of Deputies shall perform such *ad interim* duties as may appertain to the office of President until the next meeting of the General Convention or until such disability is removed.

i. If, during recess, a vacancy shall occur in the office of Secretary of the House of Deputies, the duties thereof shall devolve upon the First Assistant Secretary, or, if there be none such, upon a Secretary *pro tempore* appointed by the President of the House, or if the office of President be also vacant, then by the Vice-President, and if both offices be vacant, then by the members from the House of Deputies of the Joint Committee on Planning and Arrangements for the next General Convention, appointed by the preceding General Convention.

Secretary to be Secretary of Convention.

j. At every regular meeting of the General Convention, the Secretary elected by the House of Deputies shall, by concurrent action of the two Houses of the General Convention, also be made the Secretary of the General Convention, who shall have responsibility for assembling and printing of the Journal of the General Convention, and for other matters specifically referred to the Secretary and shall serve until a successor is elected.

Sec. 2

a. The General Convention by Canon may establish Standing *Standing*
    Commissions to study and draft policy proposals on *Commissions.*
    major subjects considered to be of continuing concern to
    the mission of the Church. The Canon shall specify the
    duties of each Standing Commission. Standing
    Commissions shall be composed of five Bishops, five
    Priests and/or Deacons of this Church and ten Lay
    Persons, who shall be confirmed adult communicants of
    this Church in good standing. The Priests, Deacons, and
    Lay Persons are not required to be Deputies to General
    Convention.

b. The terms of all members of Standing Commissions shall *Terms.*
    be equal to the interval between the regular meeting of
    the General Convention preceding their appointment and
    the adjournment of the second succeeding regular
    meeting of the General Convention, and such terms shall
    be rotated so that, as near as may be, the term of one-
    half of the members shall expire at the conclusion of each
    regular meeting of the General Convention. The term of a
    member shall become vacant in the event of two absences
    from meetings of the Commission occurring in the
    interval between successive regular meetings of the
    General Convention unless excused by the Commission
    for good cause.

c. The Presiding Bishop shall appoint the Episcopal *Appointment of*
    members and the President of the House of Deputies *members.*
    shall appoint the Lay and other Clerical members of each
    Commission as soon as practicable after the adjournment
    of the General Convention, but not later than 90 days
    after adjournment. Episcopal members appointed after
    the adjournment of any General Convention at which a
    Presiding Bishop is elected shall be appointed by the
    Presiding Bishop-elect. Vacancies shall be filled in
    similar manner; *provided however*, that vacancies
    occurring within one year after the next regular General
    Convention shall not be filled unless requested by the
    Commission.

Liaisons and consultants.	**d.** The Presiding Bishop and the President of the House of Deputies shall jointly appoint members of the Executive Council as liaisons to facilitate communication between the Executive Council and each Standing Commission and the coordination of the work of each Standing Commission and the committees of Executive Council. Notice of such appointments shall be given to the Secretary of General Convention. These liaisons shall not be members of the Commission but shall have seat and voice. The reasonable expenses of these liaisons shall be provided for by the Executive Council. Each Commission shall have staff support from the Domestic and Foreign Missionary Society designated by the Presiding Bishop. Each Commission may constitute committees from among members or non-members of the Commission, and, subject to the Commission's budget, engage the services of consultants and coordinators necessary to complete its work.
Ex officiis members.	**e.** The Presiding Bishop and the President of the House of Deputies shall be members *ex officiis* of every Commission, or may appoint personal representatives to attend any meeting in their stead, but without vote.
Notification.	**f.** The Executive Officer of the General Convention shall, not later than 120 days following the meeting of the General Convention, notify the members of the General Convention of the Commission appointments and their duty to present reports to the next Convention and shall schedule an organizational meeting for each Commission. One year prior to the opening day of the Convention, the Executive Officer of the General Convention shall remind the Chairs and Secretaries of all Commissions of this duty.
Officers.	**g.** Every Commission shall elect a chair, vice chair, and secretary.
Referrals.	**h.** The General Convention may refer a relevant matter to a Commission for its consideration; but may not direct the Commission to reach any particular conclusion.
Public notice.	**i.** A Commission shall give timely and appropriate notice to the Church of the time, place, and agendas of meetings;

and instructions on how members of the Church may address their views to the Commission.

j. Every Commission shall prepare a report, which, together with any minority report, shall be sent, not later than 150 days prior to the opening day of each Convention, to the Executive Officer of the General Convention, who shall distribute the same to all members of the Convention.

Reports due.

k. The Report of every Commission presented at the General Convention shall:

Content of report.

1. Set forth the names of its original members, any changes in membership, the names of all those who concur in, and all those who dissent from, its recommendations.

2. Summarize the work of the Commission, including the various matters studied, the recommendations for action by the General Convention, and drafts of Resolutions proposed for adoption to implement the recommendations of the Commission.

3. Include a detailed report of all receipts and expenditures, including moneys received from any source whatsoever, and if it recommends that it be continued, the estimated requirements for the ensuing interval until the next regular meeting of the General Convention.

l. Every Commission, as a condition precedent to the presentation and reception of any report to General Convention in which such Commission proposes the adoption of any Resolution, shall, by vote, authorize a member or members of General Convention, who, if possible, shall be a member of the Commission, with such limitations as the Commission may impose, to accept or reject, on behalf of the Commission, any amendments proposed by General Convention to any such Resolution; provided, however, that no such amendment may change the substance of the proposal, but shall be primarily for the purpose of correcting errors. The name of the member or members of General Convention upon whom such authority has been

Spokespersons.

conferred, and the limitations of authority, shall be communicated in writing to the Presiding Officers of General Convention not later than the presentation of such report to the General Convention.

Budget requirement.

m. Every Commission whose Report requests expenditure out of The Episcopal Church budget (except for the printing of the Report) shall include that request in its report to the General Convention and in accordance with Canon I.4.6.

n. There shall be the following Standing Commissions:

Structure, Governance, Constitution and Canons.

1. A Standing Commission on Structure, Governance, Constitution and Canons. It shall be the duty of the Commission to:

Amendments to be in proper form.

    i. Review such proposed amendments to the Constitution and Canons as may be submitted to the Commission, placing each such proposed amendment in proper Constitutional or Canonical form, including all amendments necessary to effect the proposed change. For amendments not in proper form, the Standing Commission on Constitution and Canons may direct the submitting Commission to the canonical and Rules of Order requirements for amendments to the Constitution and Canons so the submitting Commission may revise its amendment to proper form. The Commission shall express its views with respect to the substance of any such proposal only to the proponent thereof; *provided, however*, that no member of the Commission shall, by reason of membership, be deemed to be disabled from expressing, before a Legislative Committee or on the floor of the General Convention, personal views with respect to the substance of any such proposed amendment.

Continuing comprehensive review.

    ii. Conduct a continuing comprehensive review of the Constitution and Canons with respect to their internal consistency and clarity, and on the basis of such a review, propose to the General

Convention such technical amendments to the Constitution and Canons as in the opinion of the Commission are necessary or desirable in order to achieve such consistency and clarity without altering the substance of any Constitutional and Canonical provisions; *provided, however,* that the Commission shall propose, for the consideration of the appropriate Legislative Committees of the General Convention, such amendments to the Constitution and Canons as in the opinion of the Commission are technically desirable but involve a substantive alteration of a Constitutional or Canonical provision.

iii. On the basis of such review, suggest to the Domestic and Foreign Missionary Society and to the Executive Council of the General Convention such amendments to their respective By-laws as in the opinion of the Commission are necessary or desirable in order to conform the same to the Constitution and Canons.

DFMS By-laws.

iv. Conduct a continuing and comprehensive review and update of the authorized "Annotated Constitution and Canons for the Government of the Protestant Episcopal Church in the United States of America otherwise known as The Episcopal Church" to reflect actions of General Convention which amend the Constitution and Canons and, in the discretion of the Commission, develop other materials which are appropriate to the purpose of the "Annotated Constitution and Canons," and facilitate the publication of this document and related materials. The Commission may provide or support forums to promote commentary, discussion, and understanding of the Constitution and Canons.

Update Annotated version.

v. Discharge such other duties as shall from time to time be assigned by the General Convention.

vi. Study and make recommendations concerning the structure of the General Convention and of

Recommendations on structure.

The Episcopal Church. It shall, from time to time, review the operation of the several Committees, Commissions, and Boards to determine the necessity for their continuance and the effectiveness of their functions and to bring about a coordination of their efforts. Whenever a proposal is made for the creation of a new Committee, Commission, Board or Agency, it shall, wherever feasible, be referred to this Standing Commission for its consideration and advice.

Continuing review.

vii. Conduct a continuing and comprehensive review and update of the Title IV training materials, including drafting such changes as are necessitated by changes to these Constitution and Canons, or as may be deemed appropriate to maintain such training materials in a current and effective status.

Liturgy and Music.

2. A Standing Commission on Liturgy and Music. The Custodian of the Book of Common Prayer shall be a member *ex officio* with voice, but without vote. It shall be the duty of the Commission to:

   i. Discharge such duties as shall be assigned to it by the General Convention as to policies and strategies concerning the common worship of this Church.

   ii. Collect, collate, and catalogue material bearing upon possible future revisions of the Book of Common Prayer.

   iii. Cause to be prepared and to present to the General Convention recommendations concerning the Lectionary, Psalter, and offices for special occasions as authorized or directed by the General Convention or House of Bishops.

Authorized translations.

   iv. Recommend to the General Convention authorized translations of the Holy Scripture from which the Lessons prescribed in the Book of Common Prayer are to be read.

v. Receive and evaluate requests for consideration of individuals or groups to be included in the Calendar of the Church year and make recommendations thereon to the General Convention for acceptance or rejection.

Church Calendar.

vi. Collect, collate, and catalogue material bearing upon possible future revisions of The Hymnal 1982 and other musical publications regularly in use in this Church, and encourage the composition of new musical materials.

Hymnal.

vii. Cause to be prepared and present to the General Convention recommendations concerning the musical settings of liturgical texts and rubrics, and norms as to liturgical music and the manner of its rendition.

Church music.

viii. At the direction of the General Convention, to serve the Church in matters pertaining to policies and strategies concerning Church music.

ix. Collaborate with the Secretary of General Convention to make final edits to the text of resolutions adopted by General Convention that establish new or revised liturgical materials, and to arrange for their publication. For the sole purpose of this collaboration, members of the Standing Commission on Liturgy and Music are exempt from the terms of office set forth in I.1.2.b and shall remain in office until their successors are appointed and take office.

Extension of term.

x. Oversee and maintain the official liturgical website of The Episcopal Church through a subcommittee whose members shall include the Chair of the Standing Commission on Liturgy and Music or an authorized deputy who is a member of the Standing Commission on Liturgy and Music; the Custodian of the Standard Book of Common Prayer; at least one other Standing Commission on Liturgy and Music member; the Secretary of General Convention or an authorized deputy of the Secretary; a representative from

Liturgical website.

the publisher affiliated with the Church Pension Fund; at least two members with skill in website design and coding, to be appointed by the Chair of the Standing Commission on Liturgy and Music.

World Mission.

3. A Standing Commission on World Mission. It shall be the duty of the Commission to:

    i. Identify the global mission work carried out by the Domestic and Foreign Missionary Society, dioceses, congregations and mission organizations throughout the church.

    ii. Consult with the above bodies to envision future directions for the church's global engagement.

    iii. Develop policy proposals for world mission for consideration by General Convention.

    iv. Discharge such other duties as shall from time to time be assigned by the General Convention.

Formation and Ministry Development.

4. A Standing Commission on Formation and Ministry Development. The Commission shall coordinate and encourage the development of all orders of ministry, encouraging and engaging all the baptized in the work of building up the church and developing best practices to ensure all churches benefit from the diversity of leadership gifts God has given us. It shall be the duty of the Commission to:

    i. Recommend policies and strategies to the General Convention for the affirmation, development, and exercise of ministry by all baptized persons (lay persons, bishops, priests and deacons).

Ministry of the baptized.

    ii. Support Diocesan Commissions on Ministry in their support of the ministry of all the baptized, as set forth in Canon III.1 and Canon III.2.

Daily life ministries.

    iii. Encourage the recognition of daily life ministries by Diocesan Commissions on Ministry, congregations, and dioceses, so that those ministries are celebrated as expressions of the ministry of all the baptized, worthy of equal respect with ordained vocations.

iv. In collaboration with the churchwide office overseeing formation, develop and recommend to the General Convention comprehensive and coordinated policies for people across all ages and stages of life for lifelong formation as seekers and followers of Jesus.

v. Recommend strategies to General Convention for the development and support of networks of individuals, diocesan committees and commissions, agencies and institutions engaged in recruitment, gifts of discernment, education and training for ministry, leadership development, hiring, and appointments.

Development of networks.

vi. Study the needs and trends of discernment and vocational opportunities for ordained leaders and lay professionals within the Church and the appropriate formation required to live into those opportunities.

Discernment.

vii. Collaborate with those developing lay pathways grid and the Association of Episcopal Deacons to raise awareness of the competencies promulgated by those groups as guidelines for formation for those orders of ministry.

viii. Recommend policies and strategies to the General Convention to ensure the fair hiring and compensation of lay and ordained employees in all ministry settings, with special attention to parity across those lines which have historically divided us, including but not limited to race, color, ethnic origin, national origin, sex, marital status, sexual orientation, gender identity and expression, order of ministry, disabilities, or age, except as otherwise provided by these Canons.

Fair hiring and compensation.

5. A Standing Commission on Ecumenical and Interreligious Relations. It shall be the duty of the Commission to:

Ecumenical and Interreligious Relations.

i. Coordinate and encourage the work of church unity among Christian partners and collaboration and peacebuilding with interfaith partners, conciliar, and interfaith organizations.

Development of partnerships.

ii. Recommend policies and strategies to the General Convention for the affirmation and development of ecumenical and interreligious partnerships.

Racial justice.

iii. Collaborate with ecumenical and interreligious partners, conciliar and interfaith bodies to develop tools which address issues of power, racial justice, colonialism, imperialism, and the historical racial bias in ecumenical endeavors.

iv. Support Diocesan and local engagement in interreligious and ecumenical ministry.

v. Encourage theological work that recognizes the current and future ecumenical and religious landscape, contextual theologies and partnerships with conciliar bodies and others to address the Gospel issues of unity, justice, and peace, and to respond as requested to Conciliar, ecumenical or other interreligious documents.

Guidelines for inter-religious relations.

vi. In collaboration with the churchwide Office on Ecumenical and Inter-religious relations, develop and recommend to the General Convention comprehensive and coordinated policies and guidelines for inter-religious relations and ecumenical dialogues and conversations.

Training and leadership development.

vii. Recommend strategies and policies to General Convention for training and leadership development, with networks, diocesan ecumenical officers, faith-based bodies within and beyond the Episcopal Church

viii. Study the needs and trends of the ecumenical and interreligious landscape, to support and encourage the development of resources for ecumenical and interreligious formation.

Sec. 3

a. The right of calling special meetings of the General
   Convention shall be vested in the Bishops. The Presiding
   Bishop shall issue the summons for such meetings,
   designating the time and place thereof, with the consent,
   or on the requisition, of a majority of the Bishops,
   expressed to the Presiding Bishop in writing.

Special meetings.

b. The Deputies elected to the preceding General
   Convention shall be the Deputies at such special
   meetings of the General Convention, except in those
   cases in which other Deputies shall have been chosen in
   the meantime by any of the Diocesan Conventions, and
   then such other Deputies shall represent in the special
   meeting of the General Convention the Church of the
   Diocese in which they have been chosen.

Deputies at special meetings.

c. Any vacancy in the representation of any Diocese caused
   by the death, absence, or inability of any Deputy, shall be
   supplied either temporarily or permanently in such
   manner as shall be prescribed by the Diocese, or, in the
   absence of any such provision, by appointment by the
   Ecclesiastical Authority of the Diocese. During such
   periods as shall be stated in the certificate issued to such
   person by the appointing power, the Provisional Deputy
   so appointed shall possess and shall be entitled to
   exercise the power and authority of the Deputy in place
   of whom he or she shall have been designated.

Vacancy.

Sec. 4

a. All jurisdictions of this Church entitled by the
   Constitution or Canons to choose Deputies to the General
   Convention shall be required to do so not later than
   twelve months preceding the opening date of the General
   Convention for which they are chosen. Deputies of
   jurisdictions failing so to elect may not be seated unless
   permitted by ruling of the Presiding Officer.

Election of Deputies.

b. It shall be the duty of each seated Deputy to
   communicate to the electing jurisdiction the actions
   taken and the positions established by the General
   Convention.

c. It shall be the responsibility of each Diocese to provide a forum in which the Deputies to the General Convention from that jurisdiction have opportunity to report.

Registrar. **Sec. 5**

a. The Secretary of the General Convention shall, *ex officio*, be the Registrar of the General Convention, whose duty it shall be to receive all Journals, files, papers, reports, and other documents or articles that are, or shall become, the property of either House of the General Convention, and to transmit the same to the Archives of the Church as prescribed by the Archivist.

To keep and transmit records.
b. It shall also be the duty of the said Registrar to maintain suitable records of the ordinations and consecrations of all the Bishops of this Church, designating accurately the time and place of the same, with the names of the consecrating Bishops, and of others present and assisting; to have the same authenticated in the fullest manner practicable; and to take care for the similar record and authentication of all future ordinations, consecrations and installations of Bishops in this Church; and to transmit the same to the Archives of the Church when and as prescribed by the Archivist. Due notice of the time and place of such ordinations and consecrations shall be given by the Presiding Bishop to the Registrar; and thereupon it shall be the duty of the Registrar to attend such ordinations and consecrations, either in person or by appointing a clergy or lay deputy Registrar.

Letters of Consecration.
c. The Registrar shall prepare, in such form as the House of Bishops shall prescribe, the Letters of Ordination and Consecration in duplicate, shall have the same immediately signed and sealed by the ordaining and consecrating Bishops, and by such other Bishops assisting as may be practicable, shall deliver to the newly consecrated Bishop one of the said Letters, shall carefully file and retain the other, and shall make a minute thereof in the official records.

Registrar as Historiographer.
d. The Registrar shall also be Historiographer, unless in any case the House of Bishops shall make a separate

nomination; and in this event the House of Deputies shall confirm the nomination.

e. The necessary expenses incurred under this Section shall be paid by the Treasurer of the General Convention.

f. It shall be the duty of the secretaries of both Houses to deliver to the Registrar the minutes of both Houses, together with the Journals, files, papers, reports, electronic records, and all other records of either House in a manner prescribed by the Archivist. The minutes of both Houses shall remain filed until after the adjournment of the first General Convention following that at which such minutes shall have been taken; *provided, however*, that any part of such minutes, for any reason unpublished in the Journal, shall remain filed in the Archives. The Secretary of the House of Deputies shall also deliver to the Registrar, as prescribed by the Archivist, when not otherwise expressly directed, all the Journals, files, papers, reports, and other published, unpublished or electronic documents specified in Canon I.6. The Secretaries shall require the Registrar to give them receipts for the Journals and other records. The Registrar shall transmit the records of the secretaries of both Houses to the Archivist of the Church.

Journals and papers sent to Registrar and Archives.

g. In the case of a vacancy in the office of Registrar, the Presiding Bishop shall appoint a Registrar, who shall hold office until the next General Convention.

Vacancy.

Sec. 6

Recorder.

a. The House of Deputies, upon nomination of the House of Bishops, shall elect a Recorder (who may be a natural person or an incorporated organization of this Church), whose duty is/shall be to continue the List of Ordinations and to keep a list of the Clergy in regular standing.

b. It shall be the duty of the Bishop, or, if there be no Bishop, of the President of the Standing Committee of every jurisdiction to forward to the Recorder on or before the first day of March in each and every year a report certifying the following information as of the thirty-first day of December in the preceding year: (1) the names of the Clergy canonically resident therein with their several

Information to be sent to Recorder.

charges; (2) the names of the Clergy licensed by the Bishop to officiate, but not yet transferred; (3) the names of all persons connected with the jurisdiction who have been ordered Deacons or Priests during the preceding twelve months, with the date and place of ordination and the name of the Bishop ordaining; (4) the names of the Clergy of the jurisdiction who have died during the preceding twelve months, with the date and place of death; (5) the names of the Clergy who have been received during the preceding twelve months, with the date of their reception and the name of the jurisdiction from which received, and, in the case of Clergy not received from a jurisdiction of this Church, the date and place of ordination and the name of the Bishop ordaining; (6) the names of the Clergy who have been transferred during the preceding twelve months, with the dates of the Letters Dimissory and of their acceptance, and the name of the jurisdiction to which transferred; (7) the names of the Clergy who have been suspended during the preceding twelve months, with the date and ground of suspension; (8) the names of the Clergy who have been removed or deposed during the preceding twelve months, with the date, place, and ground of removal or deposition; (9) the names of the Clergy who have been restored during the preceding twelve months, with the date; (10) the names of Deaconesses canonically resident therein.

Recorder to furnish information.

c. It shall be the duty of the Recorder to furnish, upon proper authority and at the expense of the applicant, such information as may be in the possession of the Recorder, based upon the reports required under Clause .b hereof.

Report to the General Convention.

d. The Recorder shall prepare and present to each session of the General Convention a list of all Clergy ordained, received, suspended, removed, deposed, or restored, and of all Bishops consecrated, and of all Bishops and other Clergy who have died; such list to cover the period from the last preceding similar report of the Recorder through the thirty-first day of December immediately preceding each session of the General Convention.

e. The necessary expenses incurred under this Section by the Recorder shall be paid by the Treasurer of the General Convention.

Expenses.

f. In case of a vacancy in the office of Recorder, the Presiding Bishop shall appoint a Recorder, who shall hold office until the next General Convention.

Vacancy.

Sec. 7

Treasurer of General Convention.

a. At every regular meeting of the General Convention a Treasurer (who may also be Treasurer of the Domestic & Foreign Missionary Society and the Executive Council) shall be elected by concurrent action of the two Houses, and shall remain in office until a successor shall be elected. It shall be the Treasurer's duty to receive and disburse all moneys collected under the authority of the Convention, and of which the collection and disbursement shall not otherwise be prescribed; and, with the advice and approval of the Presiding Bishop and the Treasurer of the Executive Council, to invest, from time to time, such surplus funds as may be on hand. The Treasurer's account shall be rendered to the Convention at each regular meeting, and shall be audited at the direction of a committee acting under its authority.

b. In case of a vacancy, by death, resignation, or otherwise, in the office of Treasurer of the General Convention, the Presiding Bishop and the President of the House of Deputies shall appoint a Treasurer, who shall hold office until a successor is elected. In case of temporary inability of the Treasurer to act, from illness or other cause, the same officials shall appoint an Acting Treasurer who shall perform all duties of the Treasurer until the Treasurer is able to resume them.

Vacancy.

Sec. 8. The General Convention shall adopt, at each regular meeting, a budget for The Episcopal Church, including for the contingent expenses of the General Convention, the stipend of the Presiding Bishop together with the necessary expenses of that office, the necessary expenses of the President of the House of Deputies including the staff and Advisory Council required to assist in the performance of the duties and matters related to the President's office, and the

General Convention Expense Budget.

applicable Church Pension Fund assessments. To defray the expense of this budget, an assessment shall be levied upon the Dioceses of the Church in accordance with a formula which the General Convention shall adopt as part of The Episcopal Church budget. It shall be the duty of each Diocesan Convention to pay its assessment to the Treasurer of the General Convention according to the schedule established by the Executive Council.

Treasurer may borrow.

Sec. 9. The Treasurer of the General Convention shall have authority to borrow, in behalf and in the name of the Executive Council, such a sum as may be judged by the Treasurer to be necessary to help pay the expenses of The Episcopal Church budget adopted under Canon I.1.8, with the approval of the Executive Council.

Shall give bond.

Sec. 10. The Treasurer shall give a bond conditioned on the faithful performance of assigned duties. The amount thereof and the terms on which the same shall be given shall be subject to the approval of the Presiding Bishop, the expense of such bond to be paid by the General Convention.

May appoint Assistant Treasurer.

Sec. 11. The Treasurer may appoint, subject to the approval of the Presiding Bishop, an Assistant Treasurer, who shall hold office during the pleasure of the Treasurer and shall perform such duties as shall be assigned by the Treasurer. The Assistant Treasurer shall give bond conditioned on the faithful performance of assigned duties. The amount thereof and the terms on which the same shall be given shall be subject to the approval of the Presiding Bishop, the expense of such bond to be paid by the General Convention.

General Convention Executive Office.

Sec. 12

a. There shall be an Executive Office of the General Convention, to be headed by a General Convention Executive Officer to be appointed jointly by the Presiding Bishop and the President of the House of Deputies with the advice and consent of the Executive Council. The Executive Officer shall report to and serve at the pleasure of the Executive Council.

Functions.

b. The Executive Office of the General Convention shall include the functions of the Secretary of the General Convention and the Treasurer of the General Convention and those of the Manager of the General Convention and, if the several positions are filled by different persons, such officers shall serve under the general supervision of the General Convention Executive Officer, who shall also coordinate the work of the Committees, Commissions, Boards and Agencies funded by The Episcopal Church budget.

Sec. 13   *Site selection.*

a. At each meeting of the General Convention the Joint Standing Committee on Planning and Arrangements shall submit to the General Convention its recommendations for sites for the meeting of the General Convention to be held as the second succeeding General Convention following the General Convention at which the report is made. In making such recommendations, the Committee shall certify to the Convention the willingness of the Dioceses within which recommended sites are located to have the General Convention meet within their jurisdictions.

b. From the sites recommended by the Joint Committee, the General Convention shall approve no fewer than three nor more than five sites as possible for such meeting of the General Convention.   *Approval of sites.*

c. From the sites approved by the General Convention, the Joint Committee, with the advice and consent of a majority vote of the following: The Presidents and the Vice-Presidents of both Houses of Convention, the Presidents of the Provinces and the Executive Council, shall determine the site for such General Convention and proceed to make all reasonable and necessary arrangements and commitments for that meeting of the General Convention. The site and date thus selected shall be deemed to have been appointed by the General Convention, as provided in the Constitution.   *Determination of site.*

d. Upon the final selection of and the arrangements for the site for that General Convention, the Joint Committee shall advise the Secretary of the General Convention, who shall communicate the determination to the Dioceses.   *Notice to Dioceses.*

Changes in the date and length of General Convention.

e. Within such guidelines as may have been established by the General Convention regarding the date and length of future General Conventions, and pursuant to the reasonable and necessary arrangements and commitments with the Dioceses and operators of facilities within the Diocese in which the next General Convention will be held, the Joint Committee shall fix the date and the length of the next succeeding Convention, report the same to the Secretary of the General Convention and include the same in its report to the Convention. In the event of a change of circumstances indicating the necessity or advisability of changing the date or length previously fixed, the Joint Committee shall investigate and make recommendations to the Presiding Bishop and the President of the House of Deputies, who, with the advice and consent of the Executive Council, may fix a different date or length or both.

Canon 2: Of the Presiding Bishop

Sec. 1

Members of Nominating Committee.

a. At each General Convention a Joint Nominating Committee for the election of the Presiding Bishop shall be elected. The Nominating Committee shall be comprised of 20 members, as follows: five Bishops elected by the House of Bishops; five clergy persons, including at least one deacon, and five lay persons elected by the House of Deputies who may but need not be members of that House; two persons, age 16-23, appointed by the President of the House of Deputies; and three persons appointed jointly by the Presiding Bishop and the President of the House of Deputies to ensure the cultural and geographic diversity of the Church. The Joint Standing Committee on Nominations will nominate a slate of nominees for the elected positions, in accordance with its canonical charge and procedures. In all cases, the nominees and appointees shall have the skill sets needed for effective service on the Nominating Committee.

b. In the event vacancies shall occur in the Joint
    Nominating Committee after the election of its members
    due to death, disability, resignation, or other cause
    within one year of the next General Convention, the
    vacancies shall not be filled and the remaining members
    shall constitute the Joint Nominating Committee. In the
    event such vacancies shall occur more than one year
    prior to the next General Convention, the Presiding
    Officer of the House of Bishops shall appoint Bishops and
    the President of the House of Deputies shall appoint
    Clerical and Lay Deputies. A Lay member of the
    Committee who is ordained Presbyter or Deacon, or a
    Presbyter or Deacon who is consecrated a Bishop before
    the next General Convention, shall not thereby become
    ineligible to continue to serve on the Joint Nominating
    Committee through the next succeeding General
    Convention.

Vacancies on Nominating Committee.

c. The Joint Nominating Committee shall remain in office
    until the adjournment of the next General Convention, at
    which a new Joint Nominating Committee shall be
    elected. Members of the Committee are eligible for
    reelection.

Term of Nominating Committee.

d. The Joint Nominating Committee shall develop and
    manage a process for soliciting and identifying qualified
    nominees for the office of Presiding Bishop and for
    providing the nominees to the General Convention at
    which a Presiding Bishop is to be elected. The process
    must enable the work to be done efficiently and as cost-
    effectively as practicable. This process shall be designed
    to encourage diversity that reflects the breadth of The
    Episcopal Church. The process shall include (1) the
    Nominating Committee shall inform the wider church of
    the process and timeline; (2) the Nominating Committee
    shall prepare a profile for the election of the next
    Presiding Bishop, and the profile will be distributed
    widely to the Church; (3) providing the names of not
    fewer than three members of the House of Bishops for
    consideration by the House of Bishops and the House of
    Deputies in the choice of a Presiding Bishop; (4)
    establishing a timely process for any bishop or deputy to

Nomination process.

nominate any other member of the House of Bishops through a petition process, and for each Bishop so nominated to be vetted through the same process of background and reference checks as all nominees, and for each Bishop so nominated to be included in the information distributed about the nominees; and (5) providing pastoral care for each nominee bishop and his or her family and diocese.

Transition committee.

e. A Presiding Bishop Transition Committee shall be appointed by the Presiding Bishop and the President of the House of Deputies. The members shall have the necessary skills and talents to determine the need for and provide for transition assistance to the Presiding Bishop and the Presiding Bishop-elect.

Installation committee.

f. A small Presiding Bishop Installation Committee shall be appointed by Executive Council with the necessary skills and talents to plan for and carry out a Celebration of New Ministry for the new Presiding Bishop.

Election to follow Joint Session.

g. At the General Convention at which a Presiding Bishop is to be elected, the Joint Nominating Committee shall present to the House of Bishops and the House of Deputies in Joint Session the names of not fewer than three members of the House of Bishops, along with those nominated through the petition process, for the consideration of the two Houses in the choice of a Presiding Bishop, and there may be discussion of all nominees. Commencing on the day following the Joint Session, election shall be by the House of Bishops from among such nominees. If the House of Bishops shall find itself unable to elect a Presiding Bishop from among such nominees, another Joint Session shall be held, at which additional nominations may be received, and on the following day, election shall be by the House of Bishops from among all of the nominees. After the election by the House of Bishops, report of the result thereof, including the number of votes cast for each nominee on each ballot, shall be made to the House of Deputies which shall vote to confirm or not to confirm such choice of Presiding Bishop.

h. In the event a vacancy in the office of Presiding Bishop *Vacancy*
    shall occur in the interim between meetings of the *between*
    General Convention, as specified in the second paragraph *meetings of the*
    of Article I, Section 3 of the Constitution, the Joint *General*
    Nominating Committee, subject to the said Article, shall *Conventions.*
    submit to the Secretary of the House of Bishops the
    names of not fewer than three members of the House of
    Bishops for the consideration by that House in the choice
    of a Presiding Bishop to fill the vacancy, and
    simultaneously therewith shall transmit a copy of such
    report to the Secretary of the House of Deputies for
    mailing to all Deputies. Such report shall also be released
    to the Church and secular press. Thereafter, the House of
    Bishops shall hold a special meeting for the purpose of
    electing a Presiding Bishop to fill the vacancy, and, in
    such election, the vote shall be upon the nominees of the
    Joint Nominating Committee and any further
    nominations made by any voting member of the House
    of Bishops. Immediately following the election by the
    House of Bishops, the Secretary of the House of Bishops
    shall inform the President and Secretary of each
    Diocesan Standing Committee, requesting a meeting at
    the earliest possible date to consider approval. Upon
    receipt of the approval of a majority of the Standing
    Committees of the Dioceses, the Presiding Bishop Elect
    shall be declared elected.

Sec. 2. The term of office of the Presiding Bishop, when *Term of office.*
elected according to the provisions of Article I, Section 3 of
the Constitution, shall be nine years, beginning the first day
of the month of November following the close of the
Convention at which the Presiding Bishop is elected, unless
attaining the age of seventy-two years before the term shall
have been completed; in that case the Presiding Bishop shall
resign the office to the General Convention which occurs
nearest to the date of attaining such age. At that Convention
a successor shall be elected, and shall assume office on the
first day of the month of November following the close of
that Convention or immediately upon the death, retirement,
or disability of the Presiding Bishop; except that when a
Presiding Bishop has been elected by the House of Bishops to
fill a vacancy, as provided for in the second paragraph of

Article I, Section 3 of the Constitution, the Presiding Bishop so elected shall take office immediately.

To resign previous jurisdiction.

Sec. 3

a. Upon the expiration of the term of office of the Presiding Bishop, the Bishop who is elected successor shall tender to the House of Bishops a resignation from the Bishop's previous jurisdiction to take effect upon the date of assuming the office of Presiding Bishop, or, upon good cause with the advice and consent of the Advisory Committee established under the Rules of Order of the House of Bishops, not later than six months thereafter.

b. Such resignation shall be acted upon immediately by the House of Bishops.

Chief Pastor and Primate.

Sec. 4

a. The Presiding Bishop shall be the Chief Pastor and Primate of the Church, and shall:

Policy and strategy.

1. Be charged with responsibility for leadership in initiating and developing the policy and strategy in the Church and speaking for the Church as to the policies, strategies and programs authorized by the General Convention;

Representative of Church and episcopate.

2. Speak God's words to the Church and to the world, as the representative of this Church and its episcopate in its corporate capacity;

Provide for interim in a Diocese. ·

3. In the event of an Episcopal vacancy within a Diocese, consult with the Ecclesiastical Authority to ensure that adequate interim Episcopal Services are provided;

Assemble Bishops.

4. Take order for the consecration of Bishops, when duly elected; and, from time to time, assemble the Bishops of this Church to meet, either as the House of Bishops or as a Council of Bishops, and set the time and place of such meetings;

Presiding Officer.

5. Preside over meetings of the House of Bishops; and, when the two Houses of the General Convention meet in Joint Session, have the right of presiding over such Session, of calling for such Joint Session,

of recommending legislation to either House and, upon due notification, of appearing before and addressing the House of Deputies; and whenever addressing the General Convention upon the state of the Church, it shall be incumbent upon both Houses thereof to consider and act upon any recommendations contained in such address;

6. Visit every Diocese of this Church for the purpose of: (i) Holding pastoral consultations with the Bishop or Bishops thereof and, with their advice, with the Lay and Clerical leaders of the jurisdiction; (ii) Preaching the Word; and (iii) Celebrating the Holy Eucharist.   *Visitations.*

b. The Presiding Bishop shall report annually to the Church, and may, from time to time, issue Pastoral Letters.   *Reports and Pastoral Letters.*

c. The Presiding Bishop shall perform such other functions as shall be prescribed in these Canons; and, to be enabled better to perform such duties and responsibilities, the Presiding Bishop may appoint, to positions established by the Executive Council of General Convention, officers, responsible to the Presiding Bishop, who may delegate such authority as shall seem appropriate.   *May delegate authority.*

Sec. 5. The Presiding Bishop may appoint, as Chancellor to the Presiding Bishop, a confirmed adult communicant of the Church in good standing who is learned in both ecclesiastical and secular law, to serve so long as the Presiding Bishop may desire, as counselor in matters relating to the office and the discharge of the responsibilities of that office.   *May appoint Chancellor.*

Sec. 6. The stipends of the Presiding Bishop and such personal assistants as may be necessary during the Presiding Bishop's term of office for the effective performance of the duties, and the necessary expenses of that office, shall be fixed by the General Convention and shall be provided for in the budget to be submitted by the Executive Council, as provided in Canon I.4.6.   *Stipends.*

Sec. 7. In the event of the disability of the Presiding Bishop, the Bishop who, according to the Rules of the House of Bishops, becomes its Presiding Officer, shall be substituted for the Presiding Bishop for all the purposes of these Canons,   *If disabled.*

except the Canons entitled, "Of the Domestic and Foreign Missionary Society," and "Of the Executive Council."

Disability allowance. **Sec. 8.** Upon the acceptance of the Presiding Bishop's resignation for reasons of disability prior to the expiration of the term of office, the Presiding Bishop may be granted, in addition to whatever allowance may be received from The Church Pension Fund, a disability allowance to be paid by the Treasurer of the General Convention in an amount to be fixed by the Executive Council, and ratified at the next regular meeting of the General Convention.

Canon 3: Of the Domestic and Foreign Missionary Society

The Constitution of the said Society, which was incorporated by an act of the Legislature of the State of New York, as from time to time amended, is hereby amended and established so as to read as follows: *Constitution of The Domestic and Foreign Missionary Society of the Protestant Episcopal Church in the United States of America as established in 1821, and since amended at various times.*

Name of organization. **ARTICLE I** This organization shall be called The Domestic and Foreign Missionary Society of the Protestant Episcopal Church in the United States of America, and shall be considered as comprehending all persons who are members of the Church.

Board of Directors. **ARTICLE II** The Executive Council, as constituted by Canon, shall be its Board of Directors, and shall adopt By-laws for its government not inconsistent with the Constitution and Canons.

Officers. **ARTICLE III** The officers of the Society shall be a President, Vice Presidents, a Secretary, a Treasurer, and such other officers as may be appointed in accordance with the Canons or By-laws. The Presiding Bishop of the Church shall be the President of the Society; one Vice President shall be the person who is the President of the House of Deputies; and one Vice President shall be the person who is the Chief Operating Officer; the Treasurer shall be the person who is the Chief Financial Officer of the Executive Council; and the

Secretary shall be the person who is the Secretary of the Executive Council, and shall have such powers and perform such duties as may be assigned by the By-laws. The other officers of the Society shall be such as are provided for by the By-laws of the Society. The tenure of office, compensation, powers, and duties of the officers of the Society shall be such as are prescribed by the Canons and by the By-laws of the Society not inconsistent therewith.

ARTICLE IV This Constitution of the Society may be altered or amended at any time by the General Convention of the Church.   *Amendment.*

Canon 4: Of the Executive Council

Sec. 1   *Function and responsibility.*

a. There shall be an Executive Council of the General Convention (which Council shall generally be called simply the Executive Council, or the Council) whose duty it shall be to oversee the execution of the program and policies adopted by the General Convention. The Executive Council shall have oversight of the work done by the Domestic and Foreign Missionary Society in its capacity as its Board of Directors. The Council shall have oversight responsibility for the disposition of the funds and other property of the Domestic and Foreign Missionary Society in accordance with the provisions of this Canon and the resolutions, orders, and budgets adopted or approved by the General Convention. The Executive Council shall also have oversight responsibility for the work of the Office of General Convention and the Executive Officer of General Convention who shall report directly to the Executive Council. It shall also have oversight responsibility for the disposition of the moneys of the Office of General Convention. The Council shall adopt procedures it deems appropriate for approval of expenditures by the Domestic and Foreign Missionary Society and the Office of General Convention.

b. The Executive Council shall be accountable to the General Convention and shall render a full, published report concerning the work of the bodies for which it has   *Accountability.*

oversight responsibility to each meeting of the General Convention. The report shall include information on the implementation of all resolutions adopted in the previous General Convention calling for action by the Executive Council, the Domestic and Foreign Missionary Society, and the Office of General Convention.

Authority.

c. The Council shall exercise the powers conferred upon it by Canon, and such further powers as may be designated by the General Convention, and between sessions of the General Convention may initiate and develop such new work as it may deem necessary. Subject to the provisions of these Canons, it may enact By-laws for its own government and enact procedures for its own committees.

How constituted.

d. The Executive Council shall be composed (a) of 20 members elected by the General Convention, of whom four shall be Bishops, four shall be Presbyters or Deacons, and 12 shall be Lay Persons who are confirmed adult communicants in good standing (two Bishops, two Presbyters or Deacons, and six Lay Persons to be elected by each subsequent regular meeting of the General Convention); (b) of 18 members elected by the Provincial Synods; (c) of the following *ex officiis* members: the Presiding Bishop and the President of the House of Deputies; and (d) the Chief Operating Officer, the Secretary of the General Convention, the Treasurer of the General Convention, the Chief Financial Officer of the Domestic and Foreign Missionary Society, and the Chief Legal Officer of the Executive Council, all of whom shall have seat and voice but no vote. Each Province shall be entitled to be represented by one Bishop or Presbyter or Deacon canonically resident in a Diocese which is a constituent member of the Province and one Lay Person who is a confirmed adult communicant in good standing of a Diocese which is a constituent member of the Province, and the terms of the representatives of each Province shall be so rotated that two persons shall not be simultaneously elected for equal terms.

e. The Executive Council shall appoint a committee from among its members to assist the Council to (i) advise the

Joint Standing Committee on Nominations and the Provincial Councils on what skills, gifts and experience are needed on the Executive Council to enable it to function with maximum effectiveness, and whether those skills are at that time represented on the Executive Council, and (ii) create a description of the skills, gifts and experience requisite for service on the Executive Council, including the value of cultural and geographic diversity on the Council and the value of including historically underrepresented voices in the governance of the Church.

f. Of the Executive Council members elected by the General Convention, the Bishops shall be elected by the House of Bishops subject to confirmation by the House of Deputies, and the Presbyters or Deacons and Lay Persons shall be elected by the House of Deputies subject to confirmation by the House of Bishops.

Election.

g. Except in the case of members initially elected for shorter terms in order to achieve rotation of terms, the terms of office of the members of the Council (other than *ex officiis* members) shall be equal to twice the interval between regular meetings of the General Convention. The terms of office of all members shall commence immediately upon the adjournment of the General Convention at which they were elected or, in the case of election by a Synod, upon the adjournment of the first regular meeting of General Convention following such election. The term of a member shall become vacant in the event of two absences from meetings of the Council in the interval between successive regular meetings of the General Convention unless excused by the Chair or Vice Chair for good cause. Members shall remain in office until their successors are elected and qualified. No person who has served at least three consecutive years on the Executive Council shall be eligible for immediate re-election for a term of more than three years. After any person shall have served six consecutive years on the Executive Council, a period of three years shall elapse before such person shall be eligible for re-election to the Council.

Terms of office.

Vacancy.   **h.** Should any vacancy occur in the Council through death, resignation, disability, or other reason, with respect to a member elected by the General Convention, the Council shall fill such vacancy by the election of a suitable person to serve until a successor is elected by the General Convention.

       i. Should any vacancy occur in the Council through the failure of any Provincial Synod to elect a member, or through the death, resignation, or removal from the Province of any such member, the Provincial Council of the Province shall appoint a suitable person to serve until the Provincial Synod shall by election fill the vacancy.

Officers.   **Sec. 2**

       a. The Presiding Bishop shall, *ex officio*, be the Chair and chief executive officer of the Executive Council, and as such, shall have ultimate responsibility for the oversight of the work of the Executive Council in the implementation of the ministry and mission of the Church as may be committed to the Executive Council by the General Convention.

       b. The President of the House of Deputies shall, *ex officio*, be the Vice-Chair of Executive Council.

       c. The Secretary of the General Convention shall be *ex officio* the Secretary of the Executive Council.

       d. The Treasurer of the General Convention shall be *ex officio* the Treasurer of the Executive Council.

       e. The Chair shall preside at meetings of the Council, shall perform such other duties as are customary for such office, and shall perform such other duties as may be conferred by Canon and the By-laws of the Council. In the absence of or at the request of the Chair, the Vice-Chair shall preside at meetings of the Council and shall perform such other duties as may be conferred by Canon and by the By-laws of the Council.

       f. Upon joint nomination by the Chair and the Vice-Chair, the Council shall appoint a Chief Operating Officer who shall serve at the pleasure of, and report and be accountable to, the Chair. If a vacancy should occur in the office of the Chief Operating Officer, a successor shall be appointed in like manner.

g. Upon joint nomination by the Chair and the Vice-Chair, the Council shall appoint a Chief Financial Officer who shall serve at the pleasure of, and report and be accountable to, the Chair. If a vacancy should occur in that office, a successor shall be appointed in like manner.

h. Upon joint nomination by the Chair and the Vice-Chair, the Council shall appoint a Chief Legal Officer who shall function as general counsel and serve at the pleasure of, and report and be accountable to, the Chair. If a vacancy should occur in that office, a successor shall be appointed in like manner.

i. The Chief Operating Officer, the Chief Financial Officer, and the Chief Legal Officer of the Executive Council shall participate in an annual performance review conducted by the Chair, the results of which will be presented to the Executive Committee of the Executive Council.

Performance and ministry reviews.

j. The Officers of the Domestic and Foreign Missionary Society and the Officers of the Executive Council, and a committee of six members of Executive Council who are not officers, shall engage in a mutual ministry review every eighteen months, facilitated by a consultant selected by the Chair and the Vice-Chair.

k. The Council shall elect the Church's members of the Anglican Consultative Council (ACC) and of other Anglican and ecumenical bodies for which no other procedure is provided in the Canons. Members of the ACC representing The Episcopal Church shall report to each General Convention using the schedule and format required for Standing Commissions in these Canons, and shall provide comprehensive written reports to Executive Council at the Council's next meeting following each meeting of the ACC.

Elects representatives.

Sec. 3. Upon joint nomination of the Chair and the Vice-Chair, the Executive Council shall elect an Audit Committee of the Council and the Domestic and Foreign Missionary Society. The Committee shall be composed of six members:

Audit Committee.

one member who, at the time of appointment, is a member of the Executive Council committee with primary responsibility for financial matters; and the remaining five from members of the Church-at-large having experience in general business and financial practices. The members shall serve a term beginning on January 1 following the regular meeting of the General Convention at which elected or immediately following their appointment, whichever comes later, and continuing through December 31 following the adjournment of the next regular meeting of the General Convention or until a successor is appointed, and may serve two consecutive terms, after which a full interval between regular meetings of the General Convention must elapse before being eligible for reelection. Annually the Audit Committee shall elect a Chair of the Committee from among its members. The Audit Committee shall regularly review the financial statements relating to all funds under the management or control of the Council and the Domestic and Foreign Missionary Society and shall report thereon at least annually to the Council.

External audit. Upon recommendation of the Audit Committee, the Executive Council shall employ on behalf of the Council and the Domestic and Foreign Missionary Society an independent Certified Public Accountant firm to audit annually all accounts under the management or control of the Council and Domestic and Foreign Missionary Society. After receipt of the annual audit, the Audit Committee shall recommend to the Council and the Domestic and Foreign Missionary Society what action to take as to any matters identified in the annual audit and accompanying management letter. The responsibilities of the Audit Committee shall be set out in an Audit Committee Charter. The Audit Committee shall review, at least annually, the Committee's Charter and recommend any changes to the Executive Council for approval.

Council bodies and terms. **Sec. 4.** Following the adjournment of a General Convention, and subject to budgeted funds available for the purpose, the Chair and the Vice-Chair, having reviewed the resolutions adopted by the General Convention that provide for any study or further action, shall thereupon recommend to the Executive Council, the creation of such study committees and task forces as may be necessary to complete that work. Any Executive Council resolution creating a task force or study committee shall specify the size and composition, the clear and express duties assigned, the time for completion of the work assigned, to whom the body's report is to be made, and the amount and source of the funding for the body. The members of each such body shall be jointly appointed by the Chair and Vice-Chair, and the composition of such committees and task forces shall reflect the diverse voices of the Church and a balance of the Church's orders consistent with the historic polity of the Church. Those committees and task forces so appointed shall expire at the close of the next General Convention following, unless reappointed by the Chair and Vice-Chair and reauthorized by the Executive Council.

Sec. 5   *Meetings.*

a. The Council shall meet at such place, and at such stated times, at least three times each year, as it shall appoint and at such other times as it may be convened. The Council shall be convened at the request of the Chair, or on the written request of any five members of Council.

b. A majority of the elected members of the Council shall be   *Quorum.*
necessary to constitute a quorum at any meeting of the Council. No action shall be taken in the name of the Council except when a quorum, so defined, is present and voting. A member may participate in, and vote at, Council meetings by means of technology where all participants may hear one another simultaneously and according to procedures and guidelines set forth in the Council By-laws.

c. Members of Executive Council shall be entitled to   *Expenses and*
reimbursement for their reasonable expenses of   *salaries.*
attending meetings, in accordance with procedures established and approved by Executive Council. Except as determined by General Convention, the salaries of all officers of the Council and of all agents and employees of the Council and the Domestic and Foreign Missionary Society shall be fixed by the Council.

<table>
<tr><td>Proposed
Budget.</td><td>Sec. 6</td></tr>
</table>

Proposed Budget.

Sec. 6

a. Following open and accessible budget hearings, at least four months prior to the next regular meeting of the General Convention, the Executive Council shall submit to the Secretary of the General Convention a proposed Episcopal Church budget for the ensuing budgetary period (as used in this Section 6, the "budget"). The ensuing budgetary period shall comprise the calendar years starting with the January 1st following the adjournment of the most recent regular meeting of the General Convention and ending with the December 31st following the adjournment of the next regular meeting of the General Convention.

Single assessment.

b. Revenue to support the budget shall be generated primarily by a single assessment of the Dioceses of the Church based on a formula which the General Convention shall adopt as part of its budget process. If in any year the total anticipated income for budget support is less than the amount required to support the budget approved by the General Convention, the canonical portion of the budget shall have funding priority over any other budget areas subject to any decreases necessary to maintain a balanced budget.

Presentation.

c. Following open and accessible legislative hearings on the budget held within 90 days of the General Convention and also at General Convention, there shall be joint sessions of the two Houses for the presentation of the budget; and thereafter consideration shall be given and appropriate action taken thereon by the General Convention.

Notice of assessment.

d. Upon the adoption by the General Convention of a budget and the planned assessments for the budgetary period, the Council shall formally advise each Diocese of its share of the total assessments to support the budget.

Payment.

e. Full payment of the diocesan assessment shall be required of all Dioceses, effective January 1, 2019.

f. Council shall have the power to grant waivers from the full annual assessments of Dioceses within the limit established by the General Convention. Any diocese may appeal to Executive Council for a waiver of the assessment, in full or in part, on the basis of financial hardship, a stated plan for working toward full payment, or other reasons as agreed with the Executive Council. Effective January 1, 2019, failure to make full payment or to receive a waiver shall render the diocese ineligible to receive grants or loans from the Domestic and Foreign Missionary Society unless approved by Executive Council.

Waivers.

g. The Council shall have the power to expend all sums of money covered by the budget and estimated budgets approved by the General Convention, subject to such restrictions as may be imposed by the General Convention, including but not limited to the priority declaration set forth in Section 6.b of this Canon. It shall also have power to undertake such other work provided for in the budget approved by the General Convention, or other work under the jurisdiction of the Council, the need for which may have arisen after the action of the General Convention, as in the judgment of the Council its income will warrant.

Budget authority.

h. In respect of the budget the Executive Council shall have the power to consider and vote to make such adjustments therein, or additions thereto, as it shall deem to be necessary or expedient, and which, in its judgment, available funds and anticipated income will warrant subject to such restrictions as may be imposed by the General Convention. It shall also have power to approve other initiatives proposed by the Chair or otherwise considered by Council between meetings of the General Convention, as in the judgment of the Council are prudent and which the Church revenues will be adequate to support.

Adjustments.

i. Each Diocese shall annually report to the Executive Council such financial and other information pertaining to the state of the Church in the Diocese as may be required in a form authorized by Executive Council.

Diocesan financial reports.

j. Each Diocese shall report annually to the Executive Council the name and address of each new congregation, and of each congregation closed or removed by reason of any of the following:

1. dissolution of the congregation;

2. removal of the congregation to another Diocese due to cession or retrocession of geographic territory in which the congregation is located, pursuant to Articles V.6 or VI.2 of the Constitution;

3. removal of the congregation to a new physical location or address, identifying both the location or address from which the congregation has removed, and the successor location or address; and

4. merger of the congregation into one or more other congregations, in which case, the Diocese shall include in its report the names of all congregations involved in the merger, and the physical location and address at which the merged congregations shall be located.

Bishops receiving aid.

Sec. 7

a. Every Missionary Bishop or, in case of a vacancy, the Bishop in charge of the jurisdiction, receiving aid from the General Convention Budget, shall report at the close of each fiscal year to the Council, giving account of work performed, of money received from all sources and disbursed for all purposes, and of the state of the Church in the jurisdiction at the date of such report, all in such form as the Council may prescribe.

b. The Ecclesiastical Authority of every Diocese receiving aid from the General Convention Budget shall report at the close of each fiscal year to the Council, giving account of the work in the diocese supported in whole or in part by that aid.

Reports of the Council.

Sec. 8. The Council, as soon as practicable after the close of each fiscal year, shall cause to be prepared and publish a full report of the work of the Executive Council, the Domestic and Foreign Missionary Society, and the General Convention Office to the Church. Such report shall contain an itemized statement of all receipts and disbursements and a statement of all trust funds and other property of The Domestic and Foreign Missionary Society, and of all other trust funds and property in its possession or under its oversight responsibility. The report shall include a detailed schedule of the salaries paid to all officers and principal employees of the Domestic and Foreign Missionary Society and the Executive Council.

Sec. 9   *Qualifications of*
                                                       Missionaries.

a. Ordained Ministers and Lay Communicants of this Church, or of some Church in full communion with this Church, in good standing, who qualify in accordance with the standards and procedures adopted from time to time by the Executive Council, shall be eligible for appointment as Missionaries of this Church.

b. Members in good standing of Churches not in full communion with this Church, but otherwise qualified as above, may, at the request of the Ecclesiastical Authority of the jurisdiction in which the requirement exists, be employed and assigned to positions for which they are professionally prepared; and may receive the same stipends and other allowances as appointed Missionaries. The Ecclesiastical Authority of a jurisdiction may employ any qualified person for work in the jurisdiction.

Canon 5: Of the Archives of The Episcopal Church

Sec. 1. There shall be an Archives of The Episcopal Church,   *Purpose.*
the purpose of which shall be to preserve by safekeeping, to arrange and to make available the records of the General Convention, Executive Council, and the Domestic and Foreign Missionary Society, and other important records and memorabilia of the life and work of the Church, and to carry out a program of records management, so as to further the historical dimension of the mission of the Church.

Sec. 2. For purposes of this Canon, records are defined as all   *Records defined.*
fixed evidential information regardless of method, media, format or characteristics of the recording process, which have been created, received or gathered by the Church, its

officers, agents or employees in pursuance of the legal, business and administrative function and the programmatic mission of the Church. Records include all original materials used to capture information, notwithstanding the place or conditions of creation, or the formality or informality of the characteristics of the record. The records and archives of the Church are not limited by the medium in which they are kept and include such formats as paper records, electronic records, printed records and publications, photo-reproduced images, and machine-readable tapes, film and disks.

Archivist.

Sec. 3. The Archives of The Episcopal Church shall be managed by the Archivist.

Reports to the Chair of Executive Council.

Sec. 4. After consultation with the Archives Advisory Committee, the Presiding Bishop and the President of the House of Deputies in their respective roles as the Chair and Vice-Chair of the Executive Council, shall jointly nominate and the Executive Council shall appoint the Archivist who shall serve at the pleasure of, and report and be accountable to the Chair of the Executive Council. If a vacancy should occur in that office, a successor shall be appointed in like manner.

Archives Advisory Committee.

Sec. 5

a. There shall be an Archives Advisory Committee which shall consist of the Archivist, the Registrar, the Chief Legal Officer, the Historiographer, and between eight and twelve appointed persons, two or three of whom shall be Bishops, two or three of whom shall be Clergy, and four, five or six of whom shall be Lay Persons. All appointed Members of the Advisory Committee shall serve terms beginning upon the adjournment of the General Convention at which their appointments are confirmed and ending with the close of the second regular Convention thereafter.

Membership.

b. Bishops shall be appointed by the Presiding Bishop, and other Clerical and all Lay Members shall be appointed by the President of the House of Deputies; after the initial appointments, all subsequent appointments shall be subject to the confirmation of General Convention. Consideration shall be given to assure that membership includes persons who possess knowledge either of history or archival administration, or are persons skilled in disciplines pertinent to the resolutions of the concerns of the Archives. Positions of Members of the Committee which become vacant prior to the normal expiration of such Members' terms shall be filled by appointment by the Presiding Bishop or by the President of the House of Deputies, as appropriate. Such appointments shall be for the remaining unexpired portion of such Members' terms, and if a regular meeting of the General Convention intervenes, appointments for terms extending beyond such meeting shall be subject to confirmation of the General Convention. Because of the special skills and knowledge needed by this Committtee, a Member shall be eligible for appointment for two successive terms, after which the Member may not be reappointed prior to the next meeting of the General Convention following the meeting at the close of which the second successive term of the Member expired. Members appointed to fill vacancies in unexpired terms shall not thereby be disqualified from appointment to two full terms immediately thereafter.

c. The Archives Advisory Committee shall provide advice regarding identification, collection, preservation, management, use, and accessibility of records, and establishment of best practices regarding the same to the Archivist, the Archives, and the Executive Council. *Duties.*

d. The Archives Advisory Committee shall meet at least annually, or as requested by the Archivist or the Chair and Vice-Chair of the Executive Council. *Meetings.*

Sec. 6. The expenses of the Archives of The Episcopal Church shall be included in the budget for The Episcopal Church. *Expenses.*

Canon 6: Of the Mode of Securing an Accurate View of the State of This Church

Sec. 1. A report of every Parish and other Congregation of this Church shall be prepared annually for the year ending December 31 preceding, in the form authorized by the Executive Council and approved by the Committee on the *Annual parish reports to Bishop.*

State of the Church, and shall be filed not later than March 1 with the Bishop of the Diocese, or, where there is no Bishop, with the ecclesiastical authority of the Diocese. The Bishop or the ecclesiastical authority, as the case may be, shall keep a copy and submit the report to the Executive Council not later than May 1. In every Parish and other Congregation the preparation and filing of this report shall be the joint duty of the Rector or Member of the Clergy in charge thereof and the lay leadership; and before the filing thereof the report shall be approved by the Vestry or bishop's committee or mission council. This report shall include the following information:

1. the number of baptisms, confirmations, marriages, and burials during the year; the total number of baptized members, the total number of communicants in good standing, and the total number of communicants in good standing under 16 years of age.

2. a summary of all the receipts and expenditures, from whatever source derived and for whatever purpose used.

3. such other relevant information as is needed to secure an accurate view of the state of this Church, as required by the approved form.

Non-parochial reports. **Sec. 2.** Every Bishop, Presbyter, or Deacon whose report is not included in a parochial report shall also report on the exercise of such office, and if there has been none, the causes or reasons which have prevented the same.

Sec. 3. These reports, or such parts of them as the Bishop may deem proper, shall be entered in the Journal of the convention.

Annual Diocesan Reports. **Sec. 4.** Likewise, a report of every Diocese shall be prepared annually for the year ending December 31st preceding, in the form authorized by the Executive Council and approved by the Committee on the State of the Church, and shall be filed, not later than September 1, with the Executive Council. It shall include information concerning implementation by the Diocese of resolutions of the previous General Convention which have been specifically identified by the Secretary of General Convention under Joint Rule 12 as calling for Diocesan action.

Sec. 5

a. It shall be the duty of the Secretary of the Convention of every jurisdiction to forward to the Secretary of the House of Deputies by electronic means, immediately upon publication, one (1) copy of the Journal of the Convention of the jurisdiction, together with episcopal charges, statements, and such other records in electronic format as may show the state of the Church in that jurisdiction, and one (1) copy to the Archives of the Church in electronic format as prescribed by the Archivist of the Church.

Journals to be forwarded to Secretary and Archives.

b. A Committee of the House of Deputies shall be appointed following the close of each General Convention, to serve *ad interim*, and to prepare and present to the next meeting of the House of Deputies a report on the State of the Church; which report, when agreed to by the said House, shall be sent to the House of Bishops.

Report to the House of Deputies.

Canon 7: Of Business Methods in Church Affairs

Sec. 1. In every Province, Diocese, Parish, Mission and Institution connected with this Church, the following standard business methods shall be observed:

Standards observed.

a. All accounts of Provinces shall be audited annually by an independent certified public accountant, or independent licensed accountant, or such audit committee as shall be authorized by the Provincial Council. The Audit Report shall be filed with the Provincial Council not later than September 1 of each year, covering the preceding calendar year.

Provinces to be audited.

b. Funds held in trust, endowment and other permanent funds, and securities represented by physical evidence of ownership or indebtedness, shall be deposited with a National or State Bank, or a Diocesan Corporation, or with some other agency approved in writing by the Finance Committee or the Department of Finance of the Diocese, under a deed of trust, agency or other depository agreement providing for at least two signatures on any order of withdrawal of such funds or

Deposit of funds.

Proviso.   securities. But this paragraph shall not apply to funds and securities refused by the depositories named as being too small for acceptance. Such small funds and securities shall be under the care of the persons or corporations properly responsible for them. This paragraph shall not be deemed to prohibit investments in securities issued in book entry form or other manner that dispenses with the delivery of a certificate evidencing the ownership of the securities or the indebtedness of the issuer.

Record of trust funds.   c.   Records shall be made and kept of all trust and permanent funds showing at least the following:

      1.   Source and date.

      2.   Terms governing the use of principal and income.

      3.   To whom and how often reports of condition are to be made.

      4.   How the funds are invested.

Treasurers to be bonded.   d.   Treasurers and custodians, other than banking institutions, shall be adequately bonded; except treasurers of funds that do not exceed five hundred dollars at any one time during the fiscal year.

Books of account.   e.   Books of account shall be so kept as to provide the basis for satisfactory accounting.

Annual audit.   f.   All accounts of the Diocese shall be audited annually by an independent Certified Public Accountant. All accounts of Parishes, Missions or other institutions shall be audited annually by an independent Certified Public Accountant, or independent Licensed Public Accountant, or such audit committee as shall be authorized by the Finance Committee, Department of Finance, or other appropriate diocesan authority.

      g.   All reports of such audits, including any memorandum issued by the auditors or audit committee regarding internal controls or other accounting matters, together with a summary of action taken or proposed to be taken to correct deficiencies or implement recommendations contained in any such memorandum, shall be filed with the Bishop or Ecclesiastical Authority not later than 30 days following the date of such report, and in no event, not later than September 1 of each year, covering the financial reports of the previous calendar year.

h. All buildings and their contents shall be kept adequately insured.

Insurance.

i. The Finance Committee or Department of Finance of the Diocese may require copies of any or all accounts described in this Section to be filed with it and shall report annually to the Convention of the Diocese upon its administration of this Canon.

Report to Convention.

j. The fiscal year shall begin January 1.

Fiscal year.

Sec. 2. The several Dioceses shall give effect to the foregoing standard business methods by the enactment of Canons appropriate thereto, which Canons shall invariably providefor a Finance Committee, a Department of Finance of the Diocese, or other appropriate diocesan body with such authority.

Dioceses to enforce by Canon.

Sec. 3. No Vestry, Trustee, or other Body, authorized by Civil or Canon law to hold, manage, or administer real property for any Parish, Mission, Congregation, or Institution, shall encumber or alienate the same or any part thereof without the written consent of the Bishop and Standing Committee of the Diocese of which the Parish, Mission, Congregation, or Institution is a part, except under such regulations as may be prescribed by Canon of the Diocese.

Encumbrance of property requires consent.

Sec. 4. All real and personal property held by or for the benefit of any Parish, Mission or Congregation is held in trust for this Church and the Diocese thereof in which such Parish, Mission or Congregation is located. The existence of this trust, however, shall in no way limit the power and authority of the Parish, Mission or Congregation otherwise existing over such property so long as the particular Parish, Mission or Congregation remains a part of, and subject to, this Church and its Constitution and Canons.

Property held in trust.

Sec. 5. The several Dioceses may, at their election, further confirm the trust declared under the foregoing Section 4 by appropriate action, but no such action shall be necessary for the existence and validity of the trust.

Canon 8: Of The Church Pension Fund

Clergy and lay pension and health plans.

Sec. 1. The Church Pension Fund, a corporation created by Chapter 97 of the Laws of 1914 of the State of New York as subsequently amended, is hereby authorized to establish and administer the clergy pension system, including life, accident and health benefits, of this Church, substantially in accordance with the principles adopted by the General Convention of 1913 and approved thereafter by the several Dioceses, with the view to providing pensions and related benefits for the Clergy who reach normal age of retirement, for the Clergy disabled by age or infirmity, and for the surviving spouses and minor children of deceased Clergy. The Church Pension Fund is also authorized to establish and administer the lay employee pension system and denominational health plan of the Church, substantially in accordance with the principles adopted by the General Convention of 2009 in Resolution 2009-A177, with the view to providing pensions, health care and related benefits for the eligible Clergy and eligible lay employees of this Church, as well as their eligible beneficiaries and dependents.

Election of Trustees.

Sec. 2. The General Convention at each regular meeting shall elect, on the nomination of a Joint Committee thereof, twelve persons to serve as Trustees of The Church Pension Fund and shall also fill such vacancies as may exist on the Board of Trustees. Except for a Trustee filling a vacancy, the term of service of a Trustee shall begin at the adjournment of the regular meeting of the General Convention at which the Trustee was elected and expire upon the adjournment of the second regular meeting of the General Convention following. Any person who has been elected as a Trustee by General Convention for twelve or more consecutive years shall not be eligible for reelection until the next regular meeting of the General Convention following the one in which that person was not eligible for reelection to the Board of Trustees. Any vacancy which occurs at a time when the General Convention is not in session may be filled by the Board of Trustees by appointment, ad interim, of a Trustee who shall serve until the next session of the General Convention thereafter shall have elected a Trustee to serve for the remainder of the unexpired term pertaining to such vacancy.

Sec. 3. For the purpose of administering the pension system, The Church Pension Fund shall be entitled to receive and to use all net royalties from publications authorized by the General Convention, and to levy upon and to collect from all Parishes, Missions, and other ecclesiastical organizations or bodies subject to the authority of this Church, and any other societies, organizations, or bodies in the Church which under the regulations of The Church Pension Fund shall elect to come into the pension system, assessments based upon the salaries and other compensation paid to Clergy by such Parishes, Missions, and other ecclesiastical organizations or bodies for services rendered currently or in the past, prior to their becoming beneficiaries of the Fund. For the purpose of administering the lay employee pension system and denominational health plan, The Church Pension Fund shall be entitled to collect from all Parishes, Missions, and other ecclesiastical organizations or bodies subject to the authority of this Church, and any other societies, organizations, or bodies in the Church which under the regulations of The Church Pension Fund shall elect to come into the lay employee pension system, assessments and/or contributions based upon the salaries and other compensation paid to eligible lay employees by such Parishes, Missions, and other ecclesiastical organizations or bodies, determine the eligibility of all Clergy and lay employees to participate in the denominational health plan through a formal benefits enrollment process, and The Church Pension Fund shall be entitled to levy upon and collect contributions for health care and related benefits under the denominational health plan from all Parishes, Missions, and other ecclesiastical organizations or bodies subject to the authority of this Church with respect to their Clergy and lay employees.

Royalties and assessments.

Sec. 4. The pension system shall be so administered that no pension shall be allotted before there shall be in the hands of The Church Pension Fund sufficient funds to meet such pension, except as directed by the General Convention in 1967.

Limit on allotment.

*Minimum
retiring
allowance.*
Sec. 5. To every Member of the Clergy who shall have been ordained in this Church or received into this Church from another Church, and who shall have remained in service in the office and work of the Ministry in this Church for a period of at least twenty-five years, and in respect of whom the conditions of this Canon shall have been fulfilled in the payment of assessments on such reasonable basis as The Church Pension Fund may establish under its Rules of Administration, The Church Pension Fund shall provide a minimum retiring allowance the amount of which shall be determined by the Trustees of the Fund, and shall also provide surviving spouses' and minor children's allowances related thereto. In the case of a Member of the Clergy in whose behalf assessments shall not have been fully paid for a period of at least twenty-five years, The Church Pension Fund shall be empowered to recompute the aforesaid minimum retiring allowance and the other allowances related thereto at a rate or rates consistent with the proper actuarial practice. The Trustees of The Church Pension Fund are hereby empowered to establish such Rules and Regulations as will fulfill the intention of this Canon and are consistent with sound actuarial practice. Subject to the provisions of this Canon, the general principle shall be observed that there shall be an actuarial relation between the several benefits; *provided, however*, that the Board of Trustees shall have power to establish such maximum of annuities greater than two thousand dollars as shall be in the best interest of the Church, within the limits of sound actuarial practice.

Sec. 6. An Initial Reserve Fund, derived from voluntary gifts, shall be administered by The Church Pension Fund so as to assure to clergy ordained prior to March 1, 1917, and their families, such addition to the support to which they may become entitled on the basis of assessments authorized by this Canon as may bring their several allowances up to the scale herein established.

Merger.
Sec. 7. The action of the Trustees of the General Clergy Relief Fund, in accepting the provisions of Chapter 239 of the Laws of 1915 of the State of New York authorizing a merger with The Church Pension Fund, upon terms agreed upon between

said two Funds, is hereby approved. Any corporation, society, or other organization, which hitherto has administered clergy relief funds, may to such extent as may be compatible with its corporate powers and its existing obligations, and in so far as may be sanctioned in the case of diocesan societies by the respective Dioceses, merge with The Church Pension Fund, or if merger be impracticable, may establish by agreement with The Church Pension Fund the closest practicable system of co-operation with that fund. Nothing herein contained shall be construed to the prejudice of existing corporations or societies whose funds are derived from payments made by members thereof.

Sec. 8. Women ordained to the Diaconate prior to January 1, 1971, who are not employed in active service on January 1, 1977, shall continue to have the benefit of their present provisions for pension protection at the expense of their employers, through the Pension Plan for Deaconesses provided by the Church Life Insurance Corporation, or through some other pension plan providing equivalent or better guarantees of a dependable retirement income, approved by proper authority. Women ordained to the Diaconate prior to January 1, 1971, and who are employed in active service on or after January 1, 1977, shall be entitled to the same provisions for pension protection as other Deacons based on prospective service on or after January 1, 1977. Women ordained to the Diaconate on or after January 1, 1971, shall be entitled to the same pension protection as other Deacons.

Pensions for women.

Sec. 9. The General Convention reserves the power to alter or amend this Canon, but no such alteration or amendment shall be made until after the same shall have been communicated to the Trustees of The Church Pension Fund and such Trustees shall have had ample opportunity to be heard with respect thereto.

General Convention reserves right to amend.

Canon 9: Of Provinces

Sec. 1. Subject to the proviso in Article VII of the Constitution, the Dioceses of this Church shall be and are hereby united into Provinces as follows:

How constituted.

The First Province shall consist of the Dioceses within the States of Maine, New Hampshire, Vermont, Massachusetts, Rhode Island, and Connecticut.

The Second Province shall consist of the Dioceses within the States of New York and New Jersey, the Dioceses of Haiti, Cuba, Puerto Rico, and the Virgin Islands, and the Convocation of Episcopal Churches in Europe.

The Third Province shall consist of the Dioceses within the States of Pennsylvania, Delaware, Maryland, Virginia, West Virginia, and the District of Columbia.

The Fourth Province shall consist of the Dioceses within the States of North Carolina, South Carolina, Georgia, Florida, Alabama, Mississippi, Tennessee, Kentucky, and Louisiana, except for the portion thereof consisting of the Diocese of Western Louisiana.

The Fifth Province shall consist of the Diocese of Missouri, and of the Dioceses within the States of Ohio, Indiana, Illinois, Michigan, and Wisconsin.

The Sixth Province shall consist of the Dioceses within the States of Minnesota, Iowa, North Dakota, South Dakota, Nebraska, Montana, Wyoming, and Colorado.

The Seventh Province shall consist of the Dioceses of Western Louisiana and of West Missouri, and of the Dioceses within the States of Arkansas, Texas, Kansas, Oklahoma, and New Mexico.

The Eighth Province shall consist of the Dioceses within the States of Idaho, Utah, Washington, Oregon, Nevada, California, Arizona, Alaska, and Hawaii, the Diocese of Taiwan and the Area Mission of Navajoland.

The Ninth Province shall consist of the Dioceses of this Church in Colombia, the Dominican Republic, Ecuador, Honduras, and Venezuela.

Purpose. **Sec 2.** The primary purposes of the Provinces are to facilitate interdiocesan collaboration to achieve Diocesan and Episcopal Church goals, and to enable more effective communications and regional advocacy of significant programmatic efforts.

Sec. 3   *New Dioceses.*

a. When a new Diocese or Area Mission shall be created wholly within any Province, such new Diocese or Area Mission shall be included in such Province. In case a new Diocese or Area Mission shall embrace territory in two or more Provinces, it shall be included in and form part of the Province wherein the greater number of Presbyters and Deacons in such new Diocese or Area Mission shall, at the time of its creation, be canonically resident. Whenever a new Diocese or Area Mission shall be formed of territory not before included in any Province, the General Convention shall designate the Province to which it shall be annexed.

b. By mutual agreement between the Synods of two adjoining Provinces, a Diocese or Area Mission may transfer itself from one of such Provinces to the other, such transfer to be considered complete upon approval thereof by the General Convention. Following such approval, Canon I.9.1 shall be appropriately amended.

Transfer of Dioceses.

Sec. 4. For the purpose of the Province the Synodical rights and privileges of the several Dioceses within the Province shall be such as from time to time shall be determined by the Synod of the Province.

Rights and privileges of Dioceses.

Sec. 5. There shall be in each Province a Synod consisting of a House of Bishops and a House of Deputies, which Houses shall sit and deliberate either separately or together. The Synod shall meet on a regular basis as determined by each Province for the purpose of organizing and carrying out the responsibilities of the Province as provided in the Canons.

Provincial Synod.

Sec. 6. Every Bishop Diocesan of this Church, having jurisdiction within the Province, every Bishop Coadjutor, Bishop Suffragan, and Assistant Bishop, and every Bishop whose episcopal work has been within the Province, but who by reason of advanced age or bodily infirmity has resigned, shall have a seat and vote in the House of Bishops of the Province.

All bishops have seat and vote.

President of Province.

Sec. 7

a. The President of each Province may be one of the Bishops, Presbyters, Deacons, or Lay Persons of the Province, elected by the Synod. The method of election and term of office shall be determined by the rules of the Synod.

b. When the person elected is not a Bishop, a Vice-President shall be elected who shall be a Bishop member of the Province. In this event the Bishop so elected shall serve, *ex officio*, as President of the House of Bishops of the Synod, and shall represent the Province in all matters requiring the participation of a Bishop.

Provincial House of Deputies.

Sec. 8. Each Diocese and Area Mission within the Province shall be entitled to representation in the Provincial House of Deputies by Presbyters or Deacons canonically resident in the Diocese or Area Mission, and Lay Persons, confirmed adult communicants of this Church in good standing but not necessarily domiciled in the Diocese or Area Mission, in such number as the Provincial Synod, by Ordinance, may provide. Each Diocese and Area Mission shall determine the manner in which its Deputies shall be elected.

Powers of Provincial Synod.

Sec. 9. The Provincial Synod shall have power: (a) to enact Ordinances for its own regulation and government; (b) to perform such duties as many be committed to it by the General Convention; (c) to deal with all matters within the Province; *provided, however,* that no Provincial Synod shall have power to regulate or control the internal policy or affairs of any constituent Diocese; and *provided, further,* that all actions and proceedings of the Synod shall be subject to and in conformity with the provisions of the Constitution and the Canons for the government of this Church; (d) to adopt a budget for the maintenance of any Provincial work undertaken by the Synod, such budget to be raised in such manner as the Synod may determine; (e) to create by Ordinance a provincial Council with power to administer and carry on such work as may be committed to it by the General Convention, or by the Presiding Bishop and the Executive Council, or by the Synod of the Province.

Sec. 10. Within sixty days after each session of the General Convention, the Presidents of the two Houses thereof shall refer to the Provincial Synods, or any of them, such subjects as the General Convention may direct, or as they may deem advisable, for consideration thereof by the Synods, and it shall be the duty of such Synods to consider the subject or subjects so referred to them at the first meeting of the Synod held after the adjournment of the General Convention, and to report their action and judgment in the matter to the Secretary of the General Convention at least six months before the date of the meeting of the next General Convention.

To consider referrals by General Convention.

Sec. 11. Each Provincial Synod shall keep minutes, journals or other records of its meetings, and shall transmit one copy of the records to the Secretary of the House of Deputies, and one copy to The Archives of The Episcopal Church. The Synod shall also transmit copies of any unpublished inactive records to the Archives.

Records to Archives.

Sec. 12. The President of each Province shall annually submit to the Executive Council a written report on the ministries, programs and other work of the Province, including a description of how funds appropriated by the General Convention have been used, and shall report on their work to the Executive Council, on the date and in the form specified by the Executive Council.

Annual report.

Canon 10: Of New Dioceses

Sec. 1. Whenever a new Diocese is proposed to be formed within the limits of any Diocese, or by the junction of two or more Dioceses, or parts of Dioceses, the Ecclesiastical Authorities and the Standing Committees of the Dioceses involved in the proposed new diocese shall submit for approval to the Conventions of each Diocese involved a joint agreement of union setting forth their agreements, including the manner of determining the Bishop Diocesan and other Bishops (if any), the provisions of the Constitution and Canons of the new Diocese, and such other matters as may be necessary or proper. Upon approval by the Conventions of each of the involved Dioceses, the joint agreement of union

Primary Convention.

shall be submitted for ratification by the General Convention no less than ninety days prior to the first legislative day of the next meeting of the General Convention.

How called with no Bishop.

Sec. 2. Promptly after ratification by the General Convention, the Ecclesiastical Authority of the new Diocese, as set forth in the joint agreement of union, shall call the Primary Convention of the new Diocese, for the purpose of enabling it to organize, and shall fix the time and place of holding the same, such place being within the territorial limits of the new Diocese.

Division of existing Diocese.

Sec. 3. Whenever one Diocese is about to be divided into two Dioceses, the Convention of such Diocese shall declare which portion thereof is to be in the new Diocese, and shall make the same known to the General Convention before the ratification of such division.

Union with General Convention.

Sec. 4. Whenever a new Diocese shall have organized in Primary Convention in accordance with the provisions of the Constitution and Canons in such case made and provided, and in the manner prescribed in the previous Sections of this Canon, and shall have chosen a name and acceded to the Constitution of the General Convention in accordance with Article V, Section 1 of the Constitution, and shall have laid before the Executive Council certified copies of the Constitution adopted at its Primary Convention, and the proceedings preparatory to the formation of the proposed new Diocese, such new Diocese shall thereupon be admitted into union with the General Convention.

Convocation may elect Deputies and Bishop.

Sec. 5. In the event of the erection of an Area Mission into a Diocese of this Church, as provided in Article V, Section 1, the Convocation of the Area Mission shall be entitled to elect Deputies to the succeeding General Convention, and also to elect a Bishop. The jurisdiction previously assigned to the Bishop in the Area Mission shall be terminated upon the admission of the new Diocese.

Provision for reunion of Dioceses.

Sec. 6 When a Diocese and one or more other Dioceses that were formed either by division therefrom or by erection into a Diocese or a Missionary Diocese formed by division therefrom, shall desire to be reunited into one Diocese, the proposed reunion must be initiated by the approval of the Conventions of the involved Dioceses of a joint agreement of union setting forth their agreements, including the manner of determining the Bishop Diocesan and other Bishops (if any), provisions of the Constitution and Canons of the new Diocese, and such other matters as may be necessary or proper. If the agreement of the Dioceses is made and the consents of their Conventions are given more than three months before the next meeting of the General Convention, the fact of the agreement and consents shall be certified by the Ecclesiastical Authority and the Secretary of the Convention of each involved Diocese to all the Bishops of the Church having jurisdiction and to the Standing Committees of all the Dioceses; and when the consents of a majority of such Bishops and of a majority of the Standing Committees to the proposed reunion shall have been received, the facts shall be similarly certified to the Secretary of the House of Deputies of the General Convention, and thereupon the reunion shall be considered complete. But if the agreement is made and the consents given within three months of the next meeting of the General Convention, the facts shall be certified instead to the Secretary of the House of Deputies, who shall lay them before the two Houses; and the reunion shall be deemed to be complete when it shall have been approved by a majority vote in the House of Bishops, and in the House of Deputies.

Sec. 7 When the union of two or more Dioceses or portions of Dioceses or the reunion of the two or more Dioceses shall have been completed, the facts shall be certified to the Presiding Bishop and to the Secretary of the House of Deputies. Thereupon the Presiding Bishop shall notify the Secretary of the House of Bishops of any alteration in the status or style of the Bishop or Bishops concerned, and the Secretary of the House of Deputies shall strike the name of any Diocese that will cease to exist or is being renamed from the roll of Dioceses in union with the General Convention and, if appropriate, amend the name of the newly united Diocese on the roll of Dioceses in union with the General Convention.

Certification and enactment.

Canon 11: Of Missionary Jurisdictions

Responsibility of the whole Church.

Sec. 1. Area Missions established in accordance with Article VI, Sec. 1 and Missionary Dioceses organized in accordance with Article VI, Sec. 3 shall constitute jurisdictions for which this Church as a whole assumes a special responsibility.

House of Bishops may establish Area Missions.

Sec. 2

a. The House of Bishops may establish a Mission in any Area not included within the boundaries of a Diocese of this Church, or of a Church in full communion with this Church, under such conditions and agreements, not inconsistent with the Constitution and Canons of this Church, as shall be approved by the House of Bishops from time to time.

May be ecumenical.

b. Such Area Mission may be undertaken under the sole auspices of this Church, or it may be undertaken jointly with another Christian body or bodies, on such terms as shall not compromise the doctrines of the Christian faith as this Church has received the same.

Bishops to be assigned to oversee Area Missions.

c. For every such Area Mission, a Bishop of this Church, or of a Church in full communion with this Church, shall be assigned by the House of Bishops to give episcopal oversight. The person so assigned, if a Bishop of this Church, shall, for the duration of such assignment, exercise jurisdiction as a Missionary Bishop under these Canons, so far as they are applicable to the Area Mission; and should occasion arise for the function of a Standing Committee or a Commission on Ministry, the Bishop shall appoint a board or boards of Clergy and Lay Persons resident in the area, to fulfill such functions as may be required.

d. Except as may be expressly provided otherwise in the agreements referred to in paragraph a. of this Section, the Bishop having jurisdiction in an Area Mission may authorize the use of such forms of worship as the Bishop may judge appropriate to the circumstances.

May be terminated by House of Bishops.

e. (An Area Mission may be terminated by the House of Bishops as a mission of this Church; or it may be transferred by them to become a mission of another Church, or to become a constituent part of an autonomous Province in full communion with this Church; or it may organize itself as an extra-provincial Diocese.

f. An Area Mission which shall have been undertaken under the sole auspices of this Church, with a Bishop of this Church assigned to give episcopal oversight, shall be entitled to representation in the Provincial House of Bishops and the Provincial House of Deputies in the Province of which it is a part.

Representation in its Province.

g. In the event of a vacancy in the office of Bishop assigned jurisdiction in an Area Mission, the charge thereof shall devolve upon the Presiding Bishop, with the power of appointing some other Bishop as his substitute in such charge, until the vacancy is filled by the House of Bishops.

Episcopal vacancy.

Sec. 3

May be organized as Missionary Diocese.

a. An Area not previously organized as a Diocese, and not under the permanent jurisdiction of a Bishop in full communion with this Church, may, upon application for admission, in accordance with the procedures of Article V, Section 1, be admitted as a Diocese, and may be accepted as a Missionary Diocese within the meaning of Sec. 1 of this Canon. Such Missionary Diocese, and every present Missionary Diocese organized by the House of Bishops under previously existing Canons and admitted into union with the General Convention, shall be governed by a Constitution and Canons, adopted by the Convention of the said Diocese, which acknowledge the authority of the Constitution and Canons of the General Convention, and incorporate the provisions set forth in the subsequent paragraphs of this section.

To adopt a Constitution and Canons.

b. In the event a Missionary Diocese beyond the territory of the United States of America is incapable of functioning as a jurisdiction in union with The Episcopal Church, and the Bishop, or if there be none the Ecclesiastical Authority, of such Diocese, after consultation with appropriate diocesan authorities and the Presiding

Transfer to another Province.

Bishop agree that continuation in union with this Church is no longer feasible, the Presiding Bishop is authorized, after consultation with the appropriate authorities in the Anglican Communion, to take such action as needed for such Diocese to become a constituent part of another Province or Regional Council in full communion with this Church.

Convention to elect officials.

c. In every Missionary Diocese there shall be an annual Convention, composed of the Bishop or Bishops, the other Clergy of the Diocese, and Lay Delegates from the organized Congregations. Such Convention shall elect a Standing Committee, in accordance with the diocesan Canons, which shall have the powers and duties set forth for Standing Committees in Canon I.12 and in other Canons of the General Convention. It shall also elect Clerical and Lay Deputies and alternate Deputies to the General Convention, in accordance with its diocesan Canons, and the provisions of Article I.4 of the Constitution. If the Missionary Diocese is a member of a Province of this Church, it shall also provide for Clerical and Lay Deputies and alternate Deputies to the Synod, in accordance with the diocesan Canons and the provisions of the Ordinances of the Province.

Missionary Diocese to adopt a budget.

d. The Convention of a Missionary Diocese shall also adopt an annual budget and program for the Diocese, and provide for the means of its administration throughout the year; and shall make provision for the review and approval of requests for grants in aid from the Executive Council or other sources of funds, both toward current operations and for capital needs.

Election of Bishop.

e. The election of the Bishop of a Missionary Diocese, in the event of a vacancy, or, when canonical consent is given, the election of a person to be Bishop Coadjutor or Bishop Suffragan, shall be made by a Diocesan Convention in accordance with its own Canons, and the provisions of Canon III.11 of the General Convention.

General Convention may grant autonomy.

f. At the request of the Convention of a Missionary Diocese, supported by the presentation of relevant facts and a reasonable plan, the General Convention may by joint

Resolution (1) permit the Diocese seeking autonomy to unite with another Province, or Regional Council having metropolitical authority, of the Anglican Communion, or (2) permit the Diocese seeking autonomy but not planning to unite with another Province or Regional Council, to unite with no less than three other viable Dioceses at the same time which are geographically contiguous, or so located geographically as to be considered of the same region, for the purpose of establishing a new Province, or new Regional Council having metropolitical authority, of the Anglican Communion.

May transfer to another Province or Regional Council.

g. At the request of the Convention of a Missionary Diocese, accompanied by the Bishop's written resignation of permanent jurisdiction therein, the General Convention may alter the status of a Missionary Diocese to that of an Area Mission, under such terms and conditions as may be stipulated by the House of Bishops in accordance with Canon I.11.2.a; and in such case, its right to representation by Deputies in the General Convention shall cease.

Missionary Diocese may become an Area Mission.

Sec. 4. Notice shall be sent to all Archbishops and Metropolitans, and all Presiding Bishops, of Churches in full communion with this Church, of the establishment of any Area Mission, or of the organization or change of status of any Missionary Diocese outside the United States; and of the consecration, or assignment, of a Missionary Bishop therefor.

Notices to be sent to Primates.

It is hereby declared as the judgment of this Church that no two Bishops of Churches in full communion with each other should exercise jurisdiction in the same place; except as may be defined by a concordat adopted jointly by the competent authority of each of the said Churches, after consultation with the appropriate inter-Anglican body.

Exercise of jurisdiction.

Canon 12: Of Standing Committees

Sec. 1. In every Diocese the Standing Committee shall elect from their own body a President and a Secretary. They may meet in conformity with their own rules from time to time,

Meetings.

and shall keep a record of their proceedings; and they may be summoned to a special meeting whenever the President may deem it necessary. They may be summoned on the requisition of the Bishop, whenever the Bishop shall desire their advice; and they may meet of their own accord and agreeably to their own rules when they may be disposed to advise the Bishop.

Quorum. **Sec. 2.** In all cases in which a Canon of the General Convention directs a duty to be performed, or a power to be exercised, by a Standing Committee, or by the Clerical members thereof, or by any other body consisting of several members, a majority of said members, the whole having been duly cited to meet, shall be a quorum; and a majority of the quorum so convened shall be competent to act, unless the contrary is expressly required by the Canon.

Signed originals. **Sec. 3.** Any document required to be signed by members of the Standing Committee or by the Clerical members thereof, or by any other body consisting of several members may be signed in counterparts each of which shall be deemed an original.

Canon 13: Of Parishes and Congregations

Jurisdiction of Congregation and Clergy. **Sec. 1.** Every Congregation of this Church shall belong to the Church in the Diocese in which its place of worship is situated; a Member of the Clergy serving a Cure having Congregations in more than one jurisdiction shall have such rights, including vote, in the Convention of the jurisdiction in which the Member of the Clergy has canonical residence

Canonical residence. as may be provided in the Canons of that diocese and may be granted seat and voice in the jurisdiction(s) in which the Member of the Clergy does not have canonical residence.

Parish boundaries. **Sec. 2**

a. The ascertainment and defining of the boundaries of existing Parishes or Parochial Cures, as well as the establishment of a new Parish or Congregation, and the formation of a new Parish within the limits of any other Parish, is left to the action of the several Diocesan Conventions.

b. Until a Canon or other regulation of a Diocesan Convention shall have been adopted, the formation of new Parishes, or the establishment of new Parishes or Congregations within the limits of existing Parishes, shall be vested in the Bishop of the Diocese, acting by and with the advice and consent of the Standing Committee thereof, and, in case of there being no Bishop, of the Ecclesiastical Authority.

Formation of new Parish within limits of existing Parish.

Sec. 3

Boundaries of Parish when not defined by law.

a. Where Parish boundaries are not defined by law, or settled by action of the Convention of the Diocese under Section 2 of this Canon, or are not otherwise settled, they shall be defined by the civil divisions of the State as follows:

b. Parochial boundaries shall be the limits as fixed by law, of a village, town, township, incorporated borough, city, or of some division of any such civil district, which may be recognized by the Bishop, acting with the advice and consent of the Standing Committee, as constituting the boundaries of a Parish.

c. If there be but one Church or Congregation within the limits of such village, town, township, borough, city, or such division of a civil district, as herein provided, the same shall be deemed the Parochial Cure of the Member of the Clergy having charge thereof. If there be two or more Churches or Congregations therein, it shall be deemed the Cure of the Members of the Clergy thereof.

Parochial Cure.

d. This Canon shall not affect the legal rights of property of any Parish or Congregation.

Not to affect legal rights.

Canon 14: Of Parish Vestries

Sec. 1. In every Parish of this Church the number, mode of selection, and term of office of Wardens and Members of the Vestry, with the qualifications of voters, shall be such as the State or Diocesan law may permit or require, and the Wardens and Members of the Vestry selected under such law shall hold office until their successors are selected and have qualified.

Regulations left to State or Diocesan law.

As agents and legal representatives.

Sec. 2. Except as provided by the law of the State or of the Diocese, the Vestry shall be agents and legal representatives of the Parish in all matters concerning its corporate property and the relations of the Parish to its Clergy.

Rector to preside.

Sec. 3. Unless it conflicts with the law as aforesaid, the Rector, or such other member of the Vestry designated by the Rector, shall preside in all the meetings of the Vestry.

Canon 15: Of Congregations in Foreign Lands

Congregations in foreign lands.

Sec. 1. It shall be lawful, under the conditions hereinafter stated, to organize a Congregation in any foreign land and not within the jurisdiction of any Missionary Bishop of this Church nor within any Diocese, Province, or Regional Church of the Anglican Communion.

Who may officiate temporarily.

Sec. 2. The Bishop in charge of such Congregations, and the Council of Advice hereinafter provided for, may authorize any Presbyter of this Church to officiate temporarily at any place to be named by them within any such foreign land, upon being satisfied that it is expedient to establish at such place a Congregation of this Church.

Organization.

Sec. 3. Such Presbyter, after having publicly officiated at such place on four consecutive Sundays, may give notice, in the time of Divine Service, that a meeting of the persons of full age and attending the services, will be held, at a time and place to be named by the Presbyter in charge, to organize the Congregation. The said meeting may proceed to effect an organization subject to the approval of the said Bishop and Council of Advice and in conformity to such regulations as the said Council of Advice may provide.

To recognize Constitution and Canons.

Sec. 4. Before being taken under the direction of the General Convention of this Church, such Congregation shall be required, in its Constitution, or Plan, or Articles of Organization, to recognize and accede to the Constitution, Canons, Doctrine, Discipline, and Worship of this Church, and to agree to submit to and obey such directions as may be, from time to time, received from the Bishop in charge and Council of Advice.

Sec. 5. The desire of such Congregation to be taken under the direction of the General Convention shall be duly certified by the Member of the Clergy, one Warden, and two Vestry members or Trustees of said Congregation, duly elected.

To be received by General Convention.

Sec. 6. Such certificate, and the Constitution, Plan, or Articles of Organization, shall be submitted to the General Convention, if it be in session, or to the Presiding Bishop at any other time; and in case the same are found satisfactory, the Secretary of the House of Deputies of the General Convention, under written instruction from the Presiding Bishop, shall thereupon place the name of the Congregation on the list of Congregations in foreign lands under the direction of the General Convention; and a certificate of the said official action shall be forwarded to and filed by the Registrar of this Church. Such Congregations are placed under the government and jurisdiction of the Presiding Bishop.

How accepted.

Sec. 7. The Presiding Bishop may, from time to time, by written commission under the episcopal signature and seal, assign to a Bishop or Bishops of this Church, or of a Church in full communion with this Church, the care of, and responsibility for, one or more of such Congregations and the Clergy officiating therein, for such period of time as the Presiding Bishop may deem expedient; *provided* that, should such term expire in a year during which a General Convention is to be held, prior to said Convention, the commission may be extended until the adjournment of the Convention.

Presiding Bishop may assign Bishop.

Sec. 8. Nothing in this Canon is to be construed as preventing the election of a Bishop to have charge of such Congregations under the provision of Canon III.12.1-4.

Sec. 9. To aid the Presiding Bishop or the Bishop in charge of these foreign Churches in administering the affairs of the same, and in settling such questions as may, by means of their peculiar situation, arise, a Council of Advice, consisting of four Clergy and four Lay Persons, shall be constituted as follows, and shall act as a Council of Advice to the Bishop in charge of the foreign Churches. They shall be chosen to serve for two years and until their successors are elected and have

Council of Advice.

accepted election, by a Convocation duly convened, of all the Clergy of the foreign Churches or Chapels, and of two Lay representatives of each Church or Chapel, chosen by its Vestry or Committee. The Council of Advice shall be convened on the requisition of the Bishop whenever the Bishop may desire their advice, and they may meet of their own accord and agreeably to their own rules when they may wish to advise the Bishop. When a meeting is not practicable, the Bishop may ascertain their mind by letter.

It shall be lawful for the Presiding Bishop at any time to authorize by writing under the episcopal hand and seal the Council of Advice to act as the Ecclesiastical Authority.

Members of the Clergy charged with canonical offense. **Sec. 10.** In the case a Member of the Clergy in charge of a Congregation or otherwise authorized to serve the Church in a foreign land shall be accused of any offense under the Canons of this Church:

a. With the permission of the Presiding Bishop, the Bishop in Charge and the Council of Advice may (i) engage a Diocese of this Church to provide the needed Disciplinary Structures to fulfill the requirements of the Canons of this Church, or (ii) establish among the Congregations of the Convocation the needed Disciplinary Structures to fulfill the requirements of the Canons of this Church. In either case, for the purposes of implementing the provisions for Ecclesiastical Discipline (Title IV) of a member of the Clergy, the Bishop in Charge shall serve the function reserved for the Bishop Diocesan, except that the Presiding Bishop must approve any Accord, any Agreement for Discipline and the terms of any Order, and pronounce the Sentence.

b. If no other provision has been made to organize or provide the Disciplinary Structures in fulfillment of the Canons on Ecclesiastical Discipline for a Congregation in a foreign land, it shall be the duty of the Bishop in charge of such Congregations to summon the Council of Advice, and cause an inquiry to be instituted as to the truth of such accusation; and should there be reasonable grounds for believing the same to be true, the said Bishop and the Council of Advice shall appoint a

Commission, consisting of three Clergy and two Lay Persons, whose duty it shall be to meet in the place where the accused resides, and to obtain all the evidence in the case from the parties interested; they shall give to the accused all rights under the Canons of this Church which can be exercised in a foreign land. The judgment of the said Commission, solemnly made, shall then be sent to the Bishop in charge, and to the Presiding Bishop, and, if approved by them, shall be carried into effect; *provided* that no such Commission shall recommend any other discipline than admonition or removal of the Member of the Clergy from charge of said Congregation. Should the result of the inquiry of the aforesaid Commission reveal evidence tending, in their judgment, to show that said Member of the Clergy deserves a more severe discipline, all the documents in the case shall be placed in the hands of the Presiding Bishop, who may proceed against the Member of the Clergy, as far as possible, according to the Canons of the General Convention.

Proviso.

Sec. 11. If there be a Congregation within the limits of any city in a foreign land, no new Congregation shall be established in that city, except with the consent of the Bishop in charge and the Council of Advice.

Limitation on new Congregations.

Sec. 12. In case of a difference between the Member of the Clergy and a Congregation in a foreign land, the Bishop in charge shall duly examine the same, and the said Bishop shall, with the Council of Advice, have full power to settle and adjust such difference upon principles recognized in the Canons of the General Convention.

Pastoral relationship.

Sec. 13. No Member of the Clergy shall be allowed to take charge of a Congregation in a foreign land, organized under this Canon, until nominated by the Vestry thereof, or, if there be no Vestry, by the Council of Advice, and approved by the Bishop in charge; and once having accepted such appointment, the Member of the Clergy shall be transferred to the jurisdiction of the Presiding Bishop.

Appointment of Clergy.

Canon 16: Of Clergy and Congregations Seeking Affiliation with This Church

Congregation seeking affiliation with this Church.

Sec. 1. Whenever a Congregation of Christian people, holding the Christian faith as set forth in the Catholic creeds and recognizing the Scriptures as containing all things necessary to salvation, but using a rite other than that set forth by this Church, shall desire affiliation with this Church, while retaining the use of its own rite, such congregation shall, with the consent of the Bishop in whose Diocese it is situate, make application through the Bishop to the Presiding Bishop for status.

Non-episcopal ordination.

Sec. 2. Any person who has not received episcopal ordination, and desires to serve such a Congregation as a Member of the Clergy, shall conform to the provisions of Canon III.10.4.

Clergy regularly ordained.

Sec. 3. A Member of the Clergy of such Congregation who shall have been ordained by a Bishop not in full communion with this Church, but the regularity of whose ordination is approved by the Presiding Bishop, shall be admitted in the appropriate Order under the provision of Canon III.10.3.

Seat but no vote.

Sec. 4. Clergy and delegates of such Congregations may have seats but no vote in the Diocesan Convention unless by formal action of such Convention they are so admitted.

Oversight with Bishop of Diocese.

Sec. 5. The oversight of Congregations so admitted shall rest with the Bishop of the Diocese unless the Bishop delegates this authority to another Bishop who may be commissioned by the Presiding Bishop to have oversight of such Congregations.

Canon 17: Of Regulations Respecting the Laity

Baptized members.

Sec. 1

a. All persons who have received the Sacrament of Holy Baptism with water in the Name of the Father, and of the Son, and of the Holy Spirit, whether in this Church or in another Christian Church, and whose Baptisms have been duly recorded in this Church, are members thereof.

b. Members sixteen years of age and over are to be considered adult members.

Adult members.

c. It is expected that all adult members of this Church, after appropriate instruction, will have made a mature public affirmation of their faith and commitment to the responsibilities of their Baptism and will have been confirmed or received by the laying on of hands by a Bishop of this Church or by a Bishop of a Church in full communion with this Church. Those who have previously made a mature public commitment in another Church may be received by the laying on of hands by a Bishop of this Church, rather than confirmed.

Members confirmed or received.

d. Any person who is baptized in this Church as an adult and receives the laying on of hands by the Bishop at Baptism is to be considered, for the purpose of this and all other Canons, as both baptized and confirmed; also,

Adult baptism.

Any person who is baptized in this Church as an adult and at some time after the Baptism receives the laying on of hands by the Bishop in Reaffirmation of Baptismal Vows is to be considered, for the purpose of this and all other Canons, as both baptized and confirmed; also,

Any baptized person who received the laying on of hands at Confirmation (by any Bishop in historic succession) and is received into The Episcopal Church by a Bishop of this Church is to be considered, for the purpose of this and all other Canons, as both baptized and confirmed; and also,

Any baptized person who received the laying on of hands by a Bishop of this Church at Confirmation or Reception is to be considered, for the purpose of this and all other Canons, as both baptized and confirmed.

Sec. 2

Communicants.

a. All members of this Church who have received Holy Communion in this Church at least three times during the preceding year are to be considered communicants of this Church.

b. For the purposes of statistical consistency throughout the Church, communicants sixteen years of age and over are to be considered adult communicants.

Adult communicants.

Communicants in good standing.

Sec. 3. All communicants of this Church who for the previous year have been faithful in corporate worship, unless for good cause prevented, and have been faithful in working, praying, and giving for the spread of the Kingdom of God, are to be considered communicants in good standing.

Removing to another congregation.

Sec. 4

a. A member of this Church removing from the congregation in which that person's membership is recorded shall procure a certificate of membership indicating that that person is recorded as a member (or adult member) of this Church and whether or not such a member:

    1. is a communicant;

    2. is recorded as being in good standing;

    3. has been confirmed or received by a Bishop of this Church or a Bishop in full communion with this Church.

    Upon acknowledgment that a member who has received such a certificate has been enrolled in another congregation of this or another Church, the Member of the Clergy in charge or Warden issuing the certificate shall remove the name of the person from the parish register.

Recorded in Register.

b. The Member of the Clergy in charge or Warden of the congregation to which such certificate is surrendered shall record in the parish register the information contained on the presented certificate of membership, and then notify the Member of the Clergy in charge or Warden of the congregation which issued the certificate that the person has been duly recorded as a member of the new congregation. Whereupon the person's removal shall be noted in the parish register of the congregation which issued the certificate.

c. If a member of this Church, not having such a certificate, desires to become a member of a congregation in the place to which he or she has removed, that person shall be directed by the Member of the Clergy in charge of the said congregation to procure a certificate from the former congregation, although on failure to produce such a certificate through no fault of the person applying, appropriate entry may be made in the parish register upon the evidence of membership status sufficient in the judgment of the Member of the Clergy in charge or Warden.

d. Any communicant of any Church in full communion with this Church shall be entitled to the benefit of this section so far as the same can be made applicable.

Sec. 5. No one shall be denied rights, status or access to an equal place in the life, worship, governance, or employment of this Church because of race, color, ethnic origin, national origin, marital or family status (including pregnancy or child care plans), sex, sexual orientation, gender identity and expression, disabilities or age, except as otherwise specified by Canons.

Rights of Laity.

Sec. 6. A person to whom the Sacraments of the Church shall have been refused, or who has been repelled from the Holy Communion under the rubrics, or who has been informed of an intention to refuse or repel him or her from the Holy Communion under the rubrics, may appeal to the Bishop or Ecclesiastical Authority. A Priest who refuses or repels a person from the Holy Communion, or who communicates to a person an intent to repel that person from the Holy Communion shall inform that person, in writing, within fourteen days thereof of (i) the reasons therefor and (ii) his or her right to appeal to the Bishop or Ecclesiastical Authority. No Member of the Clergy of this Church shall be required to admit to the Sacraments a person so refused or repelled without the written direction of the Bishop or Ecclesiastical Authority. The Bishop or Ecclesiastical Authority may in certain circumstances see fit to require the person to be admitted or restored because of the insufficiency of the cause assigned by the member of the Clergy. If it shall appear to the Bishop or Ecclesiastical Authority that there is sufficient cause to justify refusal of the Holy Communion, however, appropriate steps shall be taken to institute such inquiry as may be directed by the Canons of the Diocese; and should no such Canon exist, the Bishop or Ecclesiastical Authority shall proceed according to

Refusal of Holy Communion.

such principles of law and equity as will ensure an impartial investigation and judgment, which judgment shall be made in writing within sixty days of the appeal and which shall also specify the steps required for readmission to Holy Communion.

Eligibility for Communion.

Sec. 7. No unbaptized person shall be eligible to receive Holy Communion in this Church.

Fiduciary responsibility.

Sec. 8. Any person accepting any office in this Church shall well and faithfully perform the duties of that office in accordance with the Constitution and Canons of this Church and of the Diocese in which the office is being exercised.

Canon 18: Of the Celebration and Blessing of Marriage

Legal and canonical requirements.

Sec. 1. Every Member of the Clergy of this Church shall conform to the laws of the State governing the creation of the civil status of marriage, and also these canons concerning the solemnization of marriage. Members of the Clergy may solemnize a marriage using any of the liturgical forms authorized by this Church.

Notice of intention.

Sec. 2. The couple shall notify the Member of the Clergy of their intent to marry at least thirty days prior to the solemnization; *provided* that if one of the parties is a member of the Congregation of the Member of the Clergy, or both parties can furnish satisfactory evidence of the need for shortening the time, this requirement can be waived for weighty cause; in which case the Member of the Clergy shall immediately report this action in writing to the Bishop.

Conditions.

Sec. 3. Prior to the solemnization, the Member of the Clergy shall determine:

a. that both parties have the right to marry according to the laws of the State and consent to do so freely, without fraud, coercion, mistake as to the identity of either, or mental reservation; and

b. that at least one of the parties is baptized; and

c. that both parties have been instructed by the Member of the Clergy, or a person known by the Member of the

Clergy to be competent and responsible, in the nature, purpose, and meaning, as well as the rights, duties and responsibilities of marriage.

Sec. 4. Prior to the solemnization, the parties shall sign the following Declaration of Intention:

We understand the teaching of the church that God's purpose for our marriage is for our mutual joy, for the help and comfort we will give to each other in prosperity and adversity, and, when it is God's will, for the gift and heritage of children and their nurture in the knowledge and love of God. We also understand that our marriage is to be unconditional, mutual, exclusive, faithful, and lifelong; and we engage to make the utmost effort to accept these gifts and fulfill these duties, with the help of God and the support of our community.

Declaration.

Sec. 5. At least two witnesses shall be present at the solemnization, and together with the Member of the Clergy and the parties, sign the record of the solemnization in the proper register; which record shall include the date and place of the solemnization, the names of the witnesses, the parties and their parents, the age of the parties, Church status, and residence(s).

Recorded in Register.

Sec. 6. A bishop or priest may pronounce a blessing upon a civil marriage using any of the liturgical forms authorized by this Church.

Blessing a civil marriage.

Sec. 7. It shall be within the discretion of any Member of the Clergy of this Church to decline to solemnize or bless any marriage.

Canon 19: Of Regulations Respecting Holy Matrimony: Concerning Preservation of Marriage, Dissolution of Marriage, and Remarriage

Sec. 1. When marital unity is imperiled by dissension, it shall be the duty, if possible, of either or both parties, before taking legal action, to lay the matter before a Member of the Clergy; it shall be the duty of such Member of the Clergy to act first to protect and promote the physical and emotional

When marriage is imperiled.

safety of those involved and only then, if it be possible, to labor that the parties may be reconciled.

Application for judgment on marital status.

Sec. 2

a. Any member of this Church whose marriage has been annulled or dissolved by a civil court may apply to the Bishop or Ecclesiastical Authority of the Diocese in which such person is legally or canonically resident for a judgment as to his or her marital status in the eyes of the Church. Such judgment may be a recognition of the nullity, or of the termination of the said marriage; *provided* that no such judgment shall be construed as affecting in any way the legitimacy of children or the civil validity of the former relationship.

Judgment in writing.

b. Every judgment rendered under this Section shall be in writing and shall be made a matter of permanent record in the records of the Diocese.

Conditions for re-marriage.

Sec. 3. No Member of the Clergy of this Church shall solemnize the marriage of any person who has been the husband or wife of any other person then living, nor shall any member of this Church enter into a marriage when either of the contracting parties has been the husband or the wife of any other person then living, except as hereinafter provided:

a. The Member of the Clergy shall be satisfied by appropriate evidence that the prior marriage has been annulled or dissolved by a final judgment or decree of a civil court of competent jurisdiction.

b. The Member of the Clergy shall have instructed the parties that continuing concern must be shown for the well-being of the former spouse, and of any children of the prior marriage.

c. The Member of the Clergy shall consult with and obtain the consent of the Bishop of the Diocese wherein the Member of the Clergy is canonically resident or the Bishop of the Diocese in which the Member of the Clergy is licensed to officiate prior to, and shall report to that Bishop, the solemnization of any marriage under this Section.

d. If the proposed marriage is to be solemnized in a jurisdiction other than the one in which the consent has been given, the consent shall be affirmed by the Bishop of that jurisdiction.

Sec. 4. All provisions of Canon I.18 shall, in all cases, apply.

Canon 20: Of Churches in Full Communion

Sec. 1. The Episcopal Church, a member of the Anglican Communion, has a relationship of full communion with (i) those Churches that are also members of the Anglican Communion by action of the Anglican Consultative Council and (ii) those Churches in the historic succession with whom it entered into covenant agreements prior to 1980 and thereafter with those Churches in historic succession with whom it has entered into covenant agreements adopted by the General Convention:

Covenant relationships.

a. the Old Catholic Churches of the Union of Utrecht (via ratification of the Bonn Agreement of 1931 by the 51st General Convention in 1934),

b. la Iglesia Filipina Independiente/the Philippine Independent Church (via The Concordat of Full Communion Between the Iglesia Filipina Independiente and The Episcopal Church of 1961 adopted by the 60th General Convention in 1961), and

c. the Mar Thoma Syrian Church of Malabar(via the Mar Thoma Church - Episcopal Church Agreement of 1979).

d. The Episcopal Church has a relationship of full communion with the Evangelical Lutheran Church in Canada under the terms of the Memorandum of Mutual Recognition of Relations of Full Communion dated September 26, 2018 by and among The Episcopal Church, the Evangelical Lutheran Church in America, the Anglican Church of Canada and the Evangelical Lutheran Church in Canada, which was accepted by the 80th General Convention of The Episcopal Church as Resolution 2022-A092.

Evangelical Lutheran Church.

Sec. 2. The Episcopal Church has a relationship of full communion with the Evangelical Lutheran Church in America under the terms of and as defined by "Called to Common Mission", which was adopted by the 73rd General Convention of The Episcopal Church as Resolution 2000–A040.

Moravian Church.

Sec. 3. The Episcopal Church has a relationship of full communion with the Northern and Southern Provinces of the Moravian Church in America under the terms of and as defined by the "Finding Our Delight in the Lord: A Proposal for Full Communion Between The Episcopal Church; the Moravian Church-Northern Province; and the Moravian Church-Southern Province", which was adopted by the 76th General Convention of The Episcopal Church as Resolution 2009-A073.

Church of Sweden.

Sec. 4. The Episcopal Church has a relationship of full communion with the Church of Sweden under the terms of the Memorandum of Understanding between The Episcopal Church and the Church of Sweden (based upon the understandings set forth in the Report on the Grounds for Future Relations between the Church of Sweden and The Episcopal Church), which was accepted by the 80th General Convention of The Episcopal Church as Resolution 2022-A137.

Title II: Worship

The Lord's Day to be observed.

Canon 1: Of the Due Celebration of Sundays

All persons within this Church shall celebrate and keep the Lord's Day, commonly called Sunday, by regular participation in the public worship of the Church, by hearing the Word of God read and taught, and by other acts of devotion and works of charity, using all godly and sober conversation.

Canon 2: Of Translations of the Bible

Sec. 1. The Lessons prescribed in the Book of Common
Prayer shall be read from the translation of the Holy
Scriptures commonly known as the King James or
Authorized Version (which is the historic Bible of this
Church) together with the Marginal Readings authorized for
use by the General Convention of 1901; or from one of the
three translations known as Revised Versions, including the
English Revision of 1881, the American Revision of 1901, and
the Revised Standard Version of 1952; from the Jerusalem
Bible of 1966; from the New English Bible with the
Apocrypha of 1970; or from The 1976 Good News Bible
(Today's English Version); or from The New American Bible
(1970); or from The Revised Standard Version, an
Ecumenical Edition, commonly known as the "R.S.V.
Common Bible" (1973); or from The New International
Version (1978); or from The New Jerusalem Bible (1987); or
from the Revised English Bible (1989); or from the New
Revised Standard Version (1989, 2022); or from the
Contemporary English Version (1995); or from the
Contemporary English Version Global (2005); or from the
Common English Bible (2011); or from The Revised New
Jerusalem Bible (2019); or from translations, authorized by
the diocesan bishop, of those approved versions published
in any other language; or from other versions of the Bible,
including those in languages other than English, which
shall be authorized by diocesan bishops for specific use in
congregations or ministries within their dioceses.

*Authorized
versions.*

Sec. 2. All translations proposed for inclusion in Canon
II.2.1 must conform to the Criteria for Recommending New
Biblical Translations for Use in Public Worship adopted by
General Convention.

Sec. 3. All translations proposed for inclusion in Canon
II.2.1 must first be referred to the Standing Commission on
Liturgy and Music for review according to the Criteria for
Recommending New Biblical Translations for Use in Public
Worship.

Canon 3: Of the Standard Book of Common Prayer

Standard Book of Common Prayer.

Sec. 1. The copy of the Book of Common Prayer accepted by the General Convention of this Church, in the year of our Lord 1979, and authenticated by the signatures of the Presiding Officers and Secretaries of the two Houses of the General Convention, is hereby declared to be the Standard Book of Common Prayer of this Church.

All copies to conform.

Sec. 2. All copies of the Book of Common Prayer to be hereafter made and published shall conform to this Standard, and shall agree therewith in paging, and, as far as it is possible, in all other matters of typographical arrangement, except that the Rubrics may be printed either in red or black, and that page numbers shall be set against the several headings in the Table of Contents. The requirement of uniformity in paging shall apply to the entire book but shall not extend to editions smaller than those known as 32mo, or to editions noted for music.

Correcting inaccuracies.

Sec. 3. In case any typographical inaccuracy shall be found in the Standard Book of Common Prayer, its correction may be ordered by a joint Resolution of any General Convention, and notice of such corrections shall be communicated by the Custodian to the Ecclesiastical Authority of each Diocese of this Church, and to actual publishers of the Book of Common Prayer.

Copies of Standard to be sent to Dioceses.

Sec. 4. Folio copies of the Standard Book of Common Prayer, duly authenticated, as in the case of the Standard Book, shall be sent to the Ecclesiastical Authority of each Diocese in trust for the use thereof, and for reference and appeal in questions as to the authorized formularies of this Church.

All editions must be authorized.

Sec. 5. No copy, translation, or edition of the Book of Common Prayer, or a part or parts thereof, shall be made, printed, published, or used as of authority in this Church, unless it contains the authorization of the Custodian of the Standard Book of Common Prayer, certifying that the Custodian or some person appointed by the Custodian has compared the said copy, translation, or edition with the said

Standard, or a certified copy thereof, and that it conforms thereto. The Custodian, or some person appointed by the Custodian, may exercise due discretion in reference to translations of the entire Standard Book or parts thereof, into other languages so that such translations reflect the idiomatic style and cultural context of those languages. And no copy, translation, or edition of the Book of Common Prayer, or a part or parts thereof, shall be made, printed, published, or used as of authority in this Church, or certified as aforesaid, which contains or is bound up with any alterations or additions thereto, or with any other matter, except the Holy Scriptures or the authorized Hymnal of this Church, or with material set forth in the Book of Occasional Services and The Proper for the Lesser Feasts and Fasts, as those books are authorized from time to time by the General Convention.

Sec. 6   *Trial use.*

a. Whenever the General Convention, pursuant to Article X of the Constitution, shall authorize for trial use a proposed revision of the Book of Common Prayer, or of a portion or portions thereof, the enabling Resolution shall specify the period of such trial use, the precise text thereof, and any special terms or conditions under which such trial use shall be carried out including translation.

b. It shall be the duty of the Custodian of the Standard Book   *Duties of*
    of Common Prayer: *Custodian.*

    1. To arrange for the publication of such proposed revision;

    2. To protect, by copyright, the authorized text of such revision, on behalf of the General Convention; which copyright shall be relinquished when such proposed revision or revisions shall have been adopted by the General Convention as an alteration of, or addition to, the Book of Common Prayer;

    3. To certify that printed copies of such revision or revisions have been duly authorized by the General Convention, and that the printed text conforms to that approved by the General Convention.

Authorized trial use texts.

c. During the said period of trial use and under the modifying conditions specified, only the material so authorized, and in the exact form in which it has been so authorized, shall be available as an alternative for the said Book of Common Prayer or the said portion or portions thereof; *provided, however,* that it shall be competent for the Presiding Bishop and the President of the House of Deputies, jointly, on recommendation by a resolution duly adopted at a meeting of the Standing Commission on Liturgy and Music communicated to the said presiding officers in writing, to authorize variations and adjustments to, or substitutions for, or alterations in, any portion of the texts under trial, which seem desirable as a result of such trial use, and which do not change the substance of a rite.

d. In the event of the authorization of such variations, adjustments, substitutions, or alternatives, as aforesaid, it shall be the duty of the Custodian of the Standard Book of Common Prayer to notify the Ecclesiastical Authority of every Diocese, and the Convocation of the Episcopal Churches in Europe, of such action, and to give notice thereof through the media of public information.

Appointment of Custodian.

Sec. 7. The appointment of the Custodian of the Standard Book of Common Prayer shall be made by nomination of the House of Bishops and confirmed by the House of Deputies at a meeting of the General Convention. The Custodian shall hold office until the second General Convention following the General Convention at which the Custodian was nominated and confirmed. A vacancy occurring in the office of Custodian when General Convention is not meeting may be filled until the next General Convention by appointment by the Presiding Bishop upon the confirmation of the Executive Council.

Action on unauthorized editions.

Sec. 8. It shall be the duty of the Ecclesiastical Authority of any Diocese in which any unauthorized edition of the Book of Common Prayer, or any part or parts thereof, shall be published or circulated, to give public notice that the said edition is not of authority in this Church.

Canon 4: Of the Authorization of Special Forms of Service

In any Congregation, worshipping in other than the English language, which shall have placed itself under the oversight of a Bishop of this Church, it shall be lawful to use a form of service in such language; *provided* that such form of service shall have previously been approved by the Bishop of the Diocese, until such time as an authorized edition of the Book of Common Prayer in such language shall be set forth by the authority of the General Convention; and *provided further*, that no Bishop shall license any such form of service until first satisfied that the same is in accordance with the Doctrine and Worship of this Church; nor in any case shall such form of service be used for the ordination or consecration of Bishops, Priests, or Deacons.

Authorized forms in a foreign language.

Canon 5: Of the Music of the Church

It shall be the duty of every Member of the Clergy to see that music is used as an offering for the glory of God and as a help to the people in their worship in accordance with the Book of Common Prayer and as authorized by the rubrics or by the General Convention of this Church. To this end the Member of the Clergy shall have final authority in the administration of matters pertaining to music. In fulfilling this responsibility the Member of the Clergy shall seek assistance from persons skilled in music. Together they shall see that music is appropriate to the context in which it is used.

Clergy responsible for music.

Canon 6: Of Dedicated and Consecrated Churches

Sec. 1. No Church or Chapel shall be consecrated until the Bishop shall have been sufficiently satisfied that the building and the ground on which it is erected are secured for ownership and use by a Parish, Mission, Congregation, or Institution affiliated with this Church and subject to its Constitution and Canons.

Evidence of affiliation.

Consent to encumber or alienate consecrated property.

Sec. 2. It shall not be lawful for any Vestry, Trustees, or other body authorized by laws of any State or Territory to hold property for any Diocese, Parish or Congregation, to encumber or alienate any dedicated and consecrated Church or Chapel, or any Church or Chapel which has been used solely for Divine Service, belonging to the Parish or Congregation which they represent, without the previous consent of the Bishop, acting with the advice and consent of the Standing Committee of the Diocese.

Consent to deconsecrate Churches.

Sec. 3. No dedicated and consecrated Church or Chapel shall be removed, taken down, or otherwise disposed of for any worldly or common use, without the previous consent of the Standing Committee of the Diocese.

All Churches to be held in trust.

Sec. 4. Any dedicated and consecrated Church or Chapel shall be subject to the trust declared with respect to real and personal property held by any Parish, Mission, or Congregation as set forth in Canon I.7.4.

Title III: Ministry

Canon 1: Of the Ministry of All Baptized Persons

Responsibility of Diocese.

Sec. 1. Each Diocese shall make provision for the affirmation and development of the ministry of all baptized persons, including:

a. Assistance in understanding that all baptized persons are called to minister in Christ's name, to identify their gifts with the help of the Church and to serve Christ's mission at all times and in all places.

b. Assistance in understanding that all baptized persons are called to sustain their ministries through commitment to life-long Christian formation.

Access to discernment process.

Sec. 2. No person shall be denied access to the discernment process or to any process for the employment, licensing, calling, or deployment for any ministry, lay or ordained, in this Church because of race, color, ethnic origin, immigration status, national origin, sex, marital or family status (including pregnancy and child care plans), sexual orientation, gender identity and expression, disabilities or age, except as otherwise provided by these Canons. No right to employment, licensing, ordination, call, deployment, or election is hereby established.

Sec. 3. The provisions of these Canons for the admission of Candidates for the Ordination to the three Orders: Bishops, Priests and Deacons shall be equally applicable to men and women.

Equal applicability.

Canon 2: Of Commissions on Ministry

Sec. 1. In each Diocese there shall be a Commission on Ministry ("Commission") consisting of Priests, Deacons, if any, and Lay Persons. The Canons of each Diocese shall provide for the number of members, terms of office, and manner of selection to the Commission. Any Diocese may agree in writing with one or more other Dioceses to share a Commission on Ministry.

Dioceses to have a Commission.

Sec. 2. The Commission shall advise and assist the Bishop:

Duties.

a. In the implementation of Title III of these Canons.

b. In the determination of present and future opportunities and needs for the ministry of all baptized persons.

c. In the design and oversight of the ongoing process for recruitment, discernment, formation for ministry, and assessment of readiness therefor.

Sec. 3. The Commission may adopt rules for its work, subject to the approval of the Bishop; *provided* that they are not inconsistent with the Constitution and Canons of this Church and of the Diocese.

May adopt rules.

Sec. 4. The Commission may establish committees consisting of members and other persons to report to the Commission or to act on its behalf.

Sec. 5. The Bishop and Commission shall ensure that the members of the Commission and its committees receive ongoing education and training for their work.

Education and training.

Canon 3: Of Discernment

Sec. 1. The Bishop and Commission shall provide encouragement, training, and necessary resources to assist each congregation in developing an ongoing process of community discernment appropriate to the cultural background, age, and life experiences of all persons seeking direction in their call to ministry.

Discernment communities.

Sec. 2. The Bishop, in consultation with the Commission, may utilize college and university campus ministry centers and other communities of faith as additional communities where discernment takes place. In cases where these discernment communities are located in another jurisdiction, the Bishop will consult with the Bishop where the discernment community is located.

Recruiting leadership.

Sec. 3. The Bishop and Commission shall actively solicit from congregations, schools and other youth organizations, college and university campus ministry centers, seminaries, and other communities of faith names of persons whose demonstrated qualities of Christian commitment and potential for leadership and vision mark them as desirable candidates for positions of leadership in the Church.

Support for discernment process.

Sec. 4. The Bishop, Commission, and the discernment community shall assist persons engaged in a process of ministry discernment to determine appropriate avenues for the expression and support of their ministries, either lay or ordained.

Canon 4: Of Licensed Ministries

Sec. 1

Selection and license.

a. A confirmed communicant in good standing or, in extraordinary circumstances, subject to guidelines established by the Bishop, a communicant in good standing, may be licensed by the Ecclesiastical Authority to serve as Pastoral Leader, Worship Leader, Preacher, Eucharistic Minister, Eucharistic Visitor, Evangelist, or Catechist. Requirements and guidelines for the selection, training, continuing education, and deployment of such persons, and the duration of licenses shall be established by the Bishop in consultation with the Commission on Ministry.

b. The Presiding Bishop or the Bishop Suffragan for the Armed Forces of the United States, Veterans' Administration Medical Centers, and Federal Correctional Institutions may authorize a member of the Armed Forces to exercise one or more of these ministries in the Armed Forces in accordance with the provisions of this Canon. Requirements and guidelines for the selection, training, continuing education and deployment of such persons shall be established by the Bishop granting the license.

Member of the Armed Forces.

Sec. 2

Terms.

a. The Member of the Clergy or other leader exercising oversight of the congregation or other community of faith may request the Ecclesiastical Authority with jurisdiction to license persons within that congregation or other community of faith to exercise such ministries. The license shall be issued for a period of time to be determined under Canon III.4.1.a and may be renewed. The license may be revoked by the Ecclesiastical Authority upon request of or upon notice to the Member of the Clergy or other leader exercising oversight of the congregation or other community of faith.

b. In renewing the license, the Ecclesiastical Authority shall consider the performance of the ministry by the person licensed, continuing education in the licensed area, and the endorsement of the Member of the Clergy or other leader exercising oversight of the congregation or other community of faith in which the person is serving.

Renewal.

c. A person licensed in any Diocese under the provisions of this Canon may serve in another congregation or other community of faith in the same or another Diocese only at the invitation of the Member of the Clergy or other leader exercising oversight, and with the consent of the Ecclesiastical Authority in whose jurisdiction the service will occur.

Pastoral Leader. **Sec. 3.** A Pastoral Leader is a lay person authorized to exercise pastoral or administrative responsibility in a congregation under special circumstances, as defined by the Bishop.

Worship Leader. **Sec. 4.** A Worship Leader is a lay person who regularly leads public worship under the direction of the Member of the Clergy or other leader exercising oversight of the congregation or other community of faith.

Preacher. **Sec. 5.** A Preacher is a lay person authorized to preach. Persons so authorized shall only preach in congregations under the direction of the Member of the Clergy or other leader exercising oversight of the congregation or other community of faith.

Eucharistic Minister. **Sec. 6.** A Eucharistic Minister is a lay person authorized to administer the Consecrated Elements at a Celebration of Holy Eucharist. A Eucharistic Minister should normally act under the direction of a Deacon, if any, or otherwise, the Member of the Clergy or other leader exercising oversight of the congregation or other community of faith.

Eucharistic Visitor. **Sec. 7.** A Eucharistic Visitor is a lay person authorized to take the Consecrated Elements in a timely manner following a Celebration of Holy Eucharist to members of the congregation who, by reason of illness or infirmity, were unable to be present at the Celebration. A Eucharistic Visitor should normally act under the direction of a Deacon, if any, or otherwise, the Member of the Clergy or other leader exercising oversight of the congregation or other community of faith.

Catechist. **Sec. 8.** A Catechist is a lay person authorized to prepare persons for Baptism, Confirmation, Reception, and the Reaffirmation of Baptismal Vows, and shall function under the direction of the Member of the Clergy or other leader exercising oversight of the congregation or other community of faith.

Evangelist. **Sec. 9.** An Evangelist is a lay person who presents the good news of Jesus Christ in such a way that people are led to receive Christ as Savior and follow Christ as Lord in the fellowship of the Church. An Evangelist assists with the community's ministry of evangelism in partnership with the

Presbyter or other leader exercising oversight of the congregation, or as directed by the Bishop.

Canon 5: Of General Provisions Respecting Ordination

Sec. 1

Episcopal authority.

a. The canonical authority assigned to the Bishop Diocesan by this Title may be exercised by a Bishop Coadjutor, when so empowered under Canon III.11.9.a, and at the request of the Bishop Diocesan, by a Bishop Suffragan, or by any other Bishop of a Church in full communion with this Church who was ordained in the historic succession, at the request of the ordinand's Bishop.

b. The Council of Advice of the Convocation of Episcopal Churches in Europe, and the board appointed by a Bishop having jurisdiction in an Area Mission in accordance with the provisions of Canon I.11.2.c, shall, for the purpose of this and other Canons of Title III have the same powers as the Standing Committee of a Diocese.

c. In case of a vacancy in the episcopate in a Diocese, as defined in Canon III.12.4.d, the Ecclesiastical Authority may authorize and request the President of the House of Bishops of the Province to take order for an ordination.

Sec. 2 No Nominee, Postulant, or Candidate for ordination shall sign any of the certificates required by this Title.

a. Testimonials required of the Standing Committee by this Title must be signed by a majority of the whole Committee, at a meeting duly convened, except that testimonials may be executed in counterparts, any of which may be delivered by facsimile or other electronic transmission, each of which shall be deemed an original.

Testimonials.

b. Whenever the letter of support of a Vestry is required, the letter must be signed and dated by at least two-thirds of all of the members of the Vestry, at a meeting duly convened, and by the Rector or Priest-in-Charge of the Parish, and attested by the Clerk of the Vestry. Should there be no Rector or Priest-in-Charge, the letter

Vestry's letter of support.

shall be signed by a Priest of the Diocese acquainted with the nominee and the Parish, the reason for the substitution being stated in the attesting clause.

c. If the congregation or other discernment community of which the nominee is a member is not a Parish, the letter of support required by Canon III.6 or Canon III.8 shall be signed and dated by the Member of the Clergy and the council of the congregation or other community of faith, and shall be attested by the secretary of the meeting at which the letter was approved. Should there be no Member of the Clergy, the letter shall be signed and dated by a Priest of the Diocese acquainted with the nominee and the congregation or other community of faith, the reason for the substitution being stated in the attesting clause.

Member of a Religious Order or Community.

d. If the applicant is a member of a Religious Order or Christian Community recognized by Canon III.14, the letters of support referred to in Canon III.5 or Canon III.6 and any other requirements imposed on a congregation or Member of the Clergy may be given by the Superior or person in charge, and Chapter, or other comparable body of the Order or Community.

Dispensations.

Sec. 3. An application for any dispensation permitted by this Title from any of the requirements for ordination must first be made to the Bishop, and if approved, referred to the Standing Committee for its advice and consent.

Canon 6: Of the Ordination of Deacons

Sec. 1. Selection

Selection and nomination of Deacons.

The Bishop, in consultation with the Commission, shall establish procedures to identify and to select persons with evident gifts and fitness for ordination to the Diaconate.

Sec. 2. Nomination

A confirmed adult communicant in good standing, may be nominated for ordination to the diaconate by the person's congregation or other community of faith.

a. The Nomination shall be in writing and shall include a letter of support by the Nominee's congregation or other community of faith committing the community to

   1. pledge to contribute financially to that preparation, and

   2. involve itself in the Nominee's preparation for ordination to the Diaconate.

   If it be a congregation, the letter shall be signed by two-thirds of the Vestry or comparable body, and by the Member of the Clergy or leader exercising oversight.

b. The Nominee, if in agreement with the nomination, shall accept the nomination in writing and shall provide the following to the Bishop:

   Application for admission as Postulant.

   1. Full name and date of birth.

   2. The length of time resident in the Diocese.

   3. Evidence of Baptism and Confirmation.

   4. Whether an application has been made previously for Postulancy or the person has been nominated in any Diocese.

   5. A description of the process of discernment by which the Nominee has been identified for ordination to the Diaconate.

   6. The level of education attained and, if any, the degrees earned, and areas of specialization, together with copies of official transcripts.

Sec. 3. Postulancy

Postulancy is the time between nomination and candidacy and may initiate the formal preparation for ordination. Postulancy involves continued exploration of and decision about the Postulant's call to the Diaconate.

Postulancy for the Diaconate.

a. Before granting admission as a Postulant, the Bishop shall

1. determine that the Nominee is a confirmed adult communicant in good standing, and

2. confer in person with the Nominee,

Application review.

b. If the Bishop approves the Nominee proceeding into Postulancy, the Commission, or a committee of the Commission, shall meet with the Nominee to review the application and prepare an evaluation of the Nominee's qualifications to pursue a program of preparation for ordination to the Diaconate. The Commission shall present its evaluation and recommendations to the Bishop.

Previous refusal or cessation.

c. No Bishop shall consider accepting as a Postulant any person who has been refused admission as a Candidate for ordination to the Diaconate in any other Diocese, or who, having been admitted, has afterwards ceased to be a Candidate, until receipt of a letter from the Bishop of the Diocese refusing admission, or in which the person has been a Candidate, declaring the cause of refusal or of cessation.

Admission to Postulancy.

d. The Bishop may admit the Nominee as a Postulant for ordination to the Diaconate. The Bishop shall record the Postulant's name and date of admission in a Register kept for that purpose. The Bishop shall inform the Postulant, the Member of the Clergy or other leader exercising oversight of the Postulant's congregation or other community of faith, the Commission, the Standing Committee, and the director of the Postulant's program of preparation, of the fact and date of such admission.

Ember Weeks.

e. Each Postulant for ordination to the Diaconate shall communicate with the Bishop in person or by letter, four times a year, in the Ember Weeks, reflecting on the Postulant's academic, diaconal, human, spiritual, and practical development.

Removal.

f. Any Postulant may be removed as a Postulant at the sole discretion of the Bishop. The Bishop shall give written notice of the removal to the Postulant and the Member of the Clergy or other leader exercising oversight of the Postulant's congregation or other community of faith,

the Commission, the Standing Committee, and the
director of the program of preparation.

Sec. 4. Candidacy

Candidacy is a time of education and formation, in *Definition of*
preparation for ordination to the Diaconate, established by a *Candidacy.*
formal commitment by the Candidate, the Bishop, the
Commission, the Standing Committee and the congregation
or other community of faith.

a. A person desiring to be considered as a Candidate for
    ordination to the Diaconate shall apply to the Bishop.
    Such application shall include the following:

    1. the Postulant's date of admission to Postulancy, and

    2. a letter of support by the Postulant's congregation or
        other community of faith. If it be a congregation the
        letter shall be signed and dated by at least two-
        thirds of the Vestry or comparable body and by the
        Member of the Clergy or other leader exercising
        oversight.

b. Upon compliance with these requirements, and receipt of *Admission to*
    a written statement from the Commission attesting to *Candidacy.*
    the continuing formation of the Postulant, and having
    received approval in writing of the Standing Committee
    who shall have interviewed the Postulant and who shall
    have had an opportunity to review the documentation
    relating to the application of the Postulant, the Bishop
    may admit the Postulant as a Candidate for ordination to
    the Diaconate. The Bishop shall record the Candidate's
    name and date of admission in a Register kept for that
    purpose. The Bishop shall inform the Candidate, the
    Member of the Clergy or other leader exercising
    oversight of the Candidate's congregation or other
    community of faith, the Commission, the Standing
    Committee, and the Dean of the seminary the Candidate
    may be attending or proposes to attend, or the director
    of the Candidate's program of preparation, of the fact
    and date of such admission.

c. A Candidate must remain in canonical relationship with *Transfers to*
    the Diocese in which admission has been granted until *another Diocese.*

ordination to the Diaconate under this Canon, except, for reasons acceptable to the Bishop, the Candidate may be transferred to another Diocese upon request, provided that the Bishop of the receiving Diocese is willing to accept the Candidate.

Candidate may be removed.

d. Any Candidate may be removed as a Candidate, at the sole discretion of the Bishop. The Bishop shall give written notice of the removal to the Candidate and the Member of the Clergy or other leader exercising oversight of the Candidate's congregation or other community of faith, the Commission, the Standing Committee, and the director of the program of preparation.

e. If a Bishop has removed the Candidate's name from the list of Candidates, except by transfer, or the Candidate's application for ordination has been rejected, no other Bishop may ordain the person without readmission to Candidacy for a period of at least twelve months.

Sec. 5. Preparation for Ordination

a. The Bishop and the Commission shall work with the Postulant or Candidate to develop and monitor a program of preparation for ordination to the Diaconate in accordance with this Canon to ensure that pastoral guidance is provided throughout the period of preparation.

Assignment.

b. The Bishop may assign the Postulant or Candidate to any congregation of the Diocese or other community of faith after consultation with the Member of the Clergy or other leader exercising oversight.

Formation.

c. Formation shall take into account the local culture and each Postulant or Candidate's background, age, occupation, and ministry.

d. Prior education and learning from life experience may be considered as part of the formation required for ordination.

e. Wherever possible, formation for the Diaconate shall take place in community, including other persons in preparation for the Diaconate, or others preparing for ministry.

f. Before ordination each Candidate shall be prepared in
    and demonstrate basic competence in five general areas:

    Competencies.

    1. Academic studies including, The Holy Scriptures,
        theology, and the tradition of the Church.

    2. Diakonia and the diaconate.

    3. Human awareness and understanding.

    4. Spiritual development and discipline.

    5. Practical training and experience.

g. Preparation for ordination shall include training
    regarding

    Training.

    1. prevention of sexual misconduct against both
        children and adults.

    2. civil requirements for reporting and pastoral
        opportunities for responding to evidence of abuse.

    3. the Constitution and Canons of The Episcopal
        Church, particularly Title IV thereof.

    4. the Church's teaching on racism.

h. Each Candidate for ordination to the Diaconate shall
    communicate with the Bishop in person or by letter, four
    times a year, in the Ember Weeks, reflecting on the
    Candidate's academic, diaconal, human, spiritual, and
    practical development.

    Ember Weeks.

i. During Candidacy each Candidate's progress shall be
    evaluated from time to time, and there shall be a written
    report of the evaluation by those authorized by the
    Commission to be in charge of the evaluation program.
    Upon certification by those in charge of the Candidate's
    program of preparation that the Candidate has
    successfully completed preparation and is ready for
    ordination, a final written assessment of readiness for
    ordination to the Diaconate shall be prepared as
    determined by the Bishop in consultation with the
    Commission. This report shall include a recommendation
    from the Commission regarding the readiness of the
    Candidate for ordination. Records shall be kept of all
    evaluations, assessments, and the recommendation, and
    shall be made available to the Standing Committee.

    Evaluation of progress.

Examinations and evaluations.

j. Within thirty-six months prior to ordination as a Deacon, the following must be accomplished

    1. a background check, according to criteria established by the Bishop and Standing Committee.

    2. medical and psychological evaluation by professionals approved by the Bishop, using forms prepared for the purpose by the Standing Commission on Ministry and Formation in accordance with principles and directions adopted by the General Convention and if desired or necessary, psychiatric referral.

k. Reports of all investigations and examinations shall be kept permanently on file by the Bishop and remain a part of the permanent diocesan record.

Sec. 6. Ordination to the Diaconate

a. A person may be ordained Deacon:

    1. after at least eighteen months from the time of written acceptance of nomination by the Nominee as provided in III.6.2.b, and

    2. upon attainment of at least twenty-four years of age.

Ordination papers.

b. The Bishop shall obtain in writing and provide to the Standing Committee:

    1. an application from the Candidate requesting ordination as a Deacon under this Canon.

    2. a letter of support from the Candidate's congregation or other community of faith, signed and dated by at least two-thirds of the Vestry and the Member of the Clergy or other leader exercising oversight.

    3. written evidence of admission of the Candidate to Postulancy and Candidacy, giving the dates of admission.

    4. a certificate from the seminary or other program of preparation showing the Candidate's scholastic record in the subjects required by the Canons, and giving an evaluation with recommendation as to the Candidate's other personal qualifications for ordination together with a recommendation

regarding ordination to the Diaconate under this Canon.

5. a certificate from the Commission giving a recommendation regarding ordination to the Diaconate under this Canon.

c. On the receipt of such certificates, the Standing Committee, if a majority of all members consent, shall certify that the Canonical requirements for ordination to the Diaconate under this Canon have been met, that there is no sufficient objection on medical, psychological, moral, or spiritual grounds and that they recommend ordination. The Standing Committee shall evidence such certification, by a testimonial, addressed to the Bishop in the form specified below and signed by the consenting members of the Standing Committee.

Standing Committee to consent.

To the Right Reverend _____ **, Bishop of** _____ **We, the Standing Committee of** _____ **, having been duly convened at** _____ **at** _____ **, do testify that A.B., desiring to be ordained to the Diaconate under Canon III.6 has presented to us the certificates as required by the Canons indicating A.B.'s preparedness for ordination to the Diaconate under Canon III.6; and we certify that all canonical requirements for ordination to the Diaconate under Canon III.6 have been met; and we find no sufficient objection to ordination. Therefore, we recommend A.B. for ordination. In witness whereof, we have hereunto set our hands this** _____ **day of** _____ **, in the year of our Lord** _____ **.**

(Signed) _____

d. The testimonial having been presented to the Bishop, and there being no sufficient objection on medical, psychological, moral, or spiritual grounds, the Bishop may ordain the Candidate to the Diaconate under this Canon; and at the time of ordination the Candidate shall subscribe publicly and make, in the presence of the Bishop, the declaration required in Article VIII of the Constitution.

Declaration of conformity.

Canon 7: Of the Life and Work of Deacons

Sec. 1. Deacons serve directly under the authority of and are accountable to the Bishop, or in the absence of the Bishop, the Ecclesiastical Authority of the Diocese.

Community of Deacons.

Sec. 2. Deacons canonically resident in each Diocese constitute a Community of Deacons, which shall meet from time to time. The Bishop may appoint one or more of such Deacons as Archdeacon(s) to assist the Bishop in the formation, deployment, supervision, and support of the Deacons or those in preparation to be Deacons, and in the implementation of this Canon.

Council on Deacons.

Sec. 3. The Bishop may establish a Council on Deacons to oversee, study, and promote the Diaconate.

Sec. 4. The Bishop, after consultation with the Deacon and the Member of the Clergy or other leader exercising oversight, may assign a Deacon to one or more congregations, other communities of faith or non-parochial ministries. Deacons assigned to a congregation or other community of faith act under the authority of the Member of the Clergy or other leader exercising oversight in all matters concerning the congregation.

Rights and responsibilities.

a. Subject to the Bishop's approval, Deacons may have a letter of agreement setting forth mutual responsibilities in the assignment, and, if such a letter exists, it is subject to renegotiation with the Vestry/Bishop's Committee after the resignation of the Rector or the Priest-in-Charge.

b. Deacons shall report annually to the Bishop or the Bishop's designee on their life and work.

c. Deacons may serve as administrators of congregations or other communities of faith, but no Deacon shall be in charge of a congregation or other community of faith.

d. Deacons may accept chaplaincies in any hospital, prison, or other institution.

e. Deacons may participate in the governance of the Church.

f. For two years following ordination, new Deacons shall continue a process of formation authorized by the Bishop.

g. The Bishop or the Bishop's designee, in consultation with the Commission, shall assign each newly ordained Deacon a mentor Deacon where a suitable mentor Deacon is available. The mentor and Deacon and shall meet regularly for at least one year to provide guidance, information, and a sustained dialogue about diaconal ministry.

Mentors.

Sec. 5. The Bishop and Commission shall require and provide for the continuing education of Deacons and keep a record of such education.

Continuing education.

Sec. 6

a. A Deacon may not serve as Deacon for more than two months in any Diocese other than the Diocese in which the Deacon is canonically resident unless the Bishop of the other Diocese shall have granted a license to the Deacon to serve in that Diocese.

License to serve in another Diocese.

b. 1. A Deacon desiring to become canonically resident within a Diocese shall request a testimonial from the Ecclesiastical Authority of the Diocese in which the Deacon is canonically resident to present to the receiving Diocese, which testimonial, if granted, shall be given by the Ecclesiastical Authority to the applicant, and a duplicate thereof may be sent to the Ecclesiastical Authority of the Diocese to which transfer is proposed. The testimonial shall be in the following words:

Letters Dimissory.

I hereby certify that A.B., who has signified to me the desire to be transferred to the Ecclesiastical Authority of _____, is a Deacon of _____ in good standing, and has not, so far as I know or believe, been justly liable to evil report for error in religion or for viciousness of life, for the last three years.

(Date) _____

(Signed) _____

2. Such testimonial shall be called Letters Dimissory. If the Ecclesiastical Authority accepts the Letters Dimissory, the canonical residence of the Deacon so transferred shall date from the acceptance of the Letters Dimissory, of which prompt notice shall be given both to the applicant and to the Ecclesiastical Authority from which it came.

3. Letters Dimissory not presented within six months from the date of transmission to the applicant shall become void.

4. A statement of the record of payments to The Church Pension Fund by or on behalf of the Deacon concerned shall accompany Letters Dimissory.

Resignation. **Sec. 7.** On reaching the age of seventy-two years, a Deacon shall resign from all positions of active service in this Church, and the resignation shall be accepted. The Bishop may, with the consent of the Deacon, assign a resigned Deacon to any congregation, other community of faith or ministry in another setting, for a term not to exceed twelve months, and this term may be renewed.

Sec. 8. Release and Removal from the Ordained Ministry of this Church

Release and removal of a Deacon. If any Deacon of The Episcopal Church shall express, in writing, to the Bishop of the Diocese in which such Deacon is canonically resident, an intention to be released and removed from the ordained Ministry of this Church and from the obligations attendant thereto, including those promises made at Ordination in the Declaration required by Article VIII of the Constitution of the General Convention, it shall be the duty of the Bishop to record the matter. The Bishop, being satisfied that the person so declaring is acting voluntarily and for causes which do not affect the person's moral character, and is neither the subject of information concerning an Offense that has been referred to an Intake Officer nor a Respondent in a pending disciplinary matter as defined in Title IV of these Canons, shall lay the matter before the Standing Committee, and with the advice and consent of a majority of the Standing Committee the Bishop may pronounce that the person is released and removed from the ordained Ministry of this Church and from the obligations attendant thereto, and is deprived of the right to exercise in The Episcopal Church the gifts and spiritual authority as a Minister of God's Word and Sacraments conferred in Ordination. The Bishop shall also declare in pronouncing and recording such action that it was for causes which do not affect the person's moral character, and shall, at the person's request, give a certificate to this effect to the person so released and removed from the ordained Ministry.

In disciplinary cases.

Sec. 9. If a Deacon submitting the writing described in Section 8 of this Canon be the subject of information concerning an Offense that has been referred to an Intake Officer or a Respondent in a pending disciplinary matter as defined in Title IV of these Canons, the Ecclesiastical Authority to whom such writing is submitted shall not consider or act upon the written request unless and until the disciplinary matter shall have been resolved by a dismissal, Accord, or Order and the time for appeal or rescission of such has expired.

Declaration.

Sec. 10. In the case of the release and removal of a Deacon from the ordained Ministry of this Church as provided in this Canon, a declaration of release and removal shall be pronounced by the Bishop in the presence of two or more Members of the Clergy, and shall be entered in the official records of the Diocese in which the Deacon being released and removed is canonically resident. The Bishop who pronounces the declaration of release and removal as provided in this Canon shall give notice thereof in writing to every Member of the Clergy, each Vestry, the Secretary of the Convention and the Standing Committee of the Diocese in which the Deacon was canonically resident; and to all Bishops of this Church, the Ecclesiastical Authority of each Diocese of this Church, the Presiding Bishop, the Recorder of Ordinations, the Secretary of the House of Bishops, the Secretary of the House of Deputies, The Church Pension Fund, and the Board for Transition Ministry.

Sec. 11. Return to the Ordained Ministry of this Church after Release and Removal.

Return to
ordained
Ministry.

a. When a Deacon who has been released and removed from the ordained Ministry of this Church under Canon III.7.8 desires to return to that Ministry, the person shall apply in writing to the Bishop of the Diocese in which the Deacon was last canonically resident, attaching the following:

1. Evidence of previous ordination in The Episcopal Church;

2. Evidence of appropriate background checks, certifications and proof of completion of applicable trainings including abuse prevention and anti-racism trainings;

3. A statement from no fewer than two members of the clergy who know the applicant in support of the application;

4. A statement of the reasons for seeking to return to the ordained Ministry of this Church.

b. If the Bishop so chooses, the Bishop may give permission for the Deacon to continue the process toward reinstatement, which may include the following:

1. Active participation in a congregation for a period of time at the Bishop's discretion;

2. Regular contact with the Bishop or the Bishop's designee during the course of the process;

3. Evaluation by a licensed mental health professional of the Bishop's choosing for the purposes of evaluation and of determining fitness for resumption of ordained ministry in this church;

4. Two references from those who are able to discuss the Deacon's former ministry;

5. Meeting with the Standing Committee, who shall have the benefit of the materials above and who shall provide to the Bishop its recommendation regarding reinstatement.

c. Before the person may be permitted to return to the ordained Ministry of this Church, the Bishop shall require the Deacon seeking to return to the ministry to sign a written declaration as required in Article VIII of the Constitution, without recourse to any other ecclesiastical jurisdiction and execute such declaration in the presence of the Bishop and two or more members of the clergy of this Church.

d. Thereafter the Bishop, taking into account the facts and circumstances surrounding the Deacon's removal and release, may permit, with the advice and consent of the Standing Committee, the return of the Deacon into the ordained Ministry of this Church.

e. The provisions of this Canon III.7.11 shall not be applicable to any Deacon who has been removed, released, or deposed from their ministry as the result of any proceeding of Title IV of these Canons.

f. Notice of the Deacon's return to the ordained Ministry of this Church shall be provided in writing to the same persons and entities receiving notice under Canon III.7.10.

Canon 8: Of the Ordination of Priests

Sec. 1. Selection

The Bishop, in consultation with the Commission, shall establish procedures to identify and select persons with evident gifts and fitness for ordination to the Priesthood.

Selection and nomination to the Priesthood.

Sec. 2. Nomination

A confirmed adult communicant in good standing may be nominated for ordination to the Priesthood by the person's congregation or other community of faith.

a. The Nomination shall be in writing and shall include a letter of support by the Nominee's congregation or other community of faith committing the community to:

Application for admission to Postulancy.

　1. pledge to contribute financially to that preparation, and

　2. involve itself in the Nominee's preparation for ordination to the Priesthood.

If it be a congregation, the letter shall be signed by two-thirds of the Vestry or comparable body, and by the Member of the Clergy or leader exercising oversight.

b. The Nominee, if agreeing, shall accept the nomination in writing, and shall provide the following to the Bishop:

1. Full name and date of birth.

2. The length of time resident in the Diocese.

3. Evidence of Baptism and Confirmation.

4. Whether an application has been made previously for Postulancy or the person has been nominated in any Diocese.

5. A description of the process of discernment by which the Nominee has been identified for ordination to the Priesthood.

6. The level of education attained and, if any, the degrees earned and areas of specialization, together with copies of official transcripts.

Sec. 3. Postulancy

Postulancy for the Priesthood.

Postulancy is the time between nomination and candidacy and may initiate the formal preparation for ordination. Postulancy involves continued exploration of and decision about the Postulant's call to the Priesthood.

a. Before granting admission as a Postulant, the Bishop shall

1. determine that the person is a confirmed adult communicant in good standing.

2. confer in person with the Nominee.

3. shall consult with the Nominee regarding financial resources which will be available for the support of the Postulant throughout preparation for ordination. During Postulancy and later Candidacy, the Bishop or someone appointed by the Bishop shall review periodically the financial condition and plans of the Postulant.

b. If the Bishop approves proceeding, the Commission, or a committee of the Commission, shall meet with the Nominee to review the application and prepare an evaluation of the Nominee's qualifications to pursue a program of preparation for ordination to the Priesthood. The Commission shall present its evaluation and recommendations to the Bishop.

Application review.

c. No Bishop shall consider accepting as a Postulant any person who has been refused admission as a Candidate for ordination to the Priesthood in any other Diocese, or who, having been admitted, has afterwards ceased to be a Candidate, until receipt of a letter from the Bishop of the Diocese refusing admission, or in which the person has been a Candidate, declaring the cause of refusal or of cessation.

Previous removal or cessation.

d. The Bishop may admit the Nominee as a Postulant for ordination to the Priesthood. The Bishop shall record the Postulant's name and date of admission in a Register kept for that purpose. The Bishop shall inform the Postulant, the Member of the Clergy or other leader exercising oversight of the Postulant's congregation or other community of faith, the Commission, the Standing Committee, and the Dean of the seminary the Postulant may be attending or proposes to attend, or the director of Postulant's program of preparation, of the fact and date of such admission.

Admission to Postulancy.

e. Each Postulant for ordination to the Priesthood shall communicate with the Bishop in person or by letter, four times a year, in the Ember Weeks, reflecting on the Postulant's academic experience and personal and spiritual development.

Ember Weeks.

f. Any Postulant may be removed as a Postulant at the sole discretion of the Bishop. The Bishop shall give written notice of the removal to the Postulant and the Member of the Clergy or other leader exercising oversight of the Postulant's congregation or other community of faith, the Commission, the Standing Committee, and the director of the program of preparation.

Removal.

Sec. 4. Candidacy

Definition of Candidacy.

Candidacy is a time of education and formation in preparation for ordination to the Priesthood, established by a formal commitment by the Candidate, the Bishop, the Commission, the Standing Committee, and the congregation or other community of faith.

Application for Candidacy.

a. A person desiring to be considered as a Candidate for ordination to the Priesthood shall apply to the Bishop. Such application shall include the following:

    1. the Postulant's date of admission to Postulancy, and

    2. a letter of support by the Postulant's congregation or other community of faith. If it be a congregation, the letter shall be signed and dated by at least two-thirds of the Vestry or comparable body and by the Member of the Clergy or other leader exercising oversight.

Admission to Candidacy.

b. Upon compliance with these requirements, and receipt of a statement from the Commission attesting to the continuing formation of the Postulant, and having received approval in writing of the Standing Committee who shall have interviewed the Postulant and who shall have had an opportunity to review the documentation relating to the application of the Postulant, the Bishop may admit the Postulant as a Candidate for ordination to the Priesthood. The Bishop shall record the Candidate's name and date of admission in a Register kept for that purpose. The Bishop shall inform the Candidate, the Member of the Clergy or leader exercising oversight of the Candidate's congregation or other community of faith, the Commission, the Standing Committee, and the Dean of the seminary the Candidate may be attending or proposes to attend, or the director of the Candidate's program of preparation, of the fact and date of such admission.

Transfer to another Diocese.

c. A Candidate must remain in canonical relationship with the Diocese in which admission has been granted until ordination to the Diaconate under this Canon, except, for reasons acceptable to the Bishop, the Candidate may be transferred to another Diocese upon request, provided that the Bishop of the receiving Diocese is willing to accept the Candidate.

d. Any Candidate may be removed as a Candidate at the sole discretion of the Bishop. The Bishop shall give written notice of the removal to the Candidate and the Member of the Clergy or other leader exercising oversight of the Candidate's congregation or other community of faith, the Commission, the Standing Committee, and the Dean of the seminary the Candidate may be attending or the director of the program of preparation.

Candidate may be removed.

e. If a Bishop has removed the Candidate's name from the list of Candidates, except by transfer, or the Candidate's application for ordination has been rejected, no other Bishop may ordain the person without readmission to Candidacy for a period of at least twelve months.

Sec. 5. Preparation for Ordination

a. The Bishop and the Commission shall work with the Postulant or Candidate to develop and monitor a program of preparation for ordination to the Priesthood and to ensure that pastoral guidance is provided throughout the period of preparation.

b. If the Postulant or Candidate has not previously obtained a baccalaureate degree, the Commission, Bishop, and Postulant or Candidate shall design a program of such additional academic work as may be necessary to prepare the Postulant or Candidate to undertake a program of theological education.

Pre-theological education.

c. Formation shall take into account the local culture and each Postulant or Candidate's background, age, occupation, and ministry.

Formation.

d. Prior education and learning from life experience may be considered as part of the formation required for the Priesthood.

e. Whenever possible, formation for the Priesthood shall take place in community, including other persons in preparation for the Priesthood, or others preparing for ministry.

f. Formation shall include theological training, practical experience, emotional development, and spiritual formation.

Theological education.

g. Subject areas for study during this program of preparation shall include:

1. The Holy Scriptures.

2. History of the Christian Church.

3. Christian Theology.

4. Christian Ethics and Moral Theology.

5. Christian Worship according to the use of the Book of Common Prayer, the Hymnal, and authorized supplemental texts.

6. The Practice of Ministry in contemporary society, including leadership, evangelism, stewardship, ecumenism, interfaith relations, mission theology, and the historical and contemporary experience of racial and minority groups.

Training.

h. Preparation for ordination shall include training regarding

1. prevention of sexual misconduct against both children and adults.

2. civil requirements for reporting and pastoral opportunities for responding to evidence of abuse.

3. the Constitution and Canons of The Episcopal Church, particularly Title IV thereof, utilizing, but not limited to use of, the Title IV training website of The Episcopal Church.

4. the Church's teaching on racism.

Ember Weeks.

i. Each Postulant or Candidate for ordination to the Priesthood shall communicate with the Bishop in person or by letter, four times a year, in the Ember Weeks, reflecting on the Candidate's academic experience and personal and spiritual development.

Evaluation of progress.

j. The seminary or other formation program shall provide for, monitor, and report on the academic performance and personal qualifications of the Postulant or Candidate for ordination. These reports will be made upon request of the Bishop and Commission, but at least once per year.

k. Within thirty-six months prior to ordination as a Deacon under this Canon, the following must be accomplished

Examinations and evaluations.

1. a background check, according to criteria established by the Bishop and Standing Committee.

2. medical and psychological evaluation by professionals approved by the Bishop, using forms prepared for the purpose by the Standing Commission on Ministry and Formation in accordance with principles and directions adopted by the General Convention, and if desired or necessary, psychiatric referral.

l. Reports of all investigations and examinations shall be kept permanently on file by the Bishop and remain a part of the permanent diocesan record.

Sec. 6. Ordination to the Diaconate for those called to the Priesthood

a. A Candidate must first be ordained Deacon before being ordained Priest.

Ordination of Deacons with a call to the Priesthood.

b. To be ordained Deacon under this Canon, a person must be at least twenty-four years of age.

c. The Bishop shall obtain in writing and provide to the Standing Committee:

Ordination papers.

1. an application from the Candidate requesting ordination as a Deacon under this Canon.

2. a letter of support from the Candidate's congregation or other community of faith, signed and dated by at least two-thirds of the Vestry and the Member of the Clergy or other leader exercising oversight.

3. written evidence of admission of the Candidate to Postulancy and Candidacy, giving the date of admission.

4. a certificate from the seminary or other program of preparation showing the Candidate's scholastic

record in the subjects required by the Canons, and giving an evaluation with recommendation as to the Candidate's other personal qualifications for ordination together with a recommendation regarding ordination to the Diaconate under this Canon.

5. a certificate from the Commission giving a recommendation regarding ordination to the Diaconate under this Canon.

Standing Committee to consent and certify Candidates.

d. On the receipt of such certificates, the Standing Committee, a majority of all the members consenting, shall certify that the canonical requirements for ordination to the Diaconate under this Canon have been met and there is no sufficient objection on medical, psychological, moral, or spiritual grounds and that they recommend ordination, by a testimonial addressed to the Bishop in the form specified below and signed by the consenting members of the Standing Committee.

To the Right Reverend _____, **Bishop of** _____ **We, the Standing Committee of** _____, **having been duly convened at** _____ **at** _____, **do testify that A.B., desiring to be ordained to the Diaconate and Priesthood under Canon III.8 has presented to us the certificates as required by the Canons indicating A.B.'s preparedness for ordination to the Diaconate under Canon III.8; and we certify that all canonical requirements for ordination to the Diaconate under Canon III.8 have been met; and we find no sufficient objection to ordination. Therefore, we recommend A.B. for ordination. In witness whereof, we have hereunto set our hands this** _____ **day of** _____, **in the year of our Lord** _____.

(Signed) _____

Declaration of conformity.

e. The testimonial having been presented to the Bishop, and there being no sufficient objection on medical, psychological, moral, or spiritual grounds, the Bishop may ordain the Candidate to the Diaconate under this Canon; and at the time of ordination the Candidate shall subscribe publicly and make, in the presence of the Bishop, the declaration required in Article VIII of the Constitution.

Sec. 7. Ordination to the Priesthood

a. A person may be ordained Priest:

1. after at least six months since ordination as a Deacon under this Canon and eighteen months from the time of acceptance of nomination by the Nominee as provided in III.8.2.b, and *Ordination requisites.*

2. upon attainment of at least twenty-four years of age, and

3. if the medical evaluation, psychological evaluation, and background check have taken place or been updated within thirty-six months prior to ordination as a Priest.

b. The Bishop shall obtain in writing and provide to the Standing Committee: *Ordination papers.*

1. an application from the Deacon requesting ordination as a Priest, including the Deacon's dates of admission to Postulancy and Candidacy and ordination as a Deacon under this Canon,

2. a letter of support from the Deacon's congregation or other community of faith, signed by at least two-thirds of the Vestry and the Member of the Clergy or other leader exercising oversight,

3. evidence of admission to Postulancy and Candidacy, including dates of admission, and ordination to the Diaconate,

4. a certificate from the seminary or other program of preparation, written at the completion of the program of preparation, showing the Deacon's scholastic record in the subjects required by the Canons, and giving an evaluation with recommendation as to the Deacon's other personal qualifications for ordination together with a recommendation regarding ordination to the Priesthood, and

5. a statement from the Commission attesting to the successful completion of the program of formation designed during Postulancy under Canon III.8.5, and proficiency in the required areas of study, and recommending the Deacon for ordination to the Priesthood.

Standing Committee to consent and certify for ordination to Priesthood.

c. On the receipt of such certificates, the Standing Committee, a majority of all the members consenting, shall certify that the canonical requirements for ordination to the Priesthood have been met and there is no sufficient objection on medical, psychological, moral, or spiritual grounds and that they recommend ordination, by a testimonial addressed to the Bishop in the form specified below and signed by the consenting members of the Standing Committee.

To the Right Reverend _____, **Bishop of** _____ **We, the Standing Committee of** _____, **having been duly convened at** _____, **do testify that A.B., desiring to be ordained to the Priesthood, has presented to us the certificates as required by the Canons indicating A.B.'s preparedness for ordination to the Priesthood have been met; and we certify that all canonical requirements for ordination to the Priesthood have been met, and we find no sufficient objection to ordination. Therefore, we recommend A.B. for ordination. In witness whereof, we have hereunto set our hands this**_____ **day of** _____, **in the year of our Lord**_____.

(Signed)_____

Declaration of conformity.

d. The testimonial having been presented to the Bishop, and there being no sufficient objection on medical, psychological, moral, or spiritual grounds, the Bishop may ordain the Deacon to the Priesthood; and at the time of ordination the Deacon shall subscribe publicly and make, in the presence of the Bishop, the declaration required in Article VIII of the Constitution.

Exercise of office before ordination.

e. No Deacon shall be ordained to the Priesthood until having been appointed to serve in a Parochial Cure within the jurisdiction of this Church, or as a Missionary under the Ecclesiastical Authority of a Diocese, or as an officer of a Missionary Society recognized by the General Convention, or as a Chaplain of the Armed Services of the United States, or as a Chaplain in a recognized hospital or other welfare institution, or as a Chaplain or instructor in a school, college, or other seminary, or with other opportunity for the exercise of the office of Priest within the Church judged appropriate by the Bishop.

f. A person ordained to the Diaconate under Canon III.6 who subsequently expresses a call to the Priesthood shall apply to the Bishop Diocesan and the Commission on Ministry. The Commission on Ministry and Bishop Diocesan shall ensure that the Deacon meets the formational requirements set forth in III.8.5.g and shall recommend such additional steps as may be necessary and required. Upon completion of these requirements and those required for Postulancy and Candidacy as set forth in Canon III.8, the Deacon may be ordained to the Priesthood.

Deacons called to the Priesthood.

Canon 9: Of the Life and Work of Priests

Sec. 1. The Bishop and Commission shall require and provide for the continuing education of Priests and keep a record of such education.

Continuing education.

Sec. 2. Mentoring for Newly Ordained Priests Each newly ordained Priest, whether employed or not, shall be assigned a mentor Priest by the Bishop in consultation with the Commission on Ministry. The mentor and new Priest shall meet regularly for at least a year to provide guidance, information, and a sustained dialogue about priestly ministry.

Mentors.

Sec. 3. The Appointment of Priests

a. Rectors.

1. When a Parish is without a Rector, the Wardens or other officers shall promptly notify the Ecclesiastical Authority in writing. If the Parish shall for thirty days fail to provide services of public worship, the Ecclesiastical Authority shall make provision for such worship.

Parish without a Rector.

Election of a Rector.

2. No Parish may elect a Rector until the names of the proposed nominees have been forwarded to the Ecclesiastical Authority and a time, not exceeding sixty days, given to the Ecclesiastical Authority to communicate with the Vestry, nor until any such communication has been considered by the Vestry at a meeting duly called and held for that purpose.

Written notice to Ecclesiastical Authority.

3. Written notice of the election of a Rector, signed by the Wardens, shall be forwarded to the Ecclesiastical Authority. If the Ecclesiastical Authority is satisfied that the person so elected is a duly qualified Priest and that such Priest has accepted the office to which elected, the notice shall be sent to the Secretary of the Convention, who shall record it. Race, color, ethnic origin, sex, national origin, marital status, sexual orientation, disabilities or age, except as otherwise specified by these Canons, shall not be a factor in the determination of the Ecclesiastical Authority as to whether such person is a duly qualified Priest. The recorded notice shall be sufficient evidence of the relationship between the Priest and the Parish.

Agreement.

4. Rectors may have a letter of agreement with the Parish setting forth mutual responsibilities, subject to the Bishop's approval.

Priests-in-Charge.

b. Priests-in-Charge.
After consultation with the Vestry, the Bishop may appoint a Priest to serve as Priest-in-Charge of any congregation in which there is no Rector. In such congregations, the Priest-in-Charge shall exercise the duties of Rector outlined in Canon III.9.6 subject to the authority of the Bishop.

c. Assistants.

Rector to select assistants.

A Priest serving as an assistant in a Parish, by whatever title designated, shall be selected by the Rector, and when required by the Canons of the Diocese, subject to the approval of the Vestry, and shall serve under the authority and direction of the Rector. Before the selection of an assistant the name of the Priest proposed for selection shall be made known to the Bishop and a time, not exceeding sixty days, given for the Bishop to communicate with the Rector and Vestry on the proposed selection. Upon resignation by the Rector, death of the Rector, or in the event of the dissolution of a pastoral relationship between the Rector and the Vestry, an assistant may continue in the service of the Parish if requested to do so by the Vestry under such conditions as the Bishop and Vestry shall determine. An assistant may continue to serve at the request of a new Rector. Assistants may have a letter of agreement with the Rector and the Vestry setting forth mutual responsibilities and containing a clearly articulated dissolution clause, subject to the Bishop's approval.

In case of vacancy.

d. Chaplains.

1. A Priest may be given ecclesiastical endorsement for service as a Chaplain in the Armed Forces of the United States of America or any other Federal Ministries including the Department of Veterans' Affairs, and the Federal Bureau of Prisons, by a Bishop Suffragan elected pursuant to Article II.7 of the Constitution, subject to the approval of the Bishop of the Diocese in which the Priest is canonically resident.

   Endorsement of Chaplains.

2. Any Priest serving as a Chaplain in an active duty, Reserve or National Guard capacity with the Armed Forces or employed as a Chaplain in the Department of Veterans' Affairs or the Federal Bureau of Prisons shall retain the Priest's canonical residence and shall be subject to the ecclesiastical authority of the Diocese in which the Priest is canonically resident, even though the Priest's work as a Chaplain shall be subject to the ecclesiastical supervision of the Bishop Suffragan elected pursuant to Article II.7 of the Constitution; *provided, however*, that in the event of a vacancy the charge thereof shall devolve upon the Presiding Bishop, with the power of appointing some other Bishop as the substitute in charge until the vacancy is filled by the House of Bishops.

   Active duty Chaplains.

Areas of service.   3. Any Priest serving as a Chaplain on a military installation, Department of Veterans' Affairs Medical Center, or Federal Bureaus of Prisons Correctional Institution shall not be subject to Canons III.9.3.e.1 or III.9.4.a. When serving other than on a military installation, Department of Veterans' Affairs Medical Center or Federal Bureau of Prisons Correctional Institution, a Chaplain shall be subject to these Sections.

    e. Employment of Priests in Other Settings.

Non-parochial Priests.   1. Any Priest who has left a position in this Church without having received a call to a new ecclesiastical position and who desires to continue the exercise of the office of Priest shall notify the Ecclesiastical Authority of the Diocese in which the Priest is canonically resident and shall advise the Bishop that reasonable opportunities for the exercise of the office of Priest exist and that use will be made of such opportunities. After having determined that the person will have and use opportunities for the exercise of the office of Priest, the Bishop, with the advice and consent of the Standing Committee, may approve the Priest's continued exercise of the office on condition that the Priest report annually in writing, in a manner prescribed by the Bishop, as provided in Canon I.6.2.

Moving to another jurisdiction.   2. a. A Priest not in parochial employment moving to another jurisdiction shall report to the Bishop of that jurisdiction within sixty days of such move.

    b. The Priest:

      i. May officiate or preach in that jurisdiction only under the terms of Canon III.9.7.a.

      ii. Shall provide notice of such move, in writing and within sixty days, to the Ecclesiastical Authority of the Diocese in which the Priest is canonically resident.

iii. Shall forward a copy of the report required by Canon I.6.2 to the Ecclesiastical Authority to whose jurisdiction the Priest has moved.

c. Upon receipt of the notice required by Canon III.9.3.e.2.b.ii, the Ecclesiastical Authority shall provide written notice thereof to the Ecclesiastical Authority into whose jurisdiction the person has moved.

3. If the Priest fails to comply with the provisions of this Canon, such failure may be considered a breach of Canon IV.4.1.h.3 occurring in the Diocese in which the Priest is canonically resident.

Failure to comply.

Sec. 4. Letters Dimissory

a. A Priest desiring to become canonically resident within a Diocese shall present to the Ecclesiastical Authority a testimonial from the Ecclesiastical Authority of the Diocese of current canonical residence, which testimonial shall be given by the Ecclesiastical Authority to the applicant, and a duplicate thereof may be sent to the Ecclesiastical Authority of the Diocese to which transfer is proposed. The testimonial shall be accompanied by a statement of the record of payments to The Church Pension Fund by or on behalf of the Priest concerned and may include a portfolio of training, continuing education and exercise of ministries. The testimonial shall be in the following form:

Testimonial for transfer.

I hereby certify that A.B., who has signified to me the desire to be transferred to the Ecclesiastical Authority of _____, is a Priest of _____ in good standing, and has not, so far as I know or believe, been justly liable to evil report, for error in religion or for viciousness of life, for the last three years.

(Date)_____

(Signed)_____

Acceptance of
Letters
Dimissory.

b. Such a testimonial shall be called Letters Dimissory. If the Ecclesiastical Authority accepts the Letters Dimissory, the canonical residence of the Priest transferred shall date from such acceptance, and prompt notice of acceptance shall be given to the applicant and to the Ecclesiastical Authority issuing the Letters Dimissory.

Voided letters
and
nonacceptance.

c. Letters Dimissory not presented within six months of their date of receipt by the applicant shall become void.

d. If a Priest has been called to a Cure in a congregation in another Diocese, the Priest shall present Letters Dimissory. The Ecclesiastical Authority of the Diocese shall accept Letters Dimissory within three months of their receipt unless the Bishop or Standing Committee has received credible information concerning the character or behavior of the Priest concerned which would form grounds for canonical inquiry and proceedings under Title IV. In such a case, the Ecclesiastical Authority shall notify the Ecclesiastical Authority of the Diocese in which the Priest is canonically resident and need not accept the Letters Dimissory unless and until the Priest shall be exculpated. The Ecclesiastical Authority shall not refuse to accept Letters Dimissory based on the applicant's race, color, ethnic origin, sex, national origin, marital status, sexual orientation, disabilities, or age.

Certificate of
transfer.

e. A Priest shall not be in charge of any congregation in the Diocese to which the person moves until obtaining from the Ecclesiastical Authority of that Diocese a certificate in the following form:

I hereby certify that A.B. has been canonically transferred to my jurisdiction and is a Priest in good standing.
(Date) _____
(Signed)_____

f. No person who has been refused ordination or reception *In case of* as a Candidate in any Diocese, and is thereafter ordained *previous refusal.* in another Diocese, shall be transferred to the Diocese in which such refusal has occurred without the consent of its Ecclesiastical Authority.

Sec. 5. Transfer to Churches in Full Communion with This Church

a. A Priest desiring to become canonically resident within a *Transfer of* Diocese or equivalent jurisdiction of a Church in full *canonical* communion with The Episcopal Church (as identified in *residency.* Canon I.20) shall request a testimonial from the Ecclesiastical Authority of the Diocese of current canonical residence, which testimonial shall be given by the Ecclesiastical Authority to the applicant, and a duplicate thereof may be sent to the Ecclesiastical Authority of the Diocese or equivalent jurisdiction to which transfer is proposed. The testimonial may include a portfolio of training, continuing education, and exercise of ministries. The testimonial shall be in the following form or in the form specified by the receiving Diocese or equivalent jurisdiction:

I hereby certify that A.B., who has signified to me the desire to be transferred to the Ecclesiastical Authority of _____, is a Priest of the Diocese of _____ of The Episcopal Church in good standing, and has not, so far as I know or believe, been justly liable to evil report, for error in religion or for viciousness of life, for the last three years.

(Date)_____

(Signed)_____

b. If the Ecclesiastical Authority of the Diocese or equivalent jurisdiction of the Church in full communion with The Episcopal Church accepts the testimonial, the canonical residence of the Priest transferred shall date from such acceptance, and notice of acceptance shall be promptly forwarded by the Priest to the Ecclesiastical Authority in the sending Diocese. Such notification from the receiving Ecclesiastical Authority may be in the following form:

I hereby certify that A.B. has been canonically transferred to my jurisdiction and is a Priest in good standing.

(Date)_____

(Signed)_____

c. Upon receipt of said acceptance, the Ecclesiastical Authority of the sending Diocese shall notify the Church Pension Fund and the Recorder of Ordinations of the priest's departure from The Episcopal Church.

Limitations.   d. This provision shall not be used for Priests who seek to enter churches not in full communion with The Episcopal Church or for those who seek transfer to another Province of the Anglican Communion while remaining geographically within the boundaries of The Episcopal Church. In such cases the provisions of Canon III.9.9 shall be followed.

Sec. 6. Rectors and Priests-in-Charge and Their Duties

Authority and responsibility.   a. 1. The Rector or Priest-in-Charge shall have full authority and responsibility for the conduct of the worship and the spiritual jurisdiction of the Parish, subject to the Rubrics of the Book of Common Prayer, the Constitution and Canons of this Church, and the pastoral direction of the Bishop.

Control of buildings.   2. For the purposes of the office and for the full and free discharge of all functions and duties pertaining thereto, the Rector or Priest-in-Charge shall at all times be entitled to the use and control of the Church and Parish buildings together with all appurtenances and furniture, and to access to all records and registers maintained by or on behalf of the congregation.

Instruction in faith and ministry.   b. 1. It shall be the duty of the Rector or Priest-in-Charge to ensure all persons in their charge receive Instruction in the Holy Scriptures; in the subjects contained in An Outline of the Faith, commonly called the Catechism; in the doctrine, discipline, and worship of this Church; and in the exercise of their ministry as baptized persons.

2. It shall be the duty of Rectors or Priests-in-Charge to ensure that all persons in their charge are instructed concerning Christian stewardship, including:

   Christian stewardship.

   i. reverence for the creation and the right use of God's gifts;

   ii. generous and consistent offering of time, talent, and treasure for the mission and ministry of the Church at home and abroad;

   iii. the biblical standard of the tithe for financial stewardship; and

   iv. the responsibility of all persons to make a will as prescribed in the Book of Common Prayer.

3. It shall be the duty of Rectors or Priests-in-Charge to ensure that persons be prepared for Baptism. Before baptizing infants or children, Rectors or Priests-in-Charge shall ensure that sponsors be prepared by instructing both the parents and the Godparents concerning the significance of Holy Baptism, the responsibilities of parents and Godparents for the Christian training of the baptized child, and how these obligations may properly be discharged.

   Preparing persons for Baptism.

4. It shall be the duty of Rectors or Priests-in-Charge to encourage and ensure the preparation of persons for Confirmation, Reception, and the Reaffirmation of Baptismal Vows, and to be ready to present them to the Bishop with a list of their names.

   Confirmation, Reception, and Reaffirmation.

5. On notice being received of the Bishop's intention to visit any congregation, the Rector or Priest-in-Charge shall announce the fact to the congregation. At every visitation it shall be the duty of the Rector or Priest-in-Charge and the Wardens, Vestry or other officers, to exhibit to the Bishop the Parish Register and to give information as to the state of the congregation, spiritual and temporal, in such

   Duty to announce and inform the Bishop.

categories as the Bishop shall have previously requested in writing.

Alms and Contributions.

6. The Alms and Contributions, not otherwise specifically designated, at the Administration of the Holy Communion on one Sunday in each calendar month, and other offerings for the poor, shall be deposited with the Rector or Priest-in-Charge or with such Church officer as the Rector or Priest-in-Charge shall appoint to be applied to such pious and charitable uses as the Rector or Priest-in-Charge shall determine. When a Parish is without a Rector or Priest-in-Charge, the Vestry shall designate a member of the Parish to fulfill this function.

Duty to read Pastoral Letters and Position Papers.

7. Whenever the House of Bishops shall publish a Pastoral Letter, it shall be the duty of the Rector or Priest-in-Charge to read it to the congregation on some occasion of public worship on a Lord's Day, or to cause copies of the same to be distributed to the members of the congregation, not later than thirty days after receipt.

8. Whenever the House of Bishops shall adopt a Position Paper, and require communication of the content of the Paper to the membership of the Church, the Rector or Priest-in-Charge shall so communicate the Paper in the manner set forth in the preceding section of this Canon.

Parish Register.

c. 1. It shall be the duty of the Rector or Priest-in-Charge to record in the Parish Register all Baptisms, Confirmations (including the canonical equivalents in Canon I.17.1.d), Marriages and Burials.

2. The registry of each Baptism shall be signed by the officiating Member of the Clergy.

Records to be entered in the Register.

3. The Rector or Priest-in-Charge shall record in the Parish Register all persons who have received Holy Baptism, all communicants, all persons who have received Confirmation (including the canonical equivalents in Canon I.17.1.d), all persons who have died, and all persons who have been received or removed by letter of transfer. The Rector or Priest-

in-Charge shall also designate in the Parish Register the names of (1) those persons whose domicile is unknown, (2) those persons whose domicile is known but are inactive, and (3) those families and persons who are active within the congregation. The Parish Register shall remain with the congregation at all times.

Sec. 7. Licenses

a. No Priest shall preach, minister the Sacraments, or hold any public service, within the limits of any Diocese other than the Diocese in which the Priest is canonically resident for more than two months without a license from the Ecclesiastical Authority of the Diocese in which the Priest desires to so officiate. No Priest shall be denied such a license on account of the Priest's race, color, ethnic origin, sex, national origin, marital status, sexual orientation, disabilities, or age, except as otherwise provided in these Canons. Upon expiration or withdrawal of a license, a priest shall cease immediately to officiate.

License to officiate in a Diocese.

b. No Priest shall preach, read prayers in public worship, or perform any similar function, in a congregation without the consent of the Rector or Priest-in-Charge of that congregation, except as follows:

Consent of Rector.

1. In the absence or impairment of the Rector or Priest-in-Charge, and if provision has not been made for the stated services of the congregation or other community of faith, a Warden may give such consent.

Exceptions.

2. If there be two or more congregations or Churches in one Cure, as provided by Canon I.13.3.b, consent may be given by the majority of the Priests-in-Charge of such congregations, or by the Bishop; *provided* that nothing in this Section shall prevent any Member of the Clergy of this Church from officiating, with the consent of the Rector or Priest-in-Charge, in the Church or place of public worship used by the congregation of the consenting Rector or Priest-in-Charge, or in private for members of the congregation; or in the absence of the Rector or

Priest-in-Charge, with the consent of the Wardens or Trustees of the congregation; *provided further*, that the license of the Ecclesiastical Authority provided in Canon III.9.7.a, if required, be obtained.

3. This Canon shall not apply to any Church, Chapel, or Oratory, which is part of the premises of an incorporated institution created by legislative authority; *provided* that such place of worship is designated and set apart for the convenience and use of such institution, and not as a place for public or parochial worship.

Evidence required to officiate.

c. No Rector or Priest-in-Charge of any congregation of this Church, or if there be none, no Wardens, Members of the Vestry, or Trustees of any congregation, shall permit any person to officiate in the congregation without sufficient evidence that such person is duly licensed and ordained and in good standing in this Church; *provided*, nothing in these Canons shall prevent:

Proviso.

1. The General Convention, by Canon or otherwise, from authorizing persons to officiate in congregations in accordance with such terms as it deems appropriate; or

2. The Bishop of any Diocese from giving permission

Bishop may authorize other officiants.

   i. To a Member of the Clergy of this Church, to invite Clergy of another Church to assist in the Book of Common Prayer Offices of Holy Matrimony or of the Burial of the Dead, or to read Morning or Evening Prayer, in the manner specified in Canon III.9.5; or

   ii. To Clergy of any other Church to preach the Gospel, or in ecumenical settings to assist in the administration of the sacraments; or

   iii. To godly persons who are not Clergy of this Church to address the Church on special occasions; or

   iv. To the Member of the Clergy or Priest-in-Charge of a congregation or if there be none, to the Wardens, to invite Clergy ordained in another

Church in full communion with this Church to officiate on an occasional basis, *provided* that such clergy are instructed to teach and act in a manner consistent with the Doctrine, Discipline, and Worship of this Church.

d. If any Member of the Clergy or Priest-in-Charge, as a result of impairment or any other cause, shall neglect to perform regular services in the congregation, and refuse, without good cause, to consent to any other duly qualified Member of the Clergy to perform such services, the Wardens, Vestry, or Trustees of the congregation shall, upon providing evidence to the Ecclesiastical Authority of the Diocese of such neglect or refusal and with the written consent of the Ecclesiastical Authority, have the authority to permit any duly qualified Member of the Clergy to officiate.

Neglect of services or refusal to officiate.

e. Any Priest desiring to officiate temporarily outside the jurisdiction of this Church but in a Church in full communion with this Church, shall obtain from the Ecclesiastical Authority of the Diocese in which the person is canonically resident, a testimonial which shall set forth the person's official standing, and which may be in the following form:

Officiating outside the Church's jurisdiction.

I hereby certify that A.B., who has signified to me the desire to be permitted to officiate temporarily in churches not under the jurisdiction of The Episcopal Church, yet in full communion with this Church, is a Priest of _____ in good standing, and as such is entitled to the rights and privileges of that Order.

(Date)_____

(Signed)_____

Such testimonial shall be valid for one year and shall be returned to the Ecclesiastical Authority at the end of that period. The Ecclesiastical Authority giving such testimonial shall record its issuance, the name of the Priest to whom issued, its date and the date of its return.

Sec. 8. Resignation

Resignation at age seventy-two.

On reaching the age of seventy-two years, a Priest shall resign from all positions in this Church, and the resignation shall be accepted. Thereafter, the Priest may accept any position in this Church, including, with the permission of the Ecclesiastical Authority, the position or positions from which resignation pursuant to this Section has occurred; *provided,*

Proviso.

a. tenure in the position shall be for a term of not more than twelve months, which term may be renewed from time to time,

b. service in the position shall have the express approval of the Bishop of the Diocese in which the service is to be performed, acting in consultation with the Ecclesiastical Authority of the Diocese in which the Priest is canonically resident.

c. Anything in this Canon to the contrary notwithstanding, a Priest who has served in a non-stipendiary capacity in a position before resignation may, at the Bishop's request, serve in the same position for a term not to exceed twelve months thereafter, and this term may be renewed.

Sec. 9. Release and Removal from the Ordained Ministry of this Church

Release and removal of a Priest.

If any Priest of The Episcopal Church shall express, in writing, to the Bishop of the Diocese in which such Priest is canonically resident, an intention to be released and removed from the ordained Ministry of this Church and from the obligations attendant thereto, including those promises made at Ordination in the Declaration required by Article VIII of the Constitution of the General Convention, it shall be the duty of the Bishop to record the matter. The Bishop, being satisfied that the person so declaring is acting voluntarily and for causes, which do not affect the person's moral character, and is neither the subject of information concerning an Offense that has been referred to an Intake Officer nor a Respondent in a pending disciplinary matter as defined in Title IV of these Canons, shall lay the matter before the Standing Committee, and with the advice and consent of a majority of the Standing Committee the Bishop may pronounce that the person is released and removed from the ordained Ministry of this Church and from the obligations attendant thereto, and is deprived of the right to exercise in The Episcopal Church the gifts and spiritual authority as a Minister of God's Word and Sacraments conferred in Ordination. The Bishop shall also declare in pronouncing and recording such action that it was for causes which do not affect the person's moral character, and shall, at the person's request, give a certificate to this effect to the person so removed and released from the ordained Ministry.

Sec. 10.

A Priest who could under this Canon be released and removed from the ordained Ministry of this Church, and who desires to enter into other than ecclesiastical employment, may express in writing to the Ecclesiastical Authority of the Diocese in which the Priest is canonically resident a desire to be released and removed from the obligations of the office and a desire to be released and removed from the exercise of the office of Priest. Upon receipt of such writing, the Ecclesiastical Authority shall proceed in the same manner as prescribed in Section 8 of this Canon.

Request for release.

Sec. 11.

If a Priest submitting the writing described in Section 8 or 9 of this Canon be the subject of information concerning an Offense that has been referred to an Intake Officer or a Respondent in a pending disciplinary matter as defined in Title IV of these Canons, the Ecclesiastical Authority to whom such writing is submitted shall not consider or act upon the written request unless and the disciplinary matter shall have been resolved by a dismissal, Accord, or Order and the time for appeal or rescission of such has expired.

In disciplinary cases.

Sec. 12.

In the case of the release and removal of a Priest from the ordained Ministry of this Church as provided in this Canon, a declaration of release and removal shall be pronounced by the Bishop in the presence of two or more Priests, and shall be entered in the official records of the Diocese in which the Priest being released and removed is canonically resident. The Bishop who pronounces the declaration of release and

Declaration.

removal as provided in this Canon shall give notice thereof in writing to every Member of the Clergy, each Vestry, the Secretary of the Convention and the Standing Committee of the Diocese in which the Priest was canonically resident; and to all Bishops of this Church, the Ecclesiastical Authority of each Diocese of this Church, the Presiding Bishop, the Recorder of Ordinations, the Secretary of the House of Bishops, the Secretary of the House of Deputies, the Church Pension Fund, and the Board for Transition Ministry.

Sec. 13. Return to the Ordained Ministry of this Church after Release and Removal.

Return to ordained Ministry.

a. When a Priest who has been released and removed from the ordained Ministry of this Church under Canon III.9.8 desires to return to that Ministry, the person shall apply in writing to the Bishop of the Diocese in which the Priest was last canonically resident, attaching the following:

1. Evidence of previous ordination in The Episcopal Church;

2. Evidence of appropriate background checks, certifications and proof of completion of applicable trainings including abuse prevention and anti-racism trainings;

3. A statement from no less than two members of the clergy known to the applicant in support of the application;

4. A statement of the reasons for seeking to return to the ordained Ministry of this Church.

b. If the Bishop so chooses, the Bishop may give permission for the Priest to continue the process toward reinstatement, which may include the following:

1. Active participation in a congregation for a period of time at the Bishop's discretion;

2. Regular contact with the Bishop or the Bishop's designee during the course of the process;

3. Evaluation by a licensed mental health professional of the Bishop's choosing for the purposes of

evaluation and of determining fitness for resumption of ordained ministry in this church;

4. Two references from those who are able to discuss the Priest's former ministry;

5. Meeting with the Standing Committee, who shall have the benefit of the materials above and who shall provide to the Bishop its recommendation regarding reinstatement.

c. Before the Priest may be permitted to return to the ordained Ministry of this Church, the Bishop shall require the Priest seeking to return to the ministry to sign a written declaration as required in Article VIII of the Constitution, without recourse to any other ecclesiastical jurisdiction and execute such declaration in the presence of the Bishop and two or more members of the clergy of this Church.

d. Thereafter the Bishop, taking into account the facts and circumstances surrounding the Priest's removal and release, may permit, with the advice and consent of the Standing Committee, the return of the person into the ordained Ministry of this Church.

e. The provisions of this Canon III.9.13 shall not be applicable to any Priest who has been removed, released, or deposed from their ministry as the result of any proceeding of Title IV of these Canons.

f. Notice of the Priest's return to the ordained Ministry of this Church shall be provided in writing to the same persons and entities receiving notice under Canon III.9.12.

Sec. 14. Reconciliation of Disagreements Affecting the Pastoral Relation

When the pastoral relationship in a parish between a Rector and the Vestry or Congregation is imperiled by disagreement or dissension, and the issues are deemed serious by a majority vote of the Vestry or the Rector, either party may petition the Ecclesiastical Authority, in writing, to intervene and assist the parties in their efforts to resolve the disagreement. The written petition shall include sufficient

Petitions to reconcile.

information to inform the Ecclesiastical Authority and the parties involved of the nature, causes, and specifics of the disagreements or dissension imperiling the pastoral relationship. The Ecclesiastical Authority shall initiate such proceedings as are deemed appropriate under the circumstances for that purpose by the Ecclesiastical Authority, which may include the appointment of a consultant or licensed mediator. The parties to the disagreement, following the recommendations of the Ecclesiastical Authority, shall labor in good faith that the parties may be reconciled. Whenever the Standing Committee is the Ecclesiastical Authority, it shall request the Bishop of a neighboring Diocese to perform the duties of the Ecclesiastical Authority under this Canon.

Sec. 15. Dissolution of the Pastoral Relation

Resignation or removal of a Rector.

a. Except upon mandatory resignation by reason of age, a Rector may not resign as Rector of a parish without the consent of its Vestry, nor may any Rector canonically or lawfully elected and in charge of a Parish be removed there from by the Vestry against the Rector's will, except as hereinafter provided.

Notice to Ecclesiastical Authority.

b. If for any urgent reason a Rector or majority of Vestry based on a vote in a duly-called meeting, desires a dissolution of the pastoral relation, and the parties cannot agree, either party may give notice in writing to the Ecclesiastical Authority of the Diocese with a copy available to the Rector or Vestry. Such notice shall include sufficient information to inform the Ecclesiastical Authority and all parties involved of the nature, causes, and specifics requiring the dissolution of the pastoral relationship. If the parties have participated in mediation or consultation processes under III.9.14, a separate report from the mediator or consultant will be submitted to the Ecclesiastical Authority with copies available to the Rector and Vestry. Whenever the Standing Committee is the Ecclesiastical Authority of the Diocese, it shall request the Bishop of another Diocese to perform the duties of the Bishop under this Canon.

c. Within sixty days of receipt of the written notice, the Bishop Diocesan or the Bishop exercising authority under this canon may initiate further mediation and reconciliation processes between Rector and Vestry in every way which the Bishop deems proper. The Bishop may appoint a committee of at least one Presbyter and one Lay Person, none of whom may be members of or related to the Parish involved, to interview the Rector and Vestry and report to the Bishop on the cooperation and responsiveness of the parties involved in the processes required by the Bishop. A copy of this report shall be available to the Vestry and Rector.

Bishop to mediate.

d. If the differences between the parties are not resolved after completion of mediation or other reconciliation efforts or actions prescribed by the Bishop, the Bishop shall proceed as follows:

Procedures for settling differences.

  1. The Bishop shall give written notice to the Rector and Vestry that a godly judgment will be rendered in the matter after consultation with the Standing Committee and that either party has the right within ten days to request in writing an opportunity to confer with the Standing Committee before it consults with the Bishop. The Bishop's written notification shall inform the Standing Committee and the parties involved of the nature, causes, and specifics of the unresolved disagreements or dissension imperiling the pastoral relationship.

  2. If a timely request is made, the President of the Standing Committee shall set a date for the conference, which shall be held within thirty days.

  3. At the conference, each party shall be entitled to attend, be represented, and present its position fully.

  4. Within thirty days after the conference or after the Bishop's notice if no conference is requested, the Bishop shall confer with and receive the recommendation of the Standing Committee; thereafter the Bishop, as final arbiter and judge, shall render a written godly judgment.

5. Upon the request of either party, the Bishop shall explain the reasons for the judgment. If the explanation is in writing, copies shall be delivered to both parties. Either party may request the explanation be in writing.

6. If the pastoral relation is to be continued, the Bishop shall require the parties to agree on definitions of responsibility and accountability for the Rector and the Vestry.

7. If the relation is to be dissolved:

   i. The Bishop shall direct the Secretary of the Convention to record the dissolution.

   ii. The judgment shall include such terms and conditions including financial settlements as shall seem to the Bishop just and compassionate.

8. In either event, the Bishop shall offer appropriate supportive services to the Priest and the Parish.

Noncompliance with judgment. **e.** In the event of the failure or refusal of either party to comply with the terms of the judgment, the Bishop may impose such penalties as may be set forth in the Constitution and Canons of the Diocese; and in default of any provisions for such penalties therein, the Bishop may act as follows:

1. In the case of a Rector, suspend the Rector from the exercise of the priestly office until the Priest shall comply with the judgment.

2. In the case of a Vestry, invoke any available sanctions including recommending to the Convention of the Diocese that the Parish be placed under the supervision of the Bishop as a Mission until it has complied with the judgment.

f. For cause, the Bishop may extend the time periods specified in this Canon, *provided* that all be done to expedite these proceedings. All parties shall be notified in writing of the length of any extension.

g. Statements made during the course of proceedings under this Canon are not discoverable nor admissible in any proceedings under Title IV *provided* that this does not require the exclusion of evidence in any proceeding under the Canons which is otherwise discoverable and admissible.

Nondiscoverable and inadmissible statements.

h. Sections 14 or 15 of this Canon shall not apply in any Diocese whose Canons are otherwise consistent with Canon III.9.

Diocesan Canons apply.

Canon 10: Of Reception of Bishops, Priests, and Deacons from other Churches

Sec. 1. Prior to reception or ordination of a priest or deacon, the following must be provided

a. a background check, according to criteria established by the Bishop and Standing Committee, and

b. medical and psychological evaluation by professionals approved by the Bishop, using forms prepared for the purpose by the Standing Commission on Ministry and Formation in accordance with principles and directions adopted by the General Convention and if desired or necessary, psychiatric referral. All such background checks and evaluations shall be conducted specifically for the ordination or reception under this Canon and not for any other process or purpose.

Examinations and evaluations.

c. evidence of training regarding

Evidence of training.

   1. prevention of sexual misconduct.

   2. civil requirements for reporting and pastoral opportunities for responding to evidence of abuse.

   3. the Constitution and Canons of The Episcopal Church, particularly Title IV thereof.

   4. training regarding the Church's teaching on racism.

d. Reports of all investigations and examinations shall be kept permanently on file by the Bishop and remain a part of the permanent diocesan record.

Diocesan records.

Mentors.   e. Prior to reception or ordination each clergy person shall be assigned a mentor Priest by the Bishop in consultation with the Commission on Ministry. The mentor and clergy person shall meet regularly to provide the clergy person an opportunity for guidance, information, and a sustained dialogue about ministry in The Episcopal Church.

Sec. 2. Clergy Ordained by Bishops of Churches in Communion with This Church

Certificate required to officiate.   a.   1. A Member of the Clergy, ordained by a Bishop of another Church in full communion with this Church, or by a Bishop consecrated for a foreign land by Bishops of this Church under Article III of the Constitution, shall, before being permitted to officiate in any Congregation of this Church, exhibit to the Member of the Clergy in charge, or, if there be no Member of the Clergy in charge, to the Vestry thereof, a certificate of recent date, signed by the Ecclesiastical Authority of the Diocese that the person's letters of Holy Orders and other credentials are valid and authentic, and given by a Bishop in full communion with this Church, and whose authority is acknowledged by this Church; and also that the person has exhibited to the Ecclesiastical Authority satisfactory evidence of (i) moral and godly character and of (ii) theological qualifications.

Letters Dimissory or equivalent credentials.   2. Before being permitted to take charge of any Congregation, or being received into any Diocese of this Church as a Member of its Clergy, the Ecclesiastical Authority shall receive Letters Dimissory or equivalent credentials under the hand and seal of the Bishop with whose Diocese the person has been last connected, which letters or credentials shall be delivered within six months from the date thereof. Before receiving the Member of the Clergy the Bishop shall require a promise in writing to submit in all things to the Discipline of this Church, without recourse to any foreign jurisdiction, civil or ecclesiastical; and shall further require the person to subscribe and make in the Bishop's presence, and in the presence of two or more Presbyters, the declaration required in Article VIII of the Constitution. The Bishop and at least one Presbyter shall examine the person as to knowledge of the history of this Church, its worship and government. The Bishop also being satisfied of the person's theological qualifications, may then receive the person into the Diocese as a Member of the Clergy of this Church.

3. The provisions of this Section shall be applicable to all Members of the Clergy ordained in any Church in full communion with this Church as specified in Canon I.20, subject to the terms of the covenant of The Episcopal Church and the other Church or Churches as adopted by the General Convention and by the denominational authority or similar body for those Churches that are not members of the Anglican Communion by action of the Anglican Consultative Council. *Churches in full communion.*

b. A Member of the Clergy who is a Deacon shall not be ordered Priest until having resided within the jurisdiction of this Church at least one year and all the requirements for ordination to the Priesthood as required by Canon III.8 have been satisfied. *Deacons.*

c. Following reception each clergy person shall be assigned a mentor Priest by the Bishop in consultation with the Commission on Ministry. The mentor and clergy person shall meet regularly to provide the clergy person an opportunity for guidance, information, and a sustained dialogue about ministry in The Episcopal Church. *Mentors.*

Sec. 3. Clergy Ordained by Bishops in Churches in the Historic Succession but Not in Full Communion with This Church

a. When a Priest or Deacon ordained in a Church by a Bishop in the Historic Succession but not in full communion with this Church, the regularity of whose ordination is approved by the Presiding Bishop as permitted by Canon I.16.3, desires to be received as a Member of the Clergy in this Church, the person shall apply in writing to a Bishop, attaching the following: *Procedures for making application.*

1. A nomination in writing for reception from the person's congregation or community of faith in this Church. The Nomination shall include a letter of support by the congregation or community of faith, committing the community to involve itself in the person's preparation for reception to the Priesthood. If it be a congregation, the letter shall be signed by two-thirds of the Vestry or comparable body, and by the Member of the Clergy or leader exercising oversight.

2. The person, if agreeing, shall accept the nomination in writing, and shall provide the following in writing to the Bishop:

    i.   Full name and date of birth.

    ii. The length of time resident in the Diocese.

    iii. Evidence that the person is a confirmed adult communicant in good standing in a Congregation of this Church.

    iv. Whether an application has been made previously for reception in any diocese.

    v.   A description of the process of discernment the person has undertaken individually and with the nominating congregation or community of faith.

    vi. A statement of reasons for seeking to enter Holy Orders in this Church.

3. Evidence of previous ordained Ministry and that all other credentials are valid and authentic.

4. Evidence of moral and godly character; and that the person is free from any vows or other engagements inconsistent with the exercise of Holy Orders in this Church.

5. Transcripts of all academic and theological studies.

6. A certificate from at least two Presbyters in good standing of this Church stating that, from personal examination or from satisfactory evidence presented to them, they believe that the departure of the person from the Communion to which the person

has belonged has not arisen from any circumstance unfavorable to moral or religious character, or on account of which it may not be expedient to admit the person to Holy Orders in this Church.

7. Certificates in the forms provided in Canon III.8.6 and III.8.7 from the Rector or Member of the Clergy in charge and Vestry of a Parish of this Church.

b. The provisions of Canon III.8.5.a shall be applicable.

c. If the person has exercised a ministry in the previous Church with good repute and success and if the person furnishes evidence of satisfactory theological training in the previous Church, then the applicant shall be examined by the Commission and show proficiency in the following subjects: *Evidence of proficiency.*

1. Church History: the history of the Anglican Communion and The Episcopal Church.

2. Doctrine: the Church's teaching as set forth in the Creeds and in An Outline of the Faith, commonly called the Catechism.

3. Liturgics: the principles and history of Anglican worship; the contents of the Book of Common Prayer.

4. Practical Theology:

    i.   The office and work of a Deacon and Priest in this Church.

    ii. The conduct of public worship.

    iii. The Constitution and Canons of The Episcopal Church and of the Diocese in which the applicant is resident.

    iv. The use of voice in reading and speaking.

5. The points of Doctrine, Discipline, Polity, and Worship in which the Church from which the applicant has come differ from this Church. This portion of the examinations shall be conducted, in part at least, by written questions and answers, and the replies kept on file for at least three years.

d. The Commission may, with the consent of the Bishop, and with notice to the applicant, examine the latter in any other subject required by Canon III.6.5.f and g or III.8.5.g and h.

Candidate to receive endorsements.

e. Prior to being examined pursuant to Sec. 3.c of this Canon, the applicant shall have received certificates from the Bishop and from the Standing Committee that the applicant is acceptable as a Member of the Clergy of this Church, subject to the successful completion of the examination.

Declaration of conformity.

f. Before the person may be ordained or received into Holy Orders in this Church, the Bishop shall require a promise in writing to submit in all things, to the Discipline of this Church without recourse to any other ecclesiastical jurisdiction or foreign civil jurisdiction, and shall further require the person to subscribe and make in the presence of the Bishop and two or more Presbyters the declaration required in Article VIII of the Constitution.

Reception, confirmation, or ordination.

g. Thereafter the Bishop, being satisfied of the person's theological qualifications and successful completion of the examination specified in Sec. 3.c of this Canon and soundness in the faith, shall:

1. Receive, with the advice and consent of the Standing Committee, the person into this Church in the Orders to which already ordained by a Bishop in the historic succession; or

2. Confirm and make the person a Deacon and, no sooner than four months thereafter, ordain as Priest, if the person has not received such ordination; or

3. Ordain as a Deacon and no sooner than six months thereafter, ordain the person a Priest conditionally (having baptized and confirmed the person conditionally if necessary) if ordained by a Bishop whose authority to convey such orders has not been recognized by this Church.

Special prefaces authorized.

h. In the case of an ordination under this Canon, the Bishop shall, at the time of such ordination, read this preface to the Service:

The Ecclesiastical Authority of this Diocese is satisfied that A.B. accepts the Doctrine, Discipline, and Worship of this Church and now desires to be ordained a Deacon (or ordained a Priest) in this Church. We are about to confer upon A.B. the grace and authority of Holy Orders as this Church has received them and requires them for the exercise of the ministry of a Deacon (or a Priest).

The certificates of ordination in such cases shall contain the words:

Acknowledging the ministry which A.B. has already received and hereby adding to that commission the grace and authority of Holy Orders as understood and required by this Church for the exercise of the ministry of a Deacon (or a Priest).

i. In the case of a conditional ordination pursuant to this Canon, the Bishop shall at the time of such ordination, read this preface to the service:

Conditional ordination.

The Ecclesiastical Authority of this Diocese has been satisfied that A.B., who has been ordained by a Bishop whose authority has not been recognized by this Church, accepts the Doctrine, Discipline, and Worship of this Church, and now desires conditional ordination. By this service of ordination, we propose to establish that A.B. is qualified to exercise the ministry of a Deacon (or a Priest).

j. No one shall be ordained or received as a Deacon or Priest until age twenty-four.

Limitations.

k. A Deacon received under this Canon, desiring to be ordained to the Priesthood must satisfy all the requirements for ordination as set forth in Canon III.8.

l. No one shall be received or ordained under this Canon less than twelve months from the date of having become a confirmed communicant of this Church.

m. Following reception or ordination each clergy person shall be assigned a mentor Priest by the Bishop in consultation with the Commission on Ministry. The mentor and clergy person shall meet regularly to provide

Mentors.

guidance, information, and a sustained dialogue about ministry in The Episcopal Church.

Sec. 4. Clergy Ordained in Churches Not in the Historic Succession

a. If a person ordained or licensed by other than a Bishop in historic succession to minister in a Church not in full communion with this Church desires to be ordained, the person shall follow the procedures and requirements set forth in Canon III.6 if the person desires to be ordained to the diaconate or Canon III.8 if the person desires to be ordained to the priesthood.

b. The Commission shall examine the applicant and report to the Bishop with respect to:

1. Whether the applicant has served in the previous Church with diligence and good reputation and has stated the causes which have impelled the applicant to leave the body and seek ordination in this Church,

2. The nature and extent of the applicant's education and theological training,

3. The preparations necessary for ordination to the Order(s) to which the applicant feels called;

Exceptions to canonical requirements.

c. The minimum period of Candidacy need not apply, if the Bishop and the Standing Committee at the recommendation of the Commission judge the Candidate to be ready for ordination to the Diaconate earlier than twelve months; the applicant shall be examined by the Commission and show proficiency in the following subjects:

Proficiencies.

1. Church History: the history of the Anglican Church and The Episcopal Church in the United States of America,

2. Doctrine: the Church's teaching as set forth in the Creeds and in An Outline of the Faith, commonly called the Catechism;

3. Liturgics: the principles and history of Anglican worship; the contents of the Book of Common Prayer;

4. Practical Theology:

    i. The office and work of a Deacon and Priest in this Church,

    ii. The conduct of public worship,

    iii. The Constitution and Canons of the General Convention, and of the Diocese in which the applicant is resident,

    iv. The use of voice in reading and speaking;

5. The points of Doctrine, Discipline, Polity, and Worship in which the Church from which the applicant has come differs from this Church. This portion of the examinations shall be conducted, in part at least, by written questions and answers, and the replies kept on file for at least three years.

d. If all the requirements of this Canon have been fulfilled, the Bishop may ordain the Candidate a Deacon under Canon III.6 or III.8, but may do so no sooner than twelve months after the Candidate became a confirmed communicant of this Church. If ordained a deacon under Canon III.8 no sooner than six months thereafter, the Candidate may be ordained a Priest at the Bishop's discretion.

Special prefaces authorized.

Sec. 5. Reception into this Church of a Bishop of a Church or Province in the Anglican Communion.

a. A Bishop in good standing of a member church or Province of the Anglican Communion, or of a national or local church with Extra-Provincial status in the Anglican Communion, who seeks to serve in this Church as an Assistant Bishop as provided in Canon III.12.5.b.3, or as a Bishop with provisional charge of a Diocese as provided in Canon III.13.1, may be received into The Episcopal Church pursuant to the requirements set out in this Section.

Bishops of Anglican Communion may be received.

b. A Bishop in good standing of a member church or Province of the Anglican Communion, or of a national or local church with Extra-Provincial status in the Anglican Communion, which church or Province is seeking admission into union with The Episcopal Church, may be received into The Episcopal Church pursuant to the requirements set out in this Section, provided that if the Bishop's selection to serve the church or Province was by a process other than election by a Convention, Synod, or other governing body, the Bishop shall provide evidence that the Convention, Synod, or other governing body has affirmed that selection;

Evidence required.

c. A Bishop seeking to be received into The Episcopal Church shall provide to the Presiding Bishop the following:

1. evidence of the Bishop's having been duly ordered Bishop in the Anglican Communion;

2. evidence of the Bishop's moral and godly character;

3. a background check, according to the criteria established by the Presiding Bishop;

4. certificates from a licensed medical doctor and a licensed psychologist authorized by the Presiding Bishop, and, as necessary, from a psychiatrist and/or a professional specializing in evaluation for substance, chemical, and alcohol use and abuse and other addictive patterns, also authorized by the Presiding Bishop, that they have thoroughly examined the Bishop as to that person's medical, psychological, and psychiatric condition and for substance, chemical and alcohol use and abuse and other addictive patterns and have not discovered any reason why the person would not be fit to undertake the work for which the person has been chosen as a Bishop in this Church. Forms and procedures agreed to by the Presiding Bishop shall be used for this purpose;

5. evidence of the Bishop having received the training set out in Section 1.c of this Canon;

6. evidence of the Bishop having been examined by at least three Bishops of this Church as to knowledge of this Church, its worship and governance, including the follow topics:

i. Church History: the history of the Anglican Communion and The Episcopal Church.

ii. Doctrine: the Church's teachings as set forth in the Creeds and in An Outline of the Faith, commonly called the Catechism.

iii. Liturgics: the principles and history of Anglican worship; the contents of the Book of Common Prayer.

iv. Practical Theology:

1. The office and work of a Deacon and Priest in this Church.

2. The conduct of public worship.

3. The Constitution and Canons of The Episcopal Church and of the Diocese in which the Bishop will serve.

4. The use of voice in reading and speaking;

7. The points of Doctrine, Discipline, Polity, and Worship in which the church or Province from the Bishop has come differ from this Church. This portion of the examinations will be conducted, in part at least, by written questions and answers, and the replies kept on file with the Office of Pastoral Development for at least three years; and

8. In the case of a Bishop seeking to be received into this Church under subsection .b of this Canon, evidence that the General Convention has consented to the admission of the church or Province pursuant to Article V, Section 1 of the Constitution.

d. Upon receipt of the items set out in subsection .c of this Canon to the satisfaction of the Presiding Bishop, the Presiding Bishop, without delay, shall notify every Bishop of this Church exercising jurisdiction and every Standing Committee of this Church of the Presiding Bishop's receipt of those items, and request from each a statement of consent, or withholding of consent, to the reception of the Bishop into The Episcopal Church. Each

Consent required.

Bishop with jurisdiction and each Standing Committee shall within 90 days of the sending of the notification respond to the Presiding Bishop or the Presiding Bishop's designee indicating their consent or their withholding of consent.

Evidence of the consent of each Standing Committee shall be a testimonial in the following words, or in similar words approved by the Presiding Bishop, signed by a majority of all the members of the Committee:

We, being a majority of all the members of the Standing Committee of _____, and having been duly convened, firmly persuaded that it is our duty to bear testimony on this solemn occasion without partiality, do, in the presence of Almighty God, testify that we know of no impediment on account of which the Right Reverend N.N. ought not to be received into The Episcopal Church to serve as a Bishop therein, and therefore consent to the reception of the Right Reverend N.N. to serve as [Assistant Bishop/Bishop with provisional charge/Bishop Diocesan] in the Diocese of _____. In witness whereof, we have hereunto set our hands this_____ day of _____ in the year of our Lord _____.

(Signed) _____

e. If a majority of the Bishops with jurisdiction and of the Standing Committees consents to the reception, the Bishop shall make the written declaration required by Article VIII of the Constitution of The Episcopal Church in the presence of the Presiding Bishop and two episcopal witnesses, at which point the Presiding Bishop shall certify that the Bishop is received into The Episcopal Church; provided that, in the case of a Bishop seeking to be received into this Church under subsection .b of this Canon, such certification shall not issue until the Executive Council has issued the approval set out on Article V, Section 1 of the Constitution.

Canon 11: Of the Ordination of Bishops

Sec. 1

a. Discernment of vocation to be a Bishop Diocesan, Coadjutor, or Suffragan occurs through a process of election in accordance with the Constitutions and Canons of this Church and the electing Diocese and any special rules adopted by the Convention of that Diocese. Unless otherwise provided in the electing Diocese's Constitution or Canons, the Standing Committee shall have oversight of, and responsibility for, any search, nomination, transition, and election processes. The Diocese shall establish a nominating process either by Canon or by the adoption of rules and procedures for the election of the Bishop at a regular or special meeting of the Convention of the Diocese with sufficient time preceding the election of the Bishop.

Discernment and election rules.

b. In lieu of electing a Bishop, the Convention of a Diocese may request that an election be made on its behalf by the House of Bishops of the Province of which the Diocese is a part, subject to confirmation by the Provincial Synod, or it may request that an election be made on its behalf by the House of Bishops of The Episcopal Church.

Other provisions for election.

1. If either option in Sec. l.b is chosen, a special Joint Nominating Committee shall be appointed unless the Diocesan Convention has otherwise provided for the nominating process. The Committee shall be composed of three persons from the Diocese, appointed by its Standing Committee, and three members of the electoral body, appointed by the President of that body. The Joint Nominating Committee shall elect its own officers and shall nominate three persons whose names it shall communicate to the Presiding Officer of the electoral body. The Presiding Officer shall communicate the names of the nominees to the electoral body at least three weeks before the election when the names shall be formally placed in nomination. Opportunity

Nomination process.

shall be given for nominations from the floor or by petition, in either case with provision for adequate background checks.

Certificate and testimonial.

2. If either option in Sec. l.b is chosen, the evidence of the election shall be a certificate signed by the Presiding Officer of the electoral body and by its Secretary, with a testimonial signed by a constitutional majority of the body, in the form required in Canon III.11.3, which shall be sent to the Standing Committee of the Diocese on whose behalf the election was held. The Standing Committee shall thereupon proceed as set forth in Canon III.11.3.

Notification of election.

c. The Secretary of the body electing a Bishop Diocesan, Bishop Coadjutor, or Bishop Suffragan, shall inform the Presiding Bishop promptly of the name of the person elected. It shall be the duty of the Bishop-elect to notify the Presiding Bishop of acceptance or declination of the election, at the same time as the Bishop-elect notifies the electing Diocese.

d. No Diocese shall elect a Bishop within thirty days before a meeting of the General Convention.

Special meeting of Diocesan Convention.

Sec. 2. A Bishop Diocesan, with the advice and consent of the Standing Committee, may call for a special meeting of the Convention of the Diocese, to be held no earlier than six months prior to the effective date of the Bishop Diocesan's resignation, to elect a successor; provided that if the Convention is to meet in regular session meanwhile, it may hold the election during the regular session. The proceedings incident to preparation for the ordination of the successor shall be as provided in this Canon; but the Presiding Bishop shall not take order for the ordination to be on any date prior to that upon which the resignation is to become effective.

Documents to be transmitted.

Sec. 3

a. The Standing Committee of the Diocese for which the Bishop has been elected shall by its President, or by some person or persons specially appointed, immediately send to the Presiding Bishop and to the Standing

Committees of the several Dioceses a certificate of the election by the Secretary of Convention of the Diocese, bearing a statement of receipt of:

1. evidence of the Bishop-elect's having been duly ordered Deacon and Priest;

2. certificates from a licensed medical doctor and licensed psychiatrist, authorized by the Presiding Bishop, that they have thoroughly examined the Bishop-elect as to that person's medical, psychological and psychiatric condition and have not discovered any reason why the person would not be fit to undertake the work for which the person has been chosen. Forms and procedures agreed to by the Presiding Bishop and the Standing Commission on Ministry and Formation in accordance with principles and directions adopted by the General Convention shall be used for this purpose; and

3. evidence that a testimonial in the following form was signed by a constitutional majority of the Convention:

We, whose names are hereunder written, fully sensible of how important it is that the Sacred Order and Office of a Bishop should not be unworthily conferred, and firmly persuaded that it is our duty to bear testimony on this solemn occasion without partiality, do, in the presence of Almighty God, testify that we know of no impediment on account of which the Reverend A.B. ought not to be ordained to that Holy Office. We do, moreover, jointly and severally declare that we believe the Reverend A.B. to have been duly and lawfully elected and to be of such sufficiency in learning, of such soundness in the Faith, and of such godly character as to be able to exercise the Office of a Bishop to the honor of God and the edifying of the Church, and to be a wholesome example to the flock of Christ.

Testimonial of election.

(Date)_____

(Signed)_____

Consent process.   The Presiding Bishop, without delay, shall notify every Bishop of this Church exercising jurisdiction of the Presiding Bishop's receipt of the certificates mentioned in this Section and request a statement of consent or withholding of consent. Each Standing Committee, in not more than one hundred and twenty days after the sending by the electing body of the certificate of the election, shall respond by sending the Standing Committee of the Diocese for which the Bishop is elected either the testimonial of consent in the form set out in paragraph b. of this Section or written notice of its refusal to give consent. If a majority of the Standing Committees of all the Dioceses consents to the ordination of the Bishop-elect, the Standing Committee of the Diocese for which the Bishop is elected shall then forward the evidence of the consent, with the other necessary certificates required in this Section (documents described in Sec. 3.a.2 of this Canon), to the Presiding Bishop. If the Presiding Bishop receives sufficient statements to indicate a majority of those Bishops consent to the ordination, the Presiding Bishop shall, without delay, notify the Standing Committee of the Diocese for which the Bishop is elected and the Bishop-elect of the consent.

Testimonials of   **b.**   Evidence of the consent of each Standing Committee
Standing   shall be a testimonial in the following words, signed by a
Committees.   majority of all the members of the Committee:

We, being a majority of all the members of the Standing Committee of _____, and having been duly convened, fully sensible how important it is that the Sacred Order and Office of a Bishop should not be unworthily conferred, and firmly persuaded that it is our duty to bear testimony on this solemn occasion without partiality, do, in the presence of Almighty God, testify that we know of no impediment on account of which the Reverend A.B. ought not to be ordained to that Holy Order. In witness whereof, we have hereunto set our hands this _____ day of _____ in the year of our Lord _____.

(Signed) _____

c. Testimonials required of the Standing Committee by this
Title must be signed by a majority of the whole
Committee, at a meeting duly convened, except that
testimonials may be executed in counterparts, any of
which may be delivered by facsimile or other electronic
transmission, each of which shall be deemed an original.

Sec. 4. In case a majority of all the Standing Committees of
the Dioceses do not consent to the ordination of the Bishop-
elect within one hundred and twenty days from the date of
the notification of the election by the Standing Committee of
the Diocese for which the Bishop was elected, or in case a
majority of all the Bishops exercising jurisdiction do not
consent within one hundred and twenty days from the date
of notification to them by the Presiding Bishop of the
election, the Presiding Bishop shall declare the election null
and void and shall give notice to the Standing Committee of
the Diocese for which the Bishop was elected and to the
Bishop-elect. The Convention of the Diocese may then
proceed to a new election.

In cases of nonconsent.

Sec. 5. Upon receipt of the consents and assurance of the
acceptance of the election by the Bishop-elect, the Presiding
Bishop shall take order for the ordination of the Bishop-elect
either by the Presiding Bishop or the President of the House
of Bishops of the Province of which the Diocese for which the
Bishop was elected is part, and two other Bishops of this
Church, or by any three Bishops to whom the Presiding
Bishop may communicate the testimonials.

Presiding Bishop to take order for ordination.

Sec. 6. In all particulars the service at the ordination of a
Bishop shall be under the direction of the Bishop presiding at
the ordination.

Ordination service.

Sec. 7. No person shall be ordained Bishop unless the person
shall at the time, and in the presence of the ordaining
Bishops and congregation, subscribe to and make the
declaration required in Article VIII of the Constitution.

Declaration of conformity.

Sec. 8

Objections to election process.

a. Within ten days after the election of a Bishop Diocesan, a
Bishop Coadjutor, or a Bishop Suffragan by a Diocesan
Convention, delegates constituting no less than ten
percent of the number of delegates casting votes on the

final ballot may file with the Secretary of the Convention written objections to the election process, setting forth in detail all alleged irregularities. Within ten days after receipt thereof, the Secretary of the Convention shall forward copies of the same to the Bishop Diocesan, the Chancellor and Standing Committee of the Diocese, and to the Presiding Bishop, who shall request the Court of

Report of the Court of Review.

Review to investigate the complaint. The Court of Review may invite response by the Bishop Diocesan, the Chancellor, the Standing Committee and any other persons within the Diocese for which the Bishop was elected. Within 45 days after receipt of the request, the Court of Review shall send a written report of its findings to the Presiding Bishop, a copy of which report the Presiding Bishop, within fifteen days, shall cause to be sent to the Bishop Diocesan, the Chancellor, the Standing Committee and the Secretary of the Convention of the electing Diocese. The Secretary shall send a copy of the report to each of the delegates who filed objection to the election process.

b. The report of the Court of Review shall be sent to the Standing Committees of the several Dioceses, with the Certificate of the Secretary of the electing Convention relating to consent to ordain. Likewise, the Presiding Bishop shall include the report in the communication to the Bishops exercising jurisdiction. The 120 day period for Standing Committees and Bishops to consent to the election begins with these communications.

Sec. 9. Other Bishops

a. Bishops Coadjutor

Bishop Coadjutor.

1. If a Diocese discerns a need for another Bishop in order to provide for orderly transition, the Diocese may elect a Bishop Coadjutor who shall have the right of succession. The election will be held in accordance with Canon III.11.1 and this Canon III.11.9.a.

Consents and duties.

2. Before an election of a Bishop Coadjutor, the Bishop Diocesan shall read, or cause to be read, to the Convention the Bishop's written consent to the

election. The consent shall state the duties to be assigned to the Bishop Coadjutor when ordained. The consent shall form part of the proceedings of the Convention. The duties assigned by the Diocesan Bishop to the Bishop Coadjutor may be enlarged by mutual consent.

3. In the case of the inability of the Bishop Diocesan to issue the required consent, the Standing Committee of the Diocese may request the Convention to act without the consent. The request shall be accompanied by a certificate by at least two licensed medical doctors, psychologists or psychiatrists as to the inability of the Diocesan Bishop to issue the written consent.

   In cases of incapacity.

4. When a Diocese desires the ordination of a Bishop Coadjutor, the Standing Committee shall forward to the Presiding Bishop, in addition to the evidence and testimonials required by Canon III.11.3.a, a certificate of the Presiding Officer and Secretary of the Convention that every requirement of this Section has been complied with.

   Required notices.

5. There shall be only one Bishop Coadjutor in any Diocese.

b. Bishops Suffragan

1. If a Diocese discerns a need for another Bishop due to the extent of diocesan work, the Diocese may elect a Bishop Suffragan in accordance with Canon III.11.1 and this Canon III.11.9.b.

   Bishop Suffragan.

2. Before the election of a Bishop Suffragan in a Diocese, the consent of a majority of the Bishops exercising jurisdiction and of the several Standing Committees must be obtained.

3. i. A Bishop Suffragan shall act as an assistant to and under the direction of the Bishop Diocesan.

   ii. Before the election of a Bishop Suffragan in a Diocese, the Bishop Diocesan shall submit a consent with a description of the role and the

   Consents and duties.

duties of the Bishop Suffragan to the Convention of the Diocese.

Tenure of office.
4. The tenure of office of a Bishop Suffragan shall not be determined by the tenure of office of the Bishop Diocesan.

5. No Bishop Suffragan, while acting as such, shall be Rector, but may serve as Member of the Clergy in charge of a Congregation.

c. Missionary Bishop

Constitution and Canons.
1. The election of a person to be a Bishop in a Missionary Diocese shall be held in accordance with the procedures set forth in the Constitution and Canon III.11 Sections 1-8, this Canon III.11.9.c and Canon III.12.6.

Provincial election.
2. The Convention of a Missionary Diocese may, in lieu of electing a Bishop, request that such election be made on its behalf by the Synod of the Province, or the House of Bishops of the Province subject to confirmation of the Provincial Council, or the Regional Council of Churches in full communion with this Church of which the Diocese is a member. A Certificate of the Election, signed by the presiding officer and the Secretary of the Synod or Provincial House of Bishops, or Regional Council, and a testimonial in the form required in Canon III.11 signed by a constitutional majority of the Synod, Provincial House of Bishops or Regional Council, shall be transmitted by its presiding officer to the Standing Committee of the Missionary Diocese on whose behalf such election was made. The Standing Committee shall thereupon proceed as set forth in Canon III.11, the above Certification of Election and Testimonial serving in lieu of evidence of election and testimonial therein required.

Election by House of Bishops.
3. The Convention of a Missionary Diocese may, in lieu of electing a Bishop, request that such election may be made on its behalf by the House of Bishops. Such choice shall be subject to confirmation by a majority of the Standing Committees of the several Dioceses.

The medical certificate as required in Canon III.11 shall also be required of Missionary Bishops-elect.

i.   When the House of Bishops is to elect a Bishop for a Missionary Diocese within a given Province, the President of the Province may convene the Synod of the Province prior to the meeting of the House of Bishops at which a Bishop for such Missionary Diocese is to be elected. The Synod of the Province may thereupon nominate not exceeding three persons to the House of Bishops for that office. It shall be the duty of the President of the Province to transmit such nominations, if any be made, to the Presiding Officer of the House of Bishops, communicate the same to the Bishops, along with other nominations that have been made, in accordance with the Rules of Order of the House. Each Province containing a Missionary Diocese shall, by Ordinance, provide the manner of convening the Synod and making such nomination.

Nominations.

ii.   The evidence of such choice shall be a certificate signed by the Bishop presiding in the House of Bishops and by its Secretary, with a testimonial, or certified copy thereof, signed by a majority of the Bishops of the House, in the form required in Canon III.11, which shall be sent to the Presiding Officer of the House of Deputies, or the Standing Committees of the several Dioceses.

iii.   When the Presiding Bishop shall have received a certificate signed by the Presidents and Secretaries of a majority of the Standing Committees, that the election has been approved, and shall have received notice of the acceptance by the Bishop-elect of the election, the Presiding Bishop shall take order for the consecration of the said Bishop-elect either by the Presiding Bishop and two other Bishops of this Church, or by three Bishops of this Church to whom the Presiding Bishop may communicate the certificates and testimonial.

Presiding Bishop to take order for ordination.

4. When a Diocese elects a Missionary Bishop as its Bishop Diocesan, or as its Bishop Coadjutor, or as a Bishop Suffragan, the Standing Committee of the Diocese electing shall give duly certified evidence of the election to every Bishop of this Church having jurisdiction, and to the Standing Committee of every Diocese. On receiving notice of the concurrence of a majority of such Bishops and of the Standing Committees in the election, and their express consent thereto, the Standing Committee of the Diocese electing shall transmit notice thereof to the Ecclesiastical Authority of every Diocese within the United States. This notice shall state what Bishops and which Standing Committees have consented to the election. On receiving this notice the Presiding Bishop shall certify to the Secretary of the House of Bishops the altered status and style of the Bishop so elected. The Standing Committee of such Diocese shall transmit to every Congregation thereof, to be publicly read therein, a notice of the election thus completed, and also cause public notice thereof to be given in such other way as they may think proper.

5. In the event of a vacancy in the episcopate of a Missionary Diocese, on account of death, resignation, or other cause, the Standing Committee shall become the Ecclesiastical Authority thereof until the vacancy is filled.

Canon 12: Of the Life and Work of a Bishop

Sec. 1. Formation

Following election or reception and continuing for three years following ordination or reception, new Bishops and Bishops received into this Church shall pursue the process of formation authorized by the House of Bishops. This process of formation shall provide a mentor for each newly ordained and received Bishop.

Sec. 2. Continuing Education

The House of Bishops shall require and provide for the continuing education of Bishops and shall keep a record of such education.

Continuing education.

Sec. 3. Duties

a. A Bishop Diocesan, Bishop Coadjutor, Bishop Suffragan, or Assistant Bishop of the Diocese shall visit the Congregations within the Diocese at least once in three years. Interim visits may be delegated to another Bishop of this Church.

Bishop to visit congregations.

 1. At every such visitation the visiting Bishop shall preside at the Holy Eucharist and at the Initiatory Rites, as required, preach the Word, examine the records of the Congregation required by Canon III.9.6.c, and examine the life and ministry of the Clergy and Congregation according to Canon III.9.6.

 2. If no visitation has occurred in a congregation for three years, the Bishop Diocesan or the Member of the Clergy in charge and Vestry or comparable body may apply to the Presiding Bishop to appoint five Bishops Diocesan who live nearest to the Diocese in which such Congregation is situated as a Council of Conciliation. The Council shall determine all matters of difference between the parties, and each party shall conform to the decision of the Council; *provided* that, in case of any subsequent disciplinary proceedings of either party for failure to conform to the decision, any right of the Respondent under the Constitutions and Canons of this Church or the Diocese holding the disciplinary proceedings may be pleaded and established as a sufficient defense, notwithstanding the former decision; and *provided further* that, in any case, the Bishop may at any time apply for such Council of Conciliation.

Council of Conciliation.

b. The Bishop Diocesan may deliver, from time to time, a Charge to the Clergy of the Diocese and a Pastoral Letter to the people of the Diocese on points of doctrine, discipline, or worship. The Bishop may require the Clergy to read the Pastoral Letter to their Congregations.

Charges and Pastoral Letters.

Record of official acts.

c. Each Bishop shall keep a record of all official acts, which record shall be the property of the Diocese and shall be transmitted to the Bishop's successor.

Bishop to make annual report.

d. At each Annual Meeting of the Diocesan Convention the Bishop Diocesan shall make a report of the State of the Diocese since the last Annual Meeting of the Convention; including the names of the Congregations visited; the number of persons confirmed and received; the names of those who have been admitted as Postulants and Candidates for Holy Orders, of those ordained, and of those suspended or deposed from Holy Orders; the changes by death, removal, or otherwise, which have taken place among the Clergy; and other matters the Bishop desires to present to the Convention; which statement shall be inserted in the Journal.

License to officiate required of visiting Bishop.

e. No Bishop shall perform episcopal acts or officiate by preaching, ministering the Sacraments, or holding any public service in a Diocese other than that in which the Bishop is canonically resident, without permission or a license to perform occasional public services from the Ecclesiastical Authority of the Diocese in which the Bishop desires to officiate or perform episcopal acts.

Sec. 4. Residency

Bishop to reside in jurisdiction.

a. Each Bishop serving in a Diocese shall maintain a residence in that Diocese, except with the consent of the Standing Committee of that Diocese.

b. The Bishop Diocesan shall not be absent from the Diocese for a period of more than three consecutive months without the consent of the Convention or the Standing Committee of the Diocese.

c. A Bishop Diocesan, whenever leaving the Diocese for six consecutive months or more, shall authorize in writing, under hand and seal, the Bishop Coadjutor, the Bishop Suffragan if the Constitution and Canons of the Diocese so provide, or, should there be none, the Standing Committee of the Diocese, to act as the Ecclesiastical Authority thereof during the absence. The Bishop Coadjutor, or the Bishop Suffragan if the Constitution and Canons of the Diocese so provide, or, should there be none, the Standing Committee may at any time serve as the Ecclesiastical Authority upon the written request of the Bishop and continue to act as such until the request is revoked by the Bishop Diocesan in writing.

d. A vacancy in the episcopate shall be deemed to exist on the occurrence of any of the following: *vacancy in the episcopate.*

   1. the death, resignation, deposition or removal of the Bishop exercising jurisdiction, or

   2. the incapacity (or inability to return from an absence within a time certain) of the Bishop exercising jurisdiction following the issuance of a court order by a court of competent jurisdiction or by determination of at least two licensed medical doctors, psychologists or psychiatrists, who have examined the case, as declared by

      i. the Presiding Bishop; or

      ii. resolution of the Standing Committee of the Diocese.

Sec. 5. Assistant Bishops

a. When a Diocese, in the opinion of its Bishop Diocesan, requires additional episcopal services, the Bishop Diocesan may, with the consent of the Standing Committee of the Diocese, ask the Convention of the Diocese to approve the creation of the position of Assistant Bishop and to authorize the Bishop Diocesan to appoint a Bishop for the position. If the Convention approves the creation of the position, the Bishop Diocesan may proceed to appoint a Bishop meeting the qualifications set forth in a Letter of Agreement approved by the Standing Committee of the Diocese. *Assistant Bishop.*

b. An Assistant Bishop may be appointed from among the following: *Eligibility.*

   1. Bishops Diocesan, Bishops Coadjutor, or Bishops Suffragan, who under the Constitution and Canons of this Church would be eligible for election in that Diocese; provided that at the time of accepting any such appointment a Bishop Diocesan, Bishop Coadjutor or Bishop Suffragan shall resign that office;

2. Bishops of this Church whose tenure as an Assistant Bishop of a Diocese has ended or who, having resigned their previous responsibilities are qualified to perform episcopal acts in this Church; and

3. Bishops in good standing of member churches or Provinces of the Anglican Communion, or of national or local churches with Extra-Provincial status in the Anglican Communion, provided they are received into this Church under Canon III.10.5.

Evidence of appointment.

c. Before an Assistant Bishop so appointed begins service in this position, the Bishop Diocesan making the appointment shall give certified evidence of the appointment to the Secretary of the House of Bishops and shall transmit notice of the appointment to the Presiding Bishop and to the Ecclesiastical Authority of every Diocese.

d. An Assistant Bishop shall serve at the discretion, and under the control and direction of, the Bishop Diocesan.

Age limit.

e. No person may serve as an Assistant Bishop of a Diocese beyond the termination of the jurisdiction of the appointing Bishop Diocesan of the Diocese or after attaining the age of seventy-two years, unless the Standing Committee and eventually, the succeeding Bishop Diocesan decide otherwise, and under the terms of a new Letter of Agreement renewable every twelve months.

Sec. 6. Missionary Bishops

As member of House of Bishops.

a. Any Bishop or Bishops elected and consecrated as a Missionary Bishop shall be entitled to a seat, voice and vote in the House of Bishops, and shall be eligible for election to the office of Bishop or Bishop Coadjutor or Bishop Suffragan in any organized Diocese within the United States; *provided* that such Bishop shall not be so eligible within five years from the date of consecration, except to the office of Bishop of Diocese formed in whole or in part out of such Missionary Diocese.

Eligibility for other episcopal office.

In cases of incapacity.

b. In the case of the permanent impairment of the Bishop of a Missionary Diocese, where the said Bishop shall not have submitted a resignation of jurisdiction, the Presiding Bishop shall, upon certification of the said permanent impairment by at least three reputable physicians, declare the jurisdiction vacant.

c. When the Bishop of a Missionary Diocese is unable, by reason of age or other permanent cause of impairment, fully to discharge the duties of office, a Bishop Coadjutor may be elected by the said Diocese, subject to the provisions of Canon III.11.9.a.

Sec. 7. Release and Removal from the Ordained Ministry of this Church

a. If any Bishop of The Episcopal Church shall express, in writing, to the Presiding Bishop, an intention to be released and removed from the ordained Ministry of this Church and from the obligations attendant thereto, including those promises made at Ordination in the Declaration required by Article VIII of the Constitution of the General Convention, it shall be the duty of the Presiding Bishop to record the matter. The Presiding Bishop, being satisfied that the person so declaring is acting voluntarily and for causes which do not affect the person's moral character, and is neither the subject of information concerning an Offense that has been referred to an Intake Officer nor a Respondent in a pending disciplinary matter as defined in Title IV of these Canons, shall lay the matter before the Advisory Council to the Presiding Bishop, and with the advice and consent of a majority of the members of the Advisory Council, the Presiding Bishop may pronounce that person is released and removed from the ordained Ministry of this Church and from the obligations attendant thereto, and is deprived of the right to exercise in The Episcopal Church the gifts and spiritual authority as a Minister of God's Word and Sacraments conferred in Ordinations. The Presiding Bishop shall also declare in pronouncing and recording such action that it was for causes which do not affect the person's moral character, and shall, at the person's request, give a certificate to this effect to the person so released and removed from the ordained Ministry.

Release and removal of a Bishop.

In disciplinary cases.

b. If a Bishop submitting the writing described in Section 7.a of this Canon be the subject of information concerning an Offense that has been referred to an Intake Officer or a Respondent in a pending disciplinary matter as defined in Title IV of these Canons, the Presiding Bishop shall not consider or act upon the written request unless and until the disciplinary matter shall have been resolved by a dismissal, Accord, or Order and the time for appeal or rescission of such has expired.

Declaration.

c. In the case of the release and removal of a Bishop from the ordained Ministry of the Church as provided in this Canon, a declaration of release and removal shall be pronounced by the Presiding Bishop in the presence of two or more Bishops, and shall be entered in the official records of the House of Bishops and of the Diocese in which the Bishop being removed and released is canonically resident. The Presiding Bishop shall give notice thereof in writing to the Secretary of the Convention and the Ecclesiastical Authority and the Standing Committee of the Diocese in which the Bishop was canonically resident, to all Bishops of this Church, the Ecclesiastical Authority of each Diocese of this Church, the Recorder, the Secretary of the House of Bishops, the Secretary of the General Convention, The Archives of The Episcopal Church, The Church Pension Fund, and the Board for Transition Ministry.

Sec. 8. Return to the Ordained Ministry of this Church after Release and Removal

Return to ordained Ministry.

a. When a Bishop who has been released and removed from the ordained Ministry of this Church under Canon III.12.7 desires to return to that Ministry, the person shall apply in writing to the Presiding Bishop, attaching the following:

1. Evidence of previous ordination in The Episcopal Church;

2. Evidence of appropriate background checks, certifications and proof of completion of applicable trainings including abuse prevention and anti-racism trainings;

3. A statement from no fewer than two Bishops who know the applicant in support of the application;

4. A statement of the reasons for seeking to return to the ordained Ministry of this Church.

b. If the Presiding Bishop so chooses, the Presiding Bishop may give permission for the Bishop to continue the process toward reinstatement, which may include the following:

1. Active participation in a congregation for a period of time at the Presiding Bishop's discretion;

2. Regular contact with the Presiding Bishop or the Presiding Bishop's designee during the course of the process;

3. Evaluation by a licensed mental health professional of the Presiding Bishop's choosing for the purposes of evaluation and of determining fitness for resumption of ordained ministry in this church;

4. Two references from those who are able to discuss the Bishop's former ministry;

5. Approval of the Presiding Bishop's Council of Advice.

c. Before the Bishop may be permitted to return to the ordained Ministry of this Church, the Presiding Bishop shall require the Bishop seeking to return to the ministry to sign a written declaration as required in Article VIII of the Constitution, without recourse to any other ecclesiastical jurisdiction and execute such declaration in the presence of the Presiding Bishop and two or more Bishops of this Church.

d. Thereafter the Presiding Bishop, taking into account the facts and circumstances surrounding the Bishop's removal and release, may permit, with the advice and consent of the Council of Advice to the Presiding Bishop, the return of the Bishop into the ordained Ministry of this Church.

e. Notice of the Bishop's return to the ordained Ministry of this Church shall be provided in writing to the same persons and entities receiving notice under Canon III.12.7.c.

f. The provisions of this Canon III.12.8 shall not be applicable to any Bishop who has been removed, released, or deposed from their ministry as the result of any proceeding of Title IV of these Canons.

Sec. 9. The Resignation or Incapacity of Bishops

Resignation at age seventy-two.

a. Each Bishop, upon attaining the age of seventy-two years, shall resign as required by Article II, Sec. 9 of the Constitution. The resignation shall be sent to the Presiding Bishop, who shall immediately communicate it to every Bishop of this Church exercising jurisdiction and shall declare the resignation accepted, effective at a designated date not later than three months from the date the resignation was tendered.

Certification.

b. The Presiding Bishop shall communicate to the resigning Bishop the acceptance of the resignation effective as of the date fixed. In the case of a Bishop Diocesan or Bishop Coadjutor, the Presiding Bishop shall certify the resignation to the Standing Committee of the Diocese concerned, and in the case of other Bishops, to the Ecclesiastical Authority of the Diocese concerned. The Presiding Bishop shall also order the Secretary of the House of Bishops to record the resignation, effective as of the date fixed, to be incorporated in the Journal of the House.

Failure to resign.

c. In the case of the release and removal of a Bishop from the ordained Ministry of this Church as provided in this Canon, a declaration of removal and release shall be pronounced by the Presiding Bishop in the presence of two or more Bishops, and shall be entered in the official records of the House of Bishops and of the Diocese in which the Bishop being removed and released is canonically resident. The Presiding Bishop shall give notice thereof in writing to the Secretary of the Convention and the Ecclesiastical Authority and the Standing Committee of the Diocese in which the Bishop was canonically resident, to all Bishops of the Church, the Ecclesiastical Authority of each Diocese of this Church, the Recorder, the Secretary of the House of Bishops, the Secretary of the General Convention, The

Church Pension Fund, and the Board for Transition Ministry.

d. Any Bishop who desires to resign shall send the resignation with the reasons therefore in writing to the Presiding Bishop at least thirty days before the date set for a meeting of the House of Bishops. The Presiding Bishop shall notify without delay every Bishop of this Church, and the Standing Committee of the Diocese of the Bishop desiring to resign, in order that the Standing Committee may be heard on behalf of the Diocese, either in person or by correspondence, upon the subject. The House during its session shall accept or refuse the resignation by a majority of those present.

Resignation procedure.

e. If a resignation has been tendered more than three months before a meeting of the House of Bishops, the Presiding Bishop shall communicate it, together with any statement from the Standing Committee of the Diocese concerned, to every Bishop of this Church. If a majority of the Bishops consents to the resignation, the Presiding Bishop, without delay, shall notify the resigning Bishop and the Standing Committee of the Diocese concerned of the acceptance of the resignation, effective as of the date fixed. The Presiding Bishop shall also order the Secretary of the House of Bishops to record the resignation, effective as of the date fixed, to be incorporated in the Journal of the House.

f. At each meeting of the General Convention, the Presiding Bishop shall communicate to the House of Deputies, when in session, a list of the resignations which have been accepted since the preceding meeting of the General Convention.

g. A resigned Bishop shall be subject in all matters to the Constitution and Canons of this Church and to the authority of the General Convention.

Resigned Bishops subject to Canons.

h. A resigned Bishop may only perform any episcopal act at the request of or with the permission of the Bishop Diocesan within that Bishop's Diocese. A resigned Bishop may, by vote of the Convention of any Diocese and with the consent of the Bishop of that Diocese, be given an

Official acts of resigned Bishops.

honorary seat in the Convention, with voice but without vote, or be given an honorary seat in the Cathedral of any Diocese, by and subject to the authority competent to grant such seat. The resigned Bishop shall report all official acts to the Bishop Diocesan and to the Diocese in which the acts are performed. These provisions shall also be applicable to a resigned Bishop of another Church in full communion with this Church, subject to the approval of competent authority within the other Church, where such approval may be required.

May be enrolled in Diocesan Clergy.

i. A resigned Bishop may, at the discretion of the Bishop of the Diocese in which the resigned Bishop resides, and upon presentation of Letters Dimissory from the Ecclesiastical Authority of the Diocese in which the resigned Bishop has had canonical residence most recently, be enrolled among the Clergy of the new Diocese, and become subject to its Constitution and Canons including being given a seat and vote in the Diocesan Convention, in accordance with its canonical provisions for qualification of clergy members.

Letters Dimissory.

j. When a resigned Bishop accepts a pastoral charge or other ministerial post within a Diocese, the Bishop Diocesan shall process the Letters Dimissory, and the resigned Bishop shall be enrolled among the Clergy of the Diocese and be given seat and vote in the Diocesan Convention in accordance with the canonical provisions of the Diocese for qualification of clergy members, and subject to the provisions of paragraph o. of this section.

May accept pastoral charge or other assignments.

k. A resigned Bishop may, with the approval of the Bishop of the Diocese in which the resigned Bishop resides, accept a pastoral charge in that Diocese, and, subject to the Diocese's canonical provisions for the filling of vacancies, may accept election as the Rector of a Parish therein.

l. A resigned Bishop may accept an appointment by a Bishop Diocesan to any position created under the authority of the Diocesan Convention, including that of Assisting Bishop, and may, at the same time, occupy a pastoral charge; provided, however, that a resigned

Bishop over the age of seventy-two may accept the appointment only for a term not to exceed twelve months, and this term may be renewed.

m. Assisting Bishops are those bishops whose primary roles are teaching, preaching or providing sacramental rites at the invitation of the Ecclesiastical Authority of the diocese where the Assisting Bishop has been invited to participate for particular times and places.

n. Enrollment among the Clergy of, or acceptance of any position within, a Diocese shall not deprive a resigned Bishop of the seat and vote in the House of Bishops to which the Bishop may be entitled under Article I, Sec. 2 of the Constitution.

Retains rights in House of Bishops.

o. The provisions of this section shall be applicable to a resigned Bishop who continues to reside within the limits of the resigned Bishop's former Diocese, except that the resigned Bishop shall not have the right to vote in the Diocesan Convention, unless the Canons of the Diocese specifically so provide.

Sec. 10. Impairment

When any of (i) a Bishop of a Diocese, including a Bishop Diocesan, a Bishop Coadjutor or a Bishop Suffragan of that Diocese, (ii) a two-thirds majority of all of the members of the Standing Committee of a Diocese, (iii) a two-thirds majority of a Diocese's Convention, or (iv) at least five Bishops conclude that a Bishop of the aforementioned Diocese is seriously impaired, either physically, psychologically, or emotionally, and that the impairment is causing substantial harm, or presents a significant risk of causing substantial harm, to the Bishop in question, his or her family, the Diocese, the Church, or any other person or community, the person or body reaching that conclusion may petition the Presiding Bishop, in writing, to intervene and assist in the matter. The written petition shall include sufficient information to inform the Presiding Bishop and the parties involved of the specifics of the purported impairment. The Presiding Bishop shall initiate such efforts as are appropriate under the circumstances to attempt to ascertain the nature and severity of any impairment and to

Impairment.

address any such impairment, which efforts may include, but are not limited to, the appointment of medical and other professionals, consultants or mediators, as well as the issuance of Pastoral Directions.

Sec. 11. Reconciliation of Disagreements Affecting the Pastoral Relation between a Bishop and Diocese

Pastoral relation.

When the pastoral relationship between a Bishop Diocesan, Bishop Coadjutor or Bishop Suffragan and the Diocese is imperiled by disagreement or dissension, and the issues are deemed serious by a Bishop of that Diocese or a two-thirds majority vote of all of the members of the Standing Committee or a two-thirds majority vote of all the members of the Diocesan Convention, any party may petition the Presiding Bishop, in writing, to intervene and assist the parties in their efforts to resolve the disagreement or dissension. The written petition shall include sufficient information to inform the Presiding Bishop and the parties involved of the nature, causes, and specifics of the disagreements or dissension imperiling the pastoral relationship. The Presiding Bishop shall initiate such proceedings as are deemed appropriate under the circumstances to attempt to reconcile the parties, which may include the appointment of a consultant or licensed mediator, and shall include appropriate pastoral care for all affected parties and individuals. The parties to the disagreement, following the recommendations of the Presiding Bishop, shall labor in good faith toward that reconciliation. If such proceedings lead to reconciliation, said reconciliation shall contain definitions of responsibility and accountability for the Bishop and the Diocese. In the event reconciliation has not been achieved within nine months from the date of the Presiding Bishop's initial receipt of communication from the Diocese, the parties to the disagreement shall meet and decide whether or not to continue attempting to reconcile under this Section or to end proceedings under this Section. If the parties do not agree, proceedings under this Section shall end. The parties shall notify the Presiding Bishop of their decision in writing. If the parties agree to continue attempting to reconcile, either party may end the further proceedings at any time by written notification to the Presiding Bishop and the other party.

Sec. 12. Reconciliation of Disagreements Affecting the Collegial Relation between Bishops in the Same Diocese

When the collegial relationship between a Bishop Diocesan, Bishop Coadjutor, or Bishop Suffragan is imperiled by disagreement or dissension, and the issues are deemed serious by a Bishop of that Diocese or a two-thirds majority vote of all of the members of the Standing Committee or a two-thirds majority vote of the Diocesan Convention, any party may petition the Presiding Bishop, in writing, to intervene and assist the parties in their efforts to resolve the disagreement or dissension. The written petition shall include sufficient information to inform the Presiding Bishop and the parties involved of the nature, causes, and specifics of the disagreements or dissension imperiling the collegial relationship. The Presiding Bishop shall initiate such proceedings as are deemed appropriate under the circumstances to attempt to reconcile the parties, which may include the appointment of a consultant or licensed mediator. The parties to the disagreement, following the recommendations of the Presiding Bishop, shall labor in good faith toward that reconciliation. If such proceedings lead to reconciliation, said reconciliation shall contain definitions of responsibility and accountability for the Bishops and the Diocese.

Collegial relation.

Sec. 13. Dissolution of the Pastoral Relation between a Bishop and Diocese

a. If for any urgent reason a Bishop or two-thirds majority of all the members of the Standing Committee or a two-thirds majority vote of Diocesan Convention, based on a vote in a duly-called meeting, desires a dissolution of the pastoral relationship, and the parties cannot agree, any party may give notice in writing to the Presiding Bishop with a copy available to the Bishop and also to the Standing Committee if the decision comes from the Diocesan Convention. Such notice shall include sufficient information to inform the Presiding Bishop and all parties involved of the nature, causes, and specifics

If parties cannot agree.

requiring the dissolution of the pastoral relationship. If the parties have participated in mediation or consultation processes, a separate report from the mediator or consultant will be submitted to the Presiding Bishop with copies available to the Bishop and Standing Committee.

b. Within thirty days of receipt of the written notice, the Presiding Bishop may initiate further mediation and reconciliation processes between the Bishop and Standing Committee in every way which the Presiding Bishop deems proper.

Procedures for irreconcilable differences.

c. If the differences between the parties are not resolved after completion of mediation or other reconciliation efforts or actions prescribed by the Presiding Bishop, the matter shall proceed as follows:

1. The Presiding Bishop shall convene a committee of one Presbyter and one Lay Person appointed by the President of the House of Deputies and one Bishop appointed by the Presiding Bishop, none of whom may be members of or related to the Diocese or Bishop involved. The committee may interview the Bishop and Standing Committee and conduct such other inquiries as it deems necessary.

2. The Presiding Bishop shall give written notice to the Bishop and Standing Committee that the committee will recommend a resolution of the matter to the House of Bishops, and that either party has the right within fifteen days to request in writing an opportunity to confer with the committee before the committee proposes a resolution for consideration of and approval by a two-thirds majority vote of the House of Bishops. The Presiding Bishop's written notification shall inform the parties involved of the nature, causes, and specifics of the unresolved disagreements or dissension imperiling the pastoral relationship.

3. If a timely request is made, the Presiding Bishop shall immediately notify the committee. The

committee shall set a date for the conference, which shall be held within fifteen days of the committee's receipt of the notification.

4. At the conference, each party shall be entitled to attend, be represented, and present its position fully.

5. Within fifteen days after the conference or after the expiration of the time to request in writing an opportunity to confer with the committee if no conference is requested, the committee shall provide its recommended resolution to the House of Bishops, the Bishop and the Standing Committee. The committee's recommended resolution of the matter shall become effective upon a two-thirds majority vote of the Bishops present and eligible to vote, at the next regular or special meeting of the House of Bishops. If a two-thirds majority of those Bishops is not obtained, the committee shall provide another recommended resolution to the Presiding Bishop for transmission and vote at the same meeting, as was the initial recommended resolution.

6. If the recommended resolution is that the pastoral relationship be continued, the recommended resolution shall contain definitions of responsibility and accountability for the Bishop and the Diocese.

7. If the relationship is to be dissolved, the dissolution shall have the effect of terminating a Bishop Diocesan or Bishop Coadjutor's jurisdiction and position in the Diocese, or a Bishop Suffragan's position in the Diocese, as if the Bishop had resigned.

   i. The Presiding Bishop shall direct the Secretary of the House of Bishops to record the dissolution.

   ii. The judgment may include terms and conditions including financial settlements.

8. In either event, the Presiding Bishop shall offer appropriate supportive services to the Bishop and the Diocese.

Canon 13: Of Dioceses without Bishops

Dioceses under provisional charge.

Sec. 1. A Diocese without a Bishop may, by an act of its Convention, and in consultation with the Presiding Bishop, be placed under the provisional charge and authority of a Bishop of another Diocese, or of a resigned Bishop, or of a Bishop who has been received into this Church under Canon III.10.5, who shall by that act be authorized to exercise all the duties and offices of the Bishop of the Diocese until a Bishop is elected and ordained for that Diocese or until the act of the Convention is revoked.

Sec. 2. Any Bishop may, on the invitation of the Convention or of the Standing Committee of any Diocese where there is no Bishop, visit and exercise episcopal offices in that Diocese or any part of it. This invitation may include a letter of agreement, shall be for a stated period and may be revoked at any time.

Sec. 3. A Diocese, while under the provisional charge of a Bishop, shall not invite any other Bishop to visit and exercise episcopal acts or authority without the consent of the Bishop in charge.

Canon 14: Of Religious Orders and Other Christian Communities

Religious Order defined.

Sec. 1

a. A Religious Order of this Church is a society of Christians (in communion with the See of Canterbury) who voluntarily commit themselves for life, or a term of years: to holding their possessions in common or in trust; to a celibate life in community; and obedience to their Rule and Constitution.

Official recognition.

b. To be officially recognized, a Religious Order must have at least six professed members, and must be approved by the Standing Committee on Religious Communities of the House of Bishops and be registered with the Committee.

c. Each Order shall have a Bishop Visitor or Protector, who need not be the Bishop of the Diocese in which the Order is established. If, however, the Bishop Visitor or Protector is not the Bishop of the Diocese in which the Mother House of the Order is situated, the Bishop Visitor or Protector shall not accept election without the consent of the Bishop of that Diocese. The Bishop Visitor or Protector shall be the guardian of the Constitution of the Order, and shall serve as an arbiter in matters which the Order or its members cannot resolve through its normal processes.

Bishop Visitor or Protector.

d. Any person under vows in a Religious Order, having exhausted the normal processes of the Order, may petition the Bishop Visitor or Protector for dispensation from those vows. In the event the petitioner is not satisfied with the ruling of the Bishop Visitor or Protector on such petition, the person may file a petition with the Presiding Bishop, who shall appoint a Board of three Bishops to review the petition and the decision thereon, and to make recommendation to the Presiding Bishop, who shall have the highest dispensing power for Religious Orders, and whose ruling on the petition shall be final.

Dispensations.

e. A Religious Order may establish a house in a Diocese only with the permission of the Bishop of the Diocese. This permission once granted shall not be withdrawn by the Bishop or any succeeding Bishop.

Permission to establish a house.

f. The Constitution of every Religious Order shall make provision for the legal ownership and administration of the temporal possessions of the Order, and in the event of dissolution of the Order, or should it otherwise cease to exist, shall provide for the disposition of its assets according to the laws governing non-profit (religious) organizations in the State wherein the Order is incorporated.

Legal ownership of property.

g. It is recognized that a Religious Order is not a Parish, Mission, Congregation or Institution of the Diocese within the meaning of Canon I.7.3, and its provisions shall not apply to Religious Orders.

Not regarded as a Parish or Institution.

<table>
<tr><td>Christian Community defined.</td><td>Sec. 2</td></tr>
</table>

Christian Community defined.

Sec. 2

a. A Christian Community of this Church under this Canon is a society of Christians (in communion with the See of Canterbury) who voluntarily commit themselves for life, or a term of years, in obedience to their Rule and Constitution.

Official recognition.

b. To be officially recognized such a Christian Community must have at least six full members in accordance with their Rule and Constitution, and must be approved by the Standing Committee on Religious Communities of the House of Bishops and be registered with the Committee.

Bishop Visitor or Protector.

c. Each such Christian Community of this Church shall have a Bishop Visitor or Protector, who need not be the Bishop of the Diocese in which the community is established. If, however, the Bishop Visitor or Protector is not the Bishop of the Diocese in which the Mother House of the Community is situated, the Bishop Visitor or Protector shall not accept election without the consent of the Bishop of that Diocese. The Bishop Visitor or Protector shall be the guardian of the Constitution of the Community, and shall serve as an arbiter in matters which the Community or its members cannot resolve through its normal processes.

Dispensations.

d. Any person under full commitment in such a Christian Community, having exhausted the normal processes of the Community, may petition the Bishop Visitor or Protector for dispensation from that full commitment. In the event the petitioner is not satisfied with the ruling of the Bishop Visitor or Protector on such petition, the person may file a petition with the Presiding Bishop of the Church, who shall appoint a Board of three Bishops to review the petition and the decision thereon, and to make recommendation to the Presiding Bishop, who shall have the highest dispensing power for Christian Communities, and whose ruling on the petition shall be final.

Permission to establish a house.

e. Each such Christian Community may establish a house in a Diocese only with the permission of the Bishop of the Diocese. This permission once granted shall not be withdrawn by the Bishop or any succeeding Bishop.

f. The Constitution of each Christian Community shall make provision for the legal ownership and administration of the temporal possessions of the Community, and in the event of dissolution of the Community, or should it otherwise cease to exist, shall provide for the disposition of its assets according to the laws governing non-profit (religious) organizations in the State wherein the Community is incorporated.

Provision for legal ownership of property.

g. It is recognized that a Christian Community is not a Parish, Mission, Congregation or Institution of the Diocese within the meaning of Canon I.7.3, and its provisions shall not apply to such Christian Communities.

Not regarded as a Parish or Institution.

Sec. 3. Any Bishop receiving vows of an individual not a member of a Religious Order or other Christian Community, using the form for "Setting Apart for a Special Vocation" in the *Book of Occasional Services* , or a similar rite, shall record the following information with the Standing Committee on Religious Communities of the House of Bishops: the name of the person making vows; the date of the service; the nature and contents of the vows made, whether temporary or permanent; and any other pastoral considerations as shall be deemed necessary.

Record to be kept of special vows.

Canon 15: Of the General Board of Examining Chaplains

Sec. 1. There shall be a General Board of Examining Chaplains, consisting of four Bishops, six Priests with pastoral cures or in specialized ministries, six members of accredited Seminary faculties or of other educational institutions, and six Lay Persons. The members of the Board shall be elected by the House of Bishops and confirmed by the House of Deputies, one-half of the members in each of the foregoing categories being elected and confirmed at each regular meeting of the General Convention for a term of two Convention periods. They shall take office at the adjournment of the meeting of the General Convention at which their elections are confirmed, and shall serve until the adjournment of the second regular meeting thereafter. No

Membership.

member shall serve more than 12 years consecutively. Additionally, the Presiding Bishop, in consultation with the Chair of the Board, may appoint up to four other members for a term. The House of Bishops, at any special meeting that may be held prior to the next meeting of the General Convention, shall fill for the unexpired portion of the term *To elect officers.* any vacancy that may have arisen in the interim. The Board shall elect its own Chair and Secretary, and shall have the power to constitute committees necessary for the carrying on of its work.

General Ordination Examination.

Sec. 2

a. The General Board of Examining Chaplains, with professional assistance, shall prepare at least annually a General Ordination Examination covering the subject matter set forth in Canon III.8.5.g, and shall conduct, administer, and evaluate it in respect to those Candidates for Holy Orders who have been identified to the Board by their several Bishops.

b. Whenever a Candidate has not demonstrated proficiency in any one or more of the canonical areas covered by the General Ordination Examination, the General Board of Examining Chaplains shall recommend to the Commission on Ministry, and through the Commission to the Board of Examining Chaplains, if one exists, of the Diocese to which the Candidate belongs, how the proficiencies might be attained.

May prepare guidelines.

Sec. 3. The General Board of Examining Chaplains may prepare, in each Convention period, guidelines based upon the subjects contained in Canon III.8.5.g, which guidelines shall be available to all persons concerned.

Examination results to be reported.

Sec. 4. The General Board of Examining Chaplains shall promptly report, in writing, to the Candidate, to the Candidate's Bishop and to the Dean of the Seminary the Candidate is attending, the results of all examinations held by them, together with the examinations themselves, whether satisfactory or unsatisfactory, making separate reports upon each person examined. The Bishop shall transmit these reports to the Standing Committee and to the Commission. Notwithstanding the results of the examinations, in no case shall the Standing Committee recommend a Candidate for Ordination under Canon III.8 until the Standing Committee has received from the Commission on Ministry a certificate to the effect that the Candidate has demonstrated a proficiency in all subjects required by Canon III.8.5.g and h.

The report of the Board shall be made in the following form:

To _____ (Candidate), the Right Reverend *Form of report.*
_____, Bishop of _____
(or in the absence of the Bishop the Standing Committee of)
_____: (Place) _____
(Date) _____ To the Dean of (Place)
_____ (Date) _____ We, having
been assigned as examiners of A.B., hereby testify that we have examined A.B. upon the subject matter prescribed in Canon III.8. Sensible of our responsibility, we give our judgment as follows: (Here specify the proficiency of A.B. in the subject matter appointed, or any deficiency therein, as made apparent by the examination.

(Signed)_____

Sec. 5. The General Board of Examining Chaplains shall make a report concerning its work to each regular meeting of the General Convention, and in years between meetings of the General Convention shall make a report to the House of Bishops.

Shall report to Convention.

Canon 16: Of the Board for Transition Ministry

Sec. 1   *Membership.*

a. There shall be a Board for Transition Ministry of the General Convention consisting of twelve members, four of whom shall be Bishops, four of whom shall be Presbyters or Deacons, and four of whom shall be Lay Persons.

b. The Bishops shall be appointed by the Presiding Bishop. *Appointment.* The Priests or Deacons and Lay Members shall be appointed by the President of the House of Deputies. All appointments to the Board shall be subject to the confirmation of the General Convention.

Terms.

c. The Members shall serve terms beginning with the adjournment of the meeting of the General Convention at which their appointments are confirmed, and ending with the adjournment of the second regular meeting thereafter. The members shall not serve successive terms.

d. At each regular meeting of the General Convention one-half of the membership shall be appointed to serve full terms.

Vacancies.

e. Vacancies shall be filled by appointment by the Presiding Bishop or by the President of the House of Deputies, as appropriate. Such appointments shall be for the remaining unexpired portion of the members' terms, and, if a regular meeting of the General Convention intervenes, appointments for terms extending beyond such meetings shall be subject to confirmation of the General Convention. Members appointed to fill the vacancies shall not thereby be disqualified from appointment to full terms thereafter.

Duties.

Sec. 2. The duties of the Board shall be:

a. To oversee the Office for Transition Ministry.

b. To provide support for the training of bishops and diocesan personnel in the transition ministry processes.

c. To study the transition ministry needs and trends in The Episcopal Church and in other Christian bodies.

d. To issue and distribute such reports and information concerning transition ministry as it deems helpful to the Church.

e. To cooperate with the Centers for Mission and the other Boards, Commissions, and Agencies which are concerned with transition ministry, and particularly with the Executive Council.

f. To report on its work and the work of the Office for Transition Ministry at each regular meeting of the General Convention.

g. To report to the Executive Council annually as a part of its accountability to the Council for the funding which the Office for Transition Ministry receives.

h. To work in cooperation with the Church Center Staff.

i. To fulfill other responsibilities assigned to it by the General Convention.

Title IV: Ecclesiastical Discipline

Canon 1: Of Accountability and Ecclesiastical Discipline

By virtue of Baptism, all members of the Church are called to holiness of life and accountability to one another. The Church and each Diocese shall support their members in their life in Christ and seek to resolve conflicts by promoting healing, repentance, forgiveness, restitution, justice, amendment of life and reconciliation among all involved or affected. This Title applies to Members of the Clergy, who have by their vows at ordination accepted additional responsibilities and accountabilities for doctrine, discipline, worship and obedience.

Accountability.

Canon 2: Of Terminology Used in This Title

Except as otherwise expressly provided or unless the context otherwise requires, as used in this Title the following terms and phrases shall have the following meanings:

Definition of terms.

Accord shall mean a written resolution, which is negotiated and agreed among the parties resulting from an agreement for discipline under Canon IV.9, conciliation under Canon IV.10 or a Conference Panel proceeding under Canon IV.12. All Accords shall meet the requirements of Canon IV.14.

Administrative Leave shall mean a restriction on ministry in which the exercise of the Respondent's ministry is suspended in its entirety during the period of the Administrative Leave and may include suspension from any ecclesiastical and related secular office.

Advisor shall mean a person familiar with the provisions and objectives of this Title who is designated to support, assist, consult with, advise and, where expressly so authorized under this Title, speak for a Complainant or Respondent in any matter of discipline under this Title, as provided in Canon IV.19.10.

Church Attorney shall mean one or more attorneys selected pursuant to Diocesan Canons to represent the Church in proceedings as provided in this Title. The Diocesan Canons may provide a process for the removal of a Church Attorney for cause. A Church Attorney shall perform all functions on behalf of the Church necessary to advance proceedings under this Title and shall have the following powers, in addition to the powers and duties otherwise provided in this Title: (a) to receive and review the Intake Officer's report; (b) to conduct investigations and oversee the Investigator and, in connection with such investigations; to have access to the personnel, books and records of the Diocese and its constituent parts; and to receive and review the reports of the Investigator; (c) to determine, in the exercise of the Church Attorney's discretion, whether the reported information, if true, would be grounds for discipline; and (d) to exercise discretion consistent with this Title and the interests of the Church by declining to advance proceedings or by referring any matter back to the Intake Officer or the Bishop Diocesan for pastoral response in lieu of disciplinary action. In representing the Church, a Church Attorney may consult with the president of the Disciplinary Board at any time after the matter has been referred out of the Reference Panel, and, when the prosecution of the case may impact the mission, life, or ministry of the Church, with the Bishop Diocesan.

Clear and Convincing shall mean proof sufficient to convince ordinarily prudent people that there is a high probability that what is claimed actually happened. More than a preponderance of the evidence is required but not proof beyond a reasonable doubt.

Community shall mean that part of the Church in which a Member of the Clergy performs his or her ministry, such as a Diocese, Parish, Mission, school, seminary, hospital, camp or any similar institution.

Complainant shall mean (a) any person or persons from whom the Intake Officer receives information concerning an alleged Offense and who, upon consent of that person(s), is designated a Complainant by the Intake Officer or (b) any Injured Person designated by the Bishop Diocesan who, in the Bishop Diocesan's discretion, should be afforded the status of a Complainant, *provided, however*, that any Injured Person so designated may decline such designation.

Conciliator shall mean a person appointed to seek the resolution of a matter under Canon IV.10.

Conduct Unbecoming a Member of the Clergy shall mean any disorder or neglect that prejudices the reputation, good order and discipline of the Church, or any conduct of a nature to bring material discredit upon the Church or the Holy Orders conferred by the Church.

Conference Panel shall mean a panel of one or more members of the Disciplinary Board selected by the president of the board, unless some other manner of selection is provided by Diocesan Canon, to serve as the body before which an informal conference is held as provided in Canon IV.12, *provided, however*, that no such member of the Conference Panel may serve as a member of the Hearing Panel in the same case. The president of the Disciplinary Board shall be ineligible to serve on the Conference Panel. If the Conference Panel consists of more than one member, it shall include both clergy and lay members.

Court of Review shall mean a court organized and existing as provided in Canon IV.5.4 to serve as the body which performs the duties prescribed in Canon IV.15.

Disciplinary Board shall mean the body provided for in Canon IV.5.1.

Discipline of the Church shall be found in the Constitution, the Canons and the Rubrics and the Ordinal of the Book of Common Prayer.

Doctrine shall mean the basic and essential teachings of the Church and is to be found in the Canon of Holy Scripture as understood in the Apostles and Nicene Creeds and in the sacramental rites, the Ordinal and Catechism of the Book of Common Prayer.

Hearing Panel shall mean a panel of three or more members of the Disciplinary Board and shall include both clergy and lay members selected by the president of the Board, unless some other manner of selection is provided by Diocesan Canon, to serve as the body before which a hearing is held as provided in Canon IV.13, *provided, however,* that no such member of the Hearing Panel may serve as a member of the Conference Panel in the same case. The president of the Disciplinary Board shall be ineligible to serve on the Hearing Panel.

Injured Person shall mean a person, group or Community who has been, is or may be affected by an Offense.

Intake Officer shall mean one or more persons designated by the Bishop Diocesan after consultation with the Disciplinary Board, unless otherwise selected pursuant to diocesan canons, to whom information regarding Offenses is reported.

Investigator shall mean a person having (a) sufficient knowledge, skill, experience and training to conduct investigations under this Title and (b) familiarity with the provisions and objectives of this Title. Investigators shall be appointed by the Bishop Diocesan in consultation with the president of the Disciplinary Board. The Investigator acts under the direction of the Reference Panel until a referral is made pursuant to Canon IV.11.3; after such referral, the Investigator shall be overseen by and report to the Church Attorney.

Member of the Clergy shall mean Bishops, Priests and Deacons of the Church.

Offense shall mean any act or omission for which a Member of the Clergy may be held accountable under Canons IV.3 or IV.4.

Order shall mean a written decision of a Conference Panel or a Hearing Panel which is issued with or without the Respondent's consent. All Orders shall meet the requirements of Canon IV.14.

Pastoral Direction shall mean a written direction given by a Bishop to a Member of the Clergy which meets the requirements of Canon IV.7.

Pastoral Relationship shall mean any relationship between a Member of the Clergy and any person to whom the Member of the Clergy provides or has provided counseling, pastoral care, spiritual direction or spiritual guidance, or from whom such Member of the Clergy has received information within the Rite of Reconciliation of a Penitent.

Privileged Communication shall mean any communication or disclosure made in confidence and with an expectation of privacy (a) within the Rite of Reconciliation of a Penitent; (b) between a client and the client's attorney; (c) between a Respondent and an Advisor or a Complainant and an Advisor; (d) between persons in a relationship in which communications are protected by secular law or Diocesan Canons; or (e) between and among a Conciliator and participants in a conciliation under Canon IV.10.

Reference Panel shall mean a panel composed of the Intake Officer, the Bishop Diocesan and the president of the Disciplinary Board to serve as the body which performs the duties prescribed in Canons IV.6 and IV.11.

Respondent shall mean any Member of the Clergy (a) who is the subject of a matter referred for conciliation or to the Conference Panel or to the Hearing Panel; (b) whose ministry has been restricted; (c) who has been placed on Administrative Leave; (d) who is the subject of an investigation and is asked by an investigator or by the Bishop Diocesan to provide information or to make a statement; (e) who agreed with the Bishop Diocesan regarding terms of discipline pursuant to Canon IV.9; or (f) any Member of the Clergy who requests a review pursuant to Canon IV.19.31.

Sentence shall mean the pronouncement of discipline of a Member of the Clergy pursuant to an Accord or Order in the form of (a) admonition, in which the conduct of such Member of the Clergy is publicly and formally censured or reprimanded, or (b) suspension, in which such Member of the Clergy is required to refrain temporarily from the exercise of the gifts of ministry conferred by ordination, or (c) deposition, in which such Member of the Clergy is deprived of the right to exercise the gifts and spiritual authority of God's word and sacraments conferred at ordination.

Sexual Abuse shall mean any Sexual Behavior at the request of, acquiesced to or by a person eighteen years of age or older and a person under eighteen years of age, in high school or legally incompetent.

Sexual Behavior shall mean any physical contact, bodily movement, speech, communication or other activity sexual in nature or that is intended to arouse or gratify erotic interest or sexual desires.

Sexual Misconduct Sexual Misconduct shall mean (a) Sexual Abuse, (b) Sexual Behavior engaged in by the Member of the Clergy with a person for whom the Sexual Behavior is unwelcome or who does not consent to the Sexual Behavior, or by force, intimidation, coercion or manipulation, or (c) Sexual Behavior at the request of, acquiesced to or by a Member of the Clergy with an employee, volunteer, student or counselee of that Member of the Clergy or in the same congregation as the Member of the Clergy, or a person with whom the Member of the Clergy has a Pastoral Relationship.

Canon 3: Of Accountability

Causes for proceedings.

Sec. 1. A Member of the Clergy shall be subject to proceedings under this Title for:

a. knowingly violating or attempting to violate, directly or through the acts of another person, the Constitution or Canons of the Church or of any Diocese;

b. failing without good cause to cooperate with any investigation or proceeding conducted under authority of this Title;

c. intentionally and maliciously bringing a false accusation or knowingly providing false testimony or false evidence in any investigation or proceeding under this Title; or

d. intentionally misrepresenting or omitting any material fact in applying for admission to Postulancy, for admission to Candidacy, for ordination as a Deacon or Priest, for reception from another Church as a Deacon or Priest, or for nomination or appointment as a Bishop.

e. discharging, demoting, or otherwise retaliating against any person because the person has opposed any practices forbidden under this Title or because the person has reported information concerning an Offense, testified, or assisted in any proceeding under this Title.

Sec. 2. A Member of the Clergy shall be accountable for any breach of the Standards of Conduct set forth in Canon IV.4.

Sec. 3. In order for any conduct or condition to be the subject of the provisions of this Title, the Offense complained of must violate applicable provisions of Canon IV.3 or IV.4 and must be material and substantial or of clear and weighty importance to the ministry of the Church.

Canon 4: Of Standards of Conduct

Sec. 1. In exercising his or her ministry, a Member of the Clergy shall:

a. respect and preserve confidences of others except that pastoral, legal or moral obligations of ministry may require disclosure of those confidences other than Privileged Communications;   *Confidences.*

b. conform to the Rubrics of the Book of Common Prayer;   *Rubrics.*

c. abide by the promises and vows made when ordained;   *Vows.*

d. abide by the requirements of any applicable Accord or Order, or any applicable Pastoral Direction, restriction on ministry, or placement on Administrative Leave issued under Canon IV.7;   *Accords or Orders.*

e. safeguard the property and funds of the Church and Community;   *Property.*

f. report to the Intake Officer all matters which may constitute an Offense as defined in Canon IV.2 meeting the standards of Canon IV.3.3, except for matters disclosed to the Member of Clergy as confessor within the Rite of Reconciliation of a Penitent;   *Reporting Offenses.*

g. exercise his or her ministry in accordance with applicable provisions of the Constitution and Canons of the Church and of the Diocese, ecclesiastical licensure or commission and Community rule or bylaws;   *Faithful exercise of Ministry.*

Restraint in conduct.

h. refrain from:

1. any act of Sexual Misconduct;

2. holding and teaching publicly or privately, and advisedly, any Doctrine contrary to that held by the Church;

3. engaging in any secular employment, calling or business without the consent of the Bishop of the Diocese in which the Member of the Clergy is canonically resident;

4. being absent from the Diocese in which the Member of the Clergy is canonically resident, except as provided in Canon III.9.3.e for more than two years without the consent of the Bishop Diocesan;

5. any criminal act that reflects adversely on the Member of the Clergy's honesty, trustworthiness or fitness as a minister of the Church;

6. conduct involving dishonesty, fraud, deceit or misrepresentation;

7. habitual neglect of the exercise of the ministerial office without good cause;

8. habitual neglect of public worship, and of the Holy Communion, according to the order and use of the Church; and

9. any Conduct Unbecoming a Member of the Clergy.

Canon 5: Of Disciplinary Structures

Disciplinary Board as Court.

Sec. 1. Each Diocese shall, by Canon, create a court to be known as the Disciplinary Board as described in this Canon. Each such Board shall consist of not fewer than seven persons to be selected as determined by Diocesan Canon. The membership of each Board shall include lay persons and Priests or Deacons, and the majority of the Board members shall be Priests or Deacons, but by no more than one. Within sixty days following each Diocesan convention, the Board shall convene to elect a president for the following year, unless another method for selection of the president is provided by Diocesan Canon.

Sec. 2. The provisions of Canon IV.19 shall apply to all Disciplinary Boards.

Sec. 3. The following rules shall govern the operations of all Disciplinary Boards:

Rules of operation.

a. In the event of any Board member's death, resignation or declination to serve, or disability rendering the member unable to act, the president shall declare a vacancy on the Board.

b. Notices of resignation or declination to serve shall be communicated in writing to the president.

c. No person serving in a Diocese as Chancellor, Vice Chancellor, Advisor, Conciliator, Church Attorney, Intake Officer or Investigator may serve on the Disciplinary Board of that Diocese, and no member of a Disciplinary Board may be selected to serve in one of those positions in the same Diocese. A member of the Standing Committee of a Diocese may serve on the Disciplinary Board if the Canons of the Diocese so provide. If any Priest elected to the Board is elected a Bishop, or any lay member is ordained prior to the commencement of a proceeding under this Title, that person shall immediately cease to be a member of the Board. If a proceeding has been commenced, that person may continue to serve on the Board for all proceedings in that matter through final disposition. A lay person ceasing to be a member under this subsection by reason of ordination may be appointed to fill a vacancy in the clergy members of the Board.

Eligibility.

d. Each Diocese shall provide by Canon for the filling of vacancies on the Board. In the event there be no such canonical provision by the Diocese, any vacancy occurring on the Board shall be filled by appointment of the Bishop Diocesan and the appointee shall be of the same order as the Board member being replaced.

e. Proceedings of the Panels of the Disciplinary Board shall be conducted within the rules provided in this Title. The Board may adopt, alter or rescind supplemental rules of procedure not inconsistent with the Constitution and Canons of the Church.

Evidence.   **f.** The rules of evidence for proceedings are as provided in Canon IV.13.10.

Clerk.   **g.** The Disciplinary Board shall appoint a clerk who may be a member of the Board, who shall be custodian of all records and files of the Disciplinary Board and who shall provide administrative services as needed for the functioning of the Board. The clerk, or an assistant clerk who may be appointed at the discretion of the Board, may be any person otherwise qualified who has no conflict of interest in the matter before the Board and who is not barred from serving on the Disciplinary Board under the provisions of IV.5.3.c or serving on the staff of persons so barred.

Records.   **h.** The Disciplinary Board shall keep a record of all proceedings before its Hearing Panels in a format that can be reduced to a transcript if necessary. The record of each proceeding shall be certified by the president of the Panel. If the record cannot be certified by the president by reason of the president's death, disability or absence, the record shall be certified by another member of the Panel selected by a majority of the remaining members of the Panel.

Sharing resources.   **i.** Any Diocese may agree in writing with one or more other Dioceses to develop and share resources necessary to implement this Title, including members of Disciplinary Boards, Church Attorneys, Intake Officers, Advisors, Investigators, Conciliators and administrative and financial support for proceedings under this Title.

   j. Church Attorneys, Intake Officers, Advisors, Investigators and Conciliators need not reside in or be members of the Diocese proceeding under this Title. Members of Disciplinary Boards shall be members of the Diocese in which they serve unless such Diocese has entered into an agreement for the sharing of resources as provided in Canon IV.5.3.i.

Court of Review.   **Sec. 4.** There shall be a court known as the Court of Review, with jurisdiction to receive and determine appeals from Hearing Panels of Dioceses as provided in Canon IV.15 and to determine venue issues as provided in Canon IV.19.5.c.

a. The Court of Review consists of: i. Three Bishops; six   *Members.*
    Members of the Clergy, who must include at least two
    Priests and at least two Deacons; and six lay persons;
    and ii. one Bishop, one Priest or Deacon, and one lay
    person to serve as alternates as provided in this Section.

b. The Joint Standing Committee on Nominations will
    nominate a slate of Clergy and lay persons for election
    to the Court of Review, in accordance with the Joint
    Standing Committee on Nominations' canonical charge
    and procedures and guided by the skill sets needed for
    effective service on the Court of Review. The Joint
    Standing Committee on Nomination may but need not
    nominate more persons than there are vacancies. The
    Clergy and lay nominees for the Court of Review may
    but need not be Deputies to General Convention. The
    Joint Standing Committee on Nominations must create
    a description of the skills, gifts, and experience
    requisite for service on the Court of Review, after
    consultation with the Court, including the value of
    cultural and geographic diversity on the Court and the
    value of including historically underrepresented voices
    in the governance of the Church.

c. The Bishop members and Bishop alternate members on
    the Court of Review will be nominated by the Presiding
    Bishop after consultation with the Joint Standing
    Committee on Nominations, and then elected by the
    House of Bishops at a regular meeting of the General
    Convention.

d. The Clergy and lay members and alternates on the
    Court of Review will be elected by the House of
    Deputies at a regular meeting of the General
    Convention.

    1. Except for a member filling a vacancy, the term of
        office of a member of the Court of Review begins at
        the adjournment of the regular meeting of the
        General Convention at which the member was
        elected and expires on the adjournment of the
        second regular meeting of the General Convention
        following

2. Members of the Court of Review will serve staggered terms of office such that the terms of half of the members expire at each regular meeting of the General Convention. The Joint Standing Committee on Nominations must make its nominations in a manner that supports this staggering of terms

3. Any member who has served 12 or more consecutive years will be ineligible for reelection to the Court of Review until the next regular meeting of the General Convention following the one at which the member was ineligible for reelection to the Court of Review. A person's service as an alternate will not count against these term limitations.

President. **e.** The Court of Review must select a President from among its members. The President must be a Priest, Deacon, or lay person.

Terms of office. **f.** The persons appointed to the Court of Review will continue to serve until their respective successors have been elected, except in case of death, resignation, or declination to serve. Members of the Court of Review who are currently appointed to a Panel will continue to serve until the Panel has completed its work.

Panels. **g.** Whenever a matter is referred to the Court of Review, the President must appoint a Panel for that case consisting of one Bishop, two Members of the Clergy, and two lay persons. No Bishop or Clergy member of the Court of Review may serve in any matter originating from the Diocese in which such Bishop or Clergy member is canonically resident or is then currently licensed to serve, and no lay member may serve in a matter originating from the Diocese of the lay member's primary residence or a Diocese in which the lay member is then currently active. In such event, the President shall appoint another member of the Court from the same Order to serve; if no other member is available to serve, the President must appoint an alternate of the same Order to serve.

Alternates. **h.** If any member of the Court of Review is excused under Canon IV.5.3.c, or, upon objection made by either party

to the appeal, is found by the other members of the Court
of Review to be disqualified, an alternate shall serve.

i. In the event of any Court of Review member's death,   *Vacancies.*
    resignation, or declination to serve, or disability
    rendering the member unable to act, and in the further
    event that no other member of the Court is available to
    serve, the President of the Court of Review must declare
    a vacancy on the Court of Review. Notices of resignation
    or declination to serve must be communicated in writing
    to the President of the Court of Review

j. Vacancies on the Court of Review must be filled by the
    President of the House of Deputies for lay and Clergy
    members and by the Presiding Bishop for Bishop
    members.

k. The Court of Review must appoint a clerk who may be a   *Clerk.*
    member of the Court, who will be custodian of all records
    and files of the Court of Review, and who will provide
    administrative services as needed for the functioning of
    the Court.

l. The rules of procedure for appeals to the Court of Review *Appeals.*
    are as provided in Canon IV.15, but the Court of Review
    may adopt, alter, or rescind supplemental rules of
    procedure not inconsistent with the Constitution and
    Canons of the Church.

m. For good cause shown, the Court of Review may extend
    any deadline in this Title pertaining to the Court of
    Review except the time to file a notice of appeal.

Canon 6: Of Intake and Referral of Information Concerning Offenses

Sec. 1. Each Diocese shall provide for and publicize methods   *Reporting*
and means of reporting information concerning Offenses.   *Offenses.*

Sec. 2. Information concerning Offenses may be submitted to   *Intake Officer.*
the Intake Officer in any manner and in any form.

Sec. 3. Any person other than the Intake Officer who receives
information regarding an Offense shall promptly forward the
information to the Intake Officer. A Bishop Diocesan shall

forward information to the Intake Officer whenever the Bishop Diocesan believes that the information may indicate conduct constituting one or more Offenses.

Initial inquiry. **Sec. 4.** Upon receipt of such information, the Intake Officer may undertake such initial inquiry as he or she deems necessary, and shall incorporate the information into a written intake report, including as much specificity as possible. The Intake Officer shall provide copies of the intake report to the other members of the Reference Panel and to the Church Attorney.

Dismissal. **Sec. 5.** If the Intake Officer determines that the information, if true, would not constitute an Offense, the Intake Officer shall inform the Bishop Diocesan of an intention to dismiss the matter. If the Bishop Diocesan does not object, the Intake Officer shall dismiss the matter. The Intake Officer shall provide written notice to the Complainant, the subject Member of the Clergy, and the Bishop Diocesan of the decision of dismissal, the reasons therefor, and the Complainant's right to appeal the decision within thirty days of the date of the notice and shall send a copy of that notice and the written intake report to the president of the Disciplinary Board. If the Complainant wishes to appeal the dismissal, the Bishop shall appoint an Advisor for the Complainant within 15 days of the date of the notice of dismissal. The Advisor shall assist the Complainant in preparing and signing a written statement of the acts complained of, which statement shall be sent by the Advisor to the president of the Disciplinary Board, along with a statement that the Complainant appeals the dismissal. The intake report and any related information, in the case of a dismissal, shall be retained by the Intake Officer and may be considered in connection with any additional information that may come to the Intake Officer thereafter concerning the subject Member of the Clergy.

Appeal of dismissal. **Sec. 6.** In the event of an appeal of a dismissal, the president of the Disciplinary Board shall, within thirty days of the receipt of the appeal, review the intake report and either affirm or overrule the dismissal. The president shall promptly notify the Complainant and the Complainant's Advisor, the subject Member of the Clergy and the subject

Member's Advisor, if any, the Intake Officer, and the Bishop Diocesan of the decision. If the decision is to overrule the dismissal, the president shall refer the intake report to the Reference Panel within 15 days.

Sec. 7. If the Intake Officer determines that the information, if true, would constitute an Offense, the Intake Officer shall promptly forward the intake report to the Reference Panel. The president shall promptly select from the Disciplinary Board, a Conference Panel and a Hearing Panel, and shall designate a president of each Panel. At the same time as forwarding the intake report to the Reference Panel, the Intake Officer shall send a notice to the subject Member of the Clergy informing him or her of the nature of the alleged Offense(s), the identity of any persons who have been designated as Complainants, and describing the next procedural steps that the Member of the Clergy can anticipate. The notice shall also remind the Member of the Clergy of his or her duty under Canon IV.3.1.b to cooperate in the subsequent proceedings.

Impanelment and notice.

Sec. 8. The Reference Panel shall meet as soon as possible after receiving the intake report to determine how to refer the report. Referral options are (a) no action required other than appropriate pastoral response pursuant to Canon IV.8; (b) Conciliation pursuant to Canon IV.10; (c) investigation pursuant to Canon IV.11; (d) to the Conference Panel pursuant to Canon IV.12; or (e) referral for possible agreement with the Bishop Diocesan regarding terms of discipline pursuant to Canon IV.9. Referral decisions shall require the approval of a majority of the Reference Panel. The Reference Panel shall establish a schedule for each approved option and the President of the Disciplinary Board shall be responsible for monitoring each such schedule.

Reference Panel.

Sec. 9. The Reference Panel shall monitor the progress of each referral on a monthly basis to ensure that the matter is progressing in a timely fashion. Until such time as the matter is referred to a Hearing Panel, if the Reference Panel determines that the matter has reached an impasse or is not progressing in a timely fashion, it may re-refer the matter. Once a matter is referred to a Hearing Panel, Canon IV.15.1 shall govern any issue regarding the progress of the matter.

Timely progress.

The Intake Officer shall report at least monthly to the Respondent, the Respondent's Advisor, the Respondent's Counsel, if any, the Complainant, the Complainant's Advisor and the Complainant's Counsel, if any, on the progress in the matter.

Determinations. **Sec. 10.** If the determination of the Reference Panel is to take no action other than an appropriate pastoral response, the Panel shall notify the Complainant and the subject Member of the Clergy of the determination and the basis for the determination to take no action other than an appropriate pastoral response. If the referral is to conciliation, the provisions of Canon IV.10 shall apply. If the referral is to investigation, the provisions of Canon IV.11 shall apply. If the referral is to the Bishop Diocesan for possible Agreement and an Agreement is not reached within 90 days of the referral, the Reference Panel will re-refer the matter, in accordance with Canon IV.6.9.

Confidentiality. **Sec. 11.** All communications and deliberations during the intake and referral stages (including the identities of any Complainants, Injured Persons, or other persons who report information concerning an Offense) shall be confidential except as the Bishop Diocesan deems to be pastorally appropriate or as required by law.

Canon 7: Of Pastoral Direction, Restricted Ministry and Administrative Leave

Pastoral Direction. **Sec. 1.** At any time the Bishop Diocesan may issue a Pastoral Direction to a Member of the Clergy, canonically resident, actually resident, or licensed in the Diocese.

Conditions. **Sec. 2.** A Pastoral Direction must (a) be made in writing; (b) set forth clearly the reasons for the Pastoral Direction; (c) set forth clearly what is required of the Member of the Clergy; (d) be issued in the Bishop Diocesan's capacity as the pastor, teacher and overseer of the Member of the Clergy; (e) be neither capricious nor arbitrary in nature nor in any way contrary to the Constitution and Canons of the General Convention or the Diocese; and (f) be directed to some matter which concerns the Doctrine, Discipline or Worship of the Church or the manner of life and behavior of the Member of the Clergy concerned; and (g) be promptly served upon the Member of the Clergy.

Sec. 3. If at any time the Bishop Diocesan determines that a Member of the Clergy may have committed any Offense, or that the good order, welfare or safety of the Church or any person or Community may be threatened by that member of the Clergy, the Bishop Diocesan may, without prior notice or hearing, (a) place restrictions upon the exercise of the ministry of such Member of the Clergy or (b) place such Member of the Clergy on Administrative Leave.

Precautionary measures.

Sec. 4. Any restriction on ministry imposed pursuant to Canon IV.7.3.a or placement on Administrative Leave pursuant to Canon IV.7.3.b must (a) be made in writing; (b) set forth clearly the reasons for which it is issued; (c) set forth clearly the limitations and conditions imposed and the duration thereof; (d) set forth clearly changes, if any, in the terms of compensation and the duration thereof; (e) be neither capricious nor arbitrary in nature nor in any way contrary to the Constitution and Canons of the General Convention or the Diocese; (f) be promptly served upon the Member of the Clergy; and (g) advise the Member of the Clergy of his or her right to be heard in the matter as provided in this Canon. A copy of such writing shall be promptly provided to the Church Attorney.

Notice of restrictions and leaves.

Sec. 5. The duration of restriction on ministry or Administrative Leave may be for a stated period or to continue until the occurrence of a specified event or the satisfaction of a specified condition.

Duration.

Sec. 6. Pastoral Directions, restrictions on ministry and Administrative Leaves (a) may be issued and imposed in any chronological order; (b) may be issued and imposed concurrently; and (c) may be modified at any time by the issuing Bishop or that Bishop's successor, *provided* that the Pastoral Direction, restriction on ministry or Administrative leave, as modified, meets the requirements of this Canon.

Bishop may modify.

Sec. 7. Any Pastoral Direction, restriction on ministry or Administrative Leave under this Canon shall be effective upon service of the writing setting it forth on the subject Member of the Clergy as provided in Canon IV.19.20.

Sec. 8. If imposition of restriction on ministry or placement on Administrative Leave occurs prior to the receipt of information by the Intake Officer, as provided in Canon IV.6, then the Bishop may forward a copy of the writing setting forth the restriction or Administrative Leave to the Intake Officer, who shall receive such information as a report of an Offense and proceed as provided in Canon IV.6.

Disclosure. **Sec. 9.** The Bishop Diocesan may disclose such information concerning any Pastoral Direction, restriction on ministry or Administrative Leave as the Bishop Diocesan deems pastorally appropriate or as necessary to seek or obtain Diocesan authority for resolution of the matter or any part thereof.

Clergy request for review. **Sec. 10.** Every imposition of restriction on ministry or placement on Administrative Leave shall be subject to review upon the request of the Member of the Clergy at any time in the duration thereof. A request for review must be in writing and addressed to the president of the Disciplinary Board and the Church Attorney, with a copy to the Bishop Diocesan. A Member of the Clergy who requests review shall become a Respondent under this Title. Reviews shall be conducted within fifteen days of the delivery of the request for review to the president of the Disciplinary Board, unless extended by consent of the Respondent. If a restriction on ministry or placement on Administrative Leave has been reviewed once, a second request for review may be made only if there has been a substantial change of circumstances from the time of the first request or if there has been a modification of the restriction on ministry or placement on Administrative Leave.

Conduct of review. **Sec. 11.** If a request for review of restriction on ministry or Administrative Leave is made prior to referral to the Conference Panel, then the review shall be conducted by the Conference Panel. If a request for review of restriction on ministry or Administrative Leave is made subsequent to referral to the Conference Panel but prior to referral to the Hearing Panel, the review shall be conducted by the Conference Panel. If a request for review of restriction on ministry or Administrative Leave is made subsequent to referral to the Hearing Panel, the review shall be conducted by the Hearing Panel. The question before a Panel reviewing a restriction on ministry or Administrative Leave is whether, at the time of the review and based upon information then available to the Panel, the restrictions on ministry or Administrative Leave and the terms and conditions thereof are warranted. The review may be conducted either personally or telephonically. The Intake Officer, the Respondent, the Respondent's Advisor, the Respondent's counsel, if any, the Bishop Diocesan, the Chancellor and the Church Attorney shall each be afforded the opportunity to be present, either personally or telephonically, at the review, and any such person present shall be heard by the Panel if such person desires to be heard. The Panel may hear from other persons at the Panel's discretion.

Sec. 12. After conducting the review and hearing from the persons designated in Canon IV.7.11 who desire to be heard, the Panel shall confer privately and make a determination to (a) dissolve the restriction on ministry or Administrative Leave; (b) affirm the restriction on ministry or Administrative Leave and the terms and conditions thereof; or (c) affirm the restriction on ministry or Administrative Leave, but with modification of the terms and conditions thereof. The Panel's determination shall be in writing and shall be delivered to the Respondent, the Church Attorney, the Bishop Diocesan and the Intake Officer, and shall be binding in the same manner as provided in Canon IV.7.7. In the event of the dissolution of the restriction on ministry or Administrative Leave, the Bishop Diocesan may give notice thereof to such persons and Communities having notice of the restriction on ministry or Administrative Leave as the Bishop Diocesan deems appropriate.

Panel to make determination.

Sec. 13. Any Accord or Order resulting from Canons IV.9, IV.10, IV.12 or IV.13, unless otherwise specified, shall supersede any restriction on ministry or Administrative Leave then in effect.

Canon 8: Of Pastoral Response

Sec. 1. The Bishop Diocesan shall provide for appropriate pastoral response whenever any report is made to the Intake

Officer. Such pastoral response shall embody respect, care, and concern for affected persons and Communities. The response shall be designed so as to promote healing, repentance, forgiveness, restitution, justice, amendment of life and reconciliation among all involved or affected. If the report involves an allegation of Sexual Misconduct, the Bishop Diocesan is encouraged to provide for a pastoral response that will include the provision of assistance by a mental health professional with appropriate skills for meaningful response to affected persons.

Available to all affected. **Sec. 2.** In each pastoral response the Bishop Diocesan shall consider offering pastoral care to all those who may be affected by an alleged Offense. Pastoral care shall be considered for the Complainant, the Complainant's family, the Respondent, the Respondent's family, Injured Persons, Injured Persons' families, any affected Community, witnesses, and the Disciplinary Board.

Disclosure. **Sec. 3.** In every case, and notwithstanding any other provision of this Title to the contrary, the Bishop Diocesan may disclose such information concerning any alleged Offense or concerning any Accord or Order as the Bishop Diocesan deems pastorally appropriate.

Privacy interests. **Sec. 4.** The Bishop Diocesan shall give consideration to the respective privacy interests and pastoral needs of all affected persons.

Sec. 5. The Bishop Diocesan may designate a person to be responsible for the implementation of the pastoral response. Such person may be the Intake Officer. The duties of such person may include coordination of pastoral care and coordination of communications between the Bishop Diocesan and Advisors.

Canon 9: Of Agreements Between Bishops Diocesan and Respondents for Discipline

Clergy may propose terms of discipline. **Sec. 1.** At any time before an Order becomes effective, the Respondent or any Member of the Clergy who has not yet become a Respondent but who is alleged to have committed an Offense may propose terms of discipline to the Bishop

Diocesan, or the Bishop Diocesan may propose terms of discipline to the Respondent or such Member of the Clergy. Before reaching agreement, the Bishop Diocesan shall consult with the Injured Persons, if any, the president of the Disciplinary Board and the Church Attorney with respect to the proposed terms of discipline. If the Respondent or such Member of the Clergy and the Bishop Diocesan reach agreement regarding terms of discipline, such terms shall be set forth in a proposed Accord. A Member of the Clergy becomes a Respondent by reaching agreement with the Bishop Diocesan regarding terms of discipline.

Sec. 2. An Accord under this Canon may be entered into if (a) the Respondent is aware of the discipline to be imposed and the effect thereof; (b) the Respondent has had adequate opportunity to consult and seek advice from, or has in fact consulted and received advice from, counsel of the Respondent's choosing; and (c) the Accord adequately considers and, where possible, provides for healing, repentance, forgiveness, restitution, justice, amendment of life and reconciliation among the Complainant, Respondent, affected Community and other persons and is otherwise an appropriate resolution of the matter. *Accord with Respondent.*

Sec. 3. An Accord under this Canon may be withdrawn by the Priest or Deacon within three days of execution thereof by the Priest or Deacon and if not withdrawn shall be effective and irrevocable thereafter.

Sec. 4. Accords under this Section shall be subject to all the provisions of Canon IV.14 regarding Accords, not inconsistent with this Section.

Canon 10: Of Conciliation

Sec. 1. Conciliation shall seek a resolution which promotes healing, repentance, forgiveness, restitution, justice, amendment of life and reconciliation among the Complainant, Respondent, affected Community, other persons and the Church.

Sec. 2. Where a matter is referred for conciliation, the Bishop Diocesan shall appoint a Conciliator to assist the *Conciliator.*

Complainant, Respondent, other affected persons and the Church in reconciling. The Bishop Diocesan or a representative appointed by the Bishop Diocesan may participate in the conciliation.

Sec. 3. If the conciliation is successful in reaching agreement among the parties on a suitable resolution of all issues, an Accord will be prepared as provided in Canon IV.14 If conciliation cannot be achieved within a reasonable time, the Conciliator will report such to the Bishop Diocesan, and the matter will be referred back to the Reference Panel.

Qualifications. **Sec. 4.** A Conciliator shall be a person skilled in dispute resolution techniques and without conflict of interest in the matter. All communications between the Complainant and the Conciliator, the Respondent and the Conciliator and other participants in the conciliation and the Conciliator shall be confidential except as the Conciliator may have the permission of the respective person to disclose the information to the other participants in the conciliation in order to promote efforts towards conciliation.

Canon 11: Of Investigations

Investigators. **Sec. 1.** In each Diocese there shall be one or more Investigators.

Sec. 2. Upon referral of an intake report, the Investigator shall investigate all facts pertinent to the factual claims of the intake report. The Investigator shall use appropriate investigative means, with due consideration to pastoral sensitivities, and shall complete the investigation as expeditiously as possible.

Report to Reference Panel. **Sec. 3.** The Investigator shall present the findings of the investigation in writing to the Reference Panel. The Reference Panel may meet with the Investigator and shall consider the report to determine whether to: (a) take no action other than appropriate pastoral responses pursuant to Canon IV.8; (b) refer the matter to the Bishop Diocesan for consideration of proceedings under Canon IV.9; (c) refer the matter to conciliation pursuant to Canon IV.10; (d) require further investigation; or (e) refer the matter to the

Conference Panel pursuant to Canon IV.12, or to the Hearing Panel pursuant to Canon IV.13. The determination shall be approved by a majority vote of the Reference Panel.

Sec. 4. If the determination is to refer for further investigation, the Investigator shall make such further investigation as the Reference Panel directs and shall submit a supplemental report of findings to the Reference Panel. The Reference Panel shall then reconvene and proceed as provided in Canon IV.11.3.

Sec. 5. All investigations shall be confidential until such time as information obtained may be utilized by the Church Attorney, the Bishop Diocesan or the Panels. All persons, prior to being interviewed by the investigator, shall be advised of the confidential nature of the investigation and when such information may be shared during the course of the proceedings.

Canon 12: Of Conference Panels

Sec. 1. Upon referral of a matter to a Conference Panel, the president of the Disciplinary Board shall forward to the Church Attorney the intake report, all of the Investigator's reports and any other writings or other file materials created or collected by the Disciplinary Board or any panel thereof during the intake, investigative or referral process. From this material the Church Attorney shall prepare a written statement, describing each alleged Offense separately, with reasonable particularity sufficient to apprise the Respondent of the acts, omissions or conditions which are the subject of the proceedings. The Church Attorney shall then forward the materials received from the president of the Disciplinary Board, together with the written statement, to the Conference Panel.

Referral to Conference Panel.

Sec. 2. The Conference Panel shall review the materials provided to determine who, in addition to those listed in Canon IV.12.3, should be directed to participate in the proceeding before the Conference Panel in order to promote the purposes of this Title. Such may include, for example, the Investigator, family members, representatives of the affected Community, or other affected persons.

Notices issued. **Sec. 3.** The Conference Panel shall issue a notice to the Respondent, the Respondent's Advisor, the Respondent's Counsel, if any, the Complainant, the Complainant's Advisor, the Complainant's Counsel, if any, the Investigator and such other persons, if any, as the Conference Panel in its discretion may determine. The notice shall describe the nature and purpose of the proceeding, shall contain a copy of the written statement prepared by the Church Attorney, shall disclose the names of all persons to whom the notice is sent, and shall establish a date, time and place for conference at which the Respondent is to appear before the Conference Panel, which date shall be not less than twenty days after service of the notice upon the Respondent. The Conference Panel shall endeavor to set the conference at a date and location reasonably convenient for the persons entitled to attend.

Attendance. **Sec. 4.** The Respondent shall attend the conference and may be accompanied by an Advisor or counsel, if any, or both.

Sec. 5. The Church Attorney shall attend the conference, shall represent the Church and shall be heard by the Conference Panel.

Sec. 6. The Complainant may attend the conference but may not be required to do so. The Complainant's Advisor may attend the conference regardless of whether the Complainant attends.

Proceedings. **Sec. 7.** The proceedings of the Conference Panel shall be informal and conversational. The Conference Panel shall describe the alleged Offense to the Respondent. The Conference Panel shall hear from the Complainant or the Complainant's Advisor or both, if either or both are present, and from the Respondent and the Respondent's Advisor or counsel, if any, or both. At its discretion, the Conference Panel may hear from the Investigator or any other persons present, and may direct the Investigator to conduct additional investigation and suspend its proceedings to allow such investigation to be completed. At its discretion, the Conference Panel may confer with any participants outside the presence of the other participants.

Sec. 8. No witnesses shall be called to testify at the proceedings before the Conference Panel. No record of the proceedings of the Conference Panel shall be made. The conference shall be closed to all except the members of the Conference Panel and invited participants. Proceedings before the Conference Panel shall be confidential except as may be provided in an Order or Accord or as provided elsewhere in this Title. No statements made by any participant in such proceeding may be used as evidence before the Hearing Panel.

Closed conference.

Sec. 9. An Accord may be entered into at a proceeding before the Conference Panel. If an Accord is not entered into, the Conference Panel shall confer privately to reach a determination of the matter, which may include (a) dismissal of the matter; (b) referral for conciliation; (c) referral to the Hearing Panel; or (d) issuance of an Order.

Determination.

Sec. 10. If the determination is to dismiss the matter, the Conference Panel shall issue an Order which shall include the reasons for dismissal and which may contain findings exonerating the Respondent. A copy of the Order shall be provided to the Bishop Diocesan, the Respondent, the Respondent's Advisor, the Complainant, the Complainant's Advisor and the Church Attorney.

Order of dismissal.

Sec. 11. If the resolution is the entry of an Accord or the issuance of an Order other than an Order of dismissal, the provisions of Canon IV.14 shall apply.

Accord or other Order.

Sec. 12. The Respondent or the Church Attorney may object to an Order issued by the Conference Panel by giving written notice of the objection to the president of the Conference Panel within fifteen days following the date on which the Order is issued. Upon receipt of the notice of objection, the president of the Conference Panel shall notify and provide copies of the notice of objection to the Bishop, president of the Disciplinary Board and the non-objecting party. The president of the Disciplinary Board shall promptly notify members of the Hearing Panel and refer the matter to the Hearing Panel.

Objection to an Order.

Canon 13: Of Hearing Panels

Referral to Hearing Panel.

Sec. 1. When the Conference Panel decides to refer a matter to the Hearing Panel, the president of the Conference Panel shall within three days of that decision notify the president of the Disciplinary Board and the Church Attorney.

Statement of Offense and notice.

Sec. 2. Within 10 days of receipt of a referral for Hearing Panel proceedings, the Church Attorney shall provide to the Hearing Panel the statement of the alleged Offense(s), updated as needed. No other material from any prior proceedings under Title IV shall be provided to the Hearing Panel. Upon receipt of the Church Attorney's communication, the Hearing Panel shall within seven days issue a notice to the Respondent, to the Respondent's Advisor, to Respondent's counsel, if any, and to the Church Attorney.

a. The notice shall describe the nature and purpose of the proceeding, contain a copy of the written statement prepared by the Church Attorney, disclose the names of all persons to whom the notice is sent, advise the Respondent that a written response to the notice must be filed by the Respondent with the Hearing Panel within thirty days of the mailing date of the notice and advise the Respondent of the provisions of Canon IV.19.6.

b. A copy of the notice shall be sent to the Complainant and to the Complainant's Advisor.

Respondent's response.

c. Unless additional time is approved for good cause by the Hearing Panel, the Respondent shall within 30 days of the mailing date of the notice file with the Hearing Panel and deliver to the Church Attorney a written response signed by the Respondent.

Document dissemination.

Sec. 3. As soon as possible, the Hearing Panel shall make documents available to members of the Church and the Church media as set forth in this Section. The documents shall be disseminated in such a way as to make them broadly known to members of the Church and the Church media. For a matter in which a Priest or Deacon is the Respondent, dissemination shall include, at a minimum, posting to the diocesan website. For a matter in which a Bishop is the

Respondent, dissemination shall include, at a minimum, posting the documents on the websites of The Episcopal Church and of the General Convention.

a. The documents covered by this Section are all documents filed with or issued by the Hearing Panel or by any party or person including but not limited to motions, briefs, affidavits, opinions, objections, decisions, notices, challenges, and Orders.

b. Notwithstanding the above, the Hearing Panel, at its discretion and for good cause to protect any Injured Person or allegedly Injured Person, may require the redaction of documents provided for in Sec. 5.a, after consultation with the Church Attorney, the Respondent's counsel, the Respondent's Advisor, the Complainant's Advisor or Complainant's counsel, if any, and, where appropriate, the Bishop Diocesan.

Sec. 4. If at any time after a matter has been referred to a Hearing Panel an Accord is reached that ends the proceedings before the Hearing Panel issues an Order, the Bishop Diocesan shall make the Notice of Accord available to the Church and Church media as provided in Sec. 3 as well as to the Hearing Panel.

Sec. 5. The Church Attorney and the Respondent shall each be afforded reasonable time and opportunity to discover evidence in preparation for the hearing as follows:

Evidence and discovery.

a. Within sixty days after the filing and delivery of the response by the Respondent, the Church Attorney and the Respondent's counsel shall each provide to the other a mandatory disclosure of all evidence known to them that would tend to prove or disprove the allegations against the Respondent, including but not limited to (1) the name and, if known, the address and telephone number of each individual likely to have direct knowledge of information which may be used to support the allegations against the Respondent or the defenses thereto, together with a detailed summary of the expected testimony of the person, if called to testify; and (2) a copy of, or a description by category and location of, all documents and tangible things that may be used to support the allegations against the Respondent or the defenses thereto, except as such disclosure would involve Privileged Communications. The parties must supplement mandatory disclosures made under this section as additional information becomes known. Documents and tangible items identified in the mandatory disclosures that are in the possession of a party shall be produced upon request, and copies of all documents provided to the requesting party. The Hearing Panel may, upon request of a party or Injured Person, enter an order limiting production of documents or tangible items of a sensitive nature.

b. If any party withholds from disclosure any relevant document on the ground of privilege, the party must provide a log containing the date of the communication, a list of all persons party to the communication, and a short description of the nature of the communication. The scope of the privilege shall be determined by the Hearing Panel, pursuant to Canon IV.19.27.

c. Within fifteen days after the delivery of the mandatory disclosures, the president of the Hearing Panel shall convene a scheduling conference with the Church Attorney and Respondent's counsel. During the scheduling conference, after the Church Attorney and Respondent's counsel have been heard, the president of the Hearing Panel shall issue a Scheduling Order to provide for (1) a calendar for discovery, including depositions and written interrogatories, as provided in this section; (2) filing deadlines and hearing dates for preliminary motions and for dispositive motions; and (3) the date of hearing before the Hearing Panel.

d. The Scheduling Order shall provide the Church Attorney and Respondent's counsel authorization to take up to two depositions and propound up to twenty written interrogatories regarding each Complainant.

e. No other discovery shall be allowed at any point during the pendency of a matter under this Title except with permission of the Hearing Panel upon a showing of good cause.

f.　Notwithstanding any provision of this section, the Hearing Panel shall take reasonable steps to assure that the discovery process will not unduly burden any person from whom information is sought or unduly adversely affect any pastoral response being offered to any such person. The Hearing Panel may impose, after reasonable notice and opportunity to be heard, reasonable sanctions on any party for failure to comply with any discovery order pursuant to the provisions of Canon IV.13.9.

Sec. 6. In all proceedings before the Hearing Panel, the Church Attorney shall appear on behalf of the Diocese, which shall then be considered the party on one side and the Respondent the party on the other.

Sec. 7. All pre-hearing motions and challenges shall be filed with the Hearing Panel within the time limits prescribed in the Scheduling Order. All responses shall be filed by the non-moving party within 15 days of receipt of the motion or challenge. Upon receipt of a motion or challenge, the Hearing Panel will promptly set the matter for hearing. The hearing may be conducted by conference call. After consideration of the argument of the parties, the Hearing Panel shall render a decision within three days of the hearing. The decision shall be final as to all procedural matters. Decisions on evidentiary matters are preliminary and may be reconsidered by the Hearing Panel during the course of the hearing if warranted by the evidence. The decision shall be provided to the parties and placed on the record of proceedings.

Procedural matters.

Sec. 8. All proceedings before the Hearing Panel except its private deliberations shall be open to the Respondent and to each Complainant, to any Injured Person, and to persons from the public. Each Complainant shall be entitled to be present throughout and observe the Hearing and each may be accompanied at the proceedings by another person of his or her own choosing in addition to his or her Advisor. Notwithstanding the above, the Hearing Panel, at its discretion and for good cause, including to protect the privacy of any person, may close any part of the proceedings to any person or group of persons, after consultation with the Church Attorney, the Respondent's counsel and, where appropriate, the Bishop Diocesan; provided, however, that no

Public proceedings and transcript.

proceedings before the Hearing Panel, except its private deliberations, shall be closed to the Respondent, Respondent's Advisor, Respondent's Counsel, the Complainant, the Complainant's Advisor, Complainant's Counsel or the Church Attorney. A record of the hearing shall be made by such means as to enable the creation of a verbatim written transcript of the hearing.

Pre-hearing disclosures.

Sec. 9. At least 15 days before the hearing, the Church Attorney and Respondent's counsel shall each provide to the other and to the Hearing Panel final pre-hearing disclosures including (1) the name, address, and telephone number of each witness expected to be called to testify at the hearing; (2) identification of each document or other tangible object expected to be used as an exhibit in the hearing; and (3) requests, if any, to have all or portions of the hearing closed to the public.

Testimony.

Sec. 10. In all proceedings of the Hearing Panel the testimony of witnesses shall be taken orally and personally or by such other means as provided by order of the Hearing Panel. All testimony shall be given under oath or solemn affirmation and be subject to cross-examination. The Hearing Panel shall determine the credibility, reliability and weight to be given to all testimony and other evidence. The proceedings shall be conducted as follows:

a.   The president shall regulate the course of the hearing so as to promote full disclosure of relevant facts.

b.   The president:

  1.   may exclude evidence that is irrelevant, immaterial or unduly repetitious;

  2.   shall exclude privileged evidence;

  3.   may receive documentary evidence in the form of a copy or excerpt if the copy or excerpt contains all pertinent portions of the original document;

  4.   may take official notice of any facts that could be judicially noticed, including records of other proceedings;

  5.   may not exclude evidence solely because it is hearsay;

6. shall afford to the Church Attorney and to the Respondent reasonable opportunity to present evidence, argue and respond to argument, conduct cross-examination and submit rebuttal evidence; and

7. may, at the discretion of the Hearing Panel, give persons other than the Church Attorney and the Respondent opportunity to present oral or written statements at the hearing.

c. Nothing in this section shall preclude the exercise of discretion by the president in taking measures appropriate to preserve the integrity of the hearing.

Sec. 11

a. The Hearing Panel shall have the authority, upon reasonable notice, to impose sanctions on the Respondent, the Respondent's counsel, or the Church Attorney, for conduct that the Hearing Panel deems to be disruptive, dilatory, or otherwise contrary to the integrity of the proceedings. If the conduct in question is that of the Respondent's counsel, notice shall be given to the following: the Respondent, Respondent's counsel, and Respondent's Advisor. If the conduct in question is that of the Church Attorney, notice shall be given to each of the Church Attorney, the Bishop Diocesan, and the person or Diocesan body with authority to remove or replace the Church Attorney. If the conduct is that of the Respondent, notice shall be given to each of the Church Attorney, the Bishop Diocesan, Respondent's counsel, Respondent's Advisor, and Respondent.

Sanctions.

b. Any sanction must be proportionate to the underlying misconduct. Sanctions that may be imposed pursuant to Canon IV.13.11.a include, but are not limited to:

1. amending a scheduling order;

2. limiting discovery;

3. refusing to allow the disobedient party to support or oppose claims or defenses;

4. refusing to allow the disobedient party to introduce certain matters into evidence;

5. striking claims or defenses or responses; or

6. disqualification of counsel.

Appeal of sanction.

c. Within 10 days of the imposition of sanctions under this section, the sanctioned party may appeal the sanction to the Disciplinary Board (excluding the members of the Hearing Panel). The standard of review for such appeal shall be *de novo*. The president of the Disciplinary Board shall establish a hearing date and convene the Disciplinary Board members, within 20 days, either personally or telephonically, to consider the appeal. The Disciplinary Board shall issue its ruling within three days of conclusion of the hearing. The ruling of the Disciplinary Board cannot be the subject of an interlocutory appeal.

d. The requirements of Sec. 3 of this Canon shall apply to the Disciplinary Board as if it were a Hearing Panel for the purpose of an appeal of sanctions under this Section.

e. If an Accord is reached that ends the proceedings before the Disciplinary Board issues an Order under this Section, the Bishop Diocesan shall make the Notice of Accord available to the Church and Church media as provided in Sec. 3 as well as to the Disciplinary Board and the Hearing Panel.

Determination.

Sec. 12. Following the conclusion of the hearing, the Hearing Panel shall confer privately to reach a determination of the matter by (a) dismissal of the matter or (b) issuance of an Order.

Order of dismissal.

Sec. 13. If the determination is to dismiss the matter, the Hearing Panel shall issue an Order which shall include the reasons for dismissal and which may contain findings exonerating the Respondent. A copy of the Order shall be provided to the Bishop Diocesan, the Respondent, the Respondent's Advisor, the Complainant, the Complainant's Advisor, and the Church Attorney, and a record copy of the Order shall be kept by transmitting a copy to The Archives of The Episcopal Church.

Sec. 14. If the resolution is the issuance of an Order other than an Order of dismissal, the provisions of Canon IV.14 shall apply.

Canon 14: Of Accords and Orders

Sec. 1. An Accord may (a) provide any terms which promote healing, repentance, forgiveness, restitution, justice, amendment of life and reconciliation among the Complainant, Respondent, affected Community and other persons; (b) place restrictions on the Respondent's exercise of ministry; (c) place the Respondent on probation; (d) recommend to the Bishop Diocesan that the Respondent be admonished, suspended or deposed from ministry; (e) limit the involvement, attendance or participation of the Respondent in the Community; or (f) any combination of the foregoing. An Accord may be conditioned on the Bishop Diocesan imposing any recommended admonition, suspension, deposition or conditions for restoration to ministry. An Accord providing for suspension from ministry shall specify on what terms or conditions and at what time the suspension shall cease. Any Accord providing for limitation upon the involvement, attendance or participation of the Respondent in the Community shall also provide conditions for restoration.

Accords.

Sec. 2. If an Accord results from a Conciliation, the Accord shall be signed by the Complainant, the Respondent and the Conciliator, *provided* that the Conciliator shall sign last.

Accords from Conciliation.

Sec. 3. If an Accord results from proceedings before a Conference Panel, the Complainant and the Complainant's Advisor shall have first been afforded an opportunity to be heard by the Panel regarding the proposed terms of the Accord. The Accord shall be signed by the Respondent, the Church Attorney and the president of the Panel, *provided* that the president shall sign last.

Complainant to be heard.

Sec. 4. In the case of any Accord that has become effective:

a. On the date when an Accord becomes effective and irrevocable, a copy of the Accord must be served on the Complainant, the Complainant's Advisor, the

Distribution of Accord.

Complainant's counsel, if any, the Respondent, the Respondent's Advisor, the Respondent's counsel, if any, the Church Attorney, the president of the Disciplinary Board, and the Bishop Diocesan. If the Accord was reached before the Conciliator, the Conciliator must serve the Accord on the persons specified above; if the Accord was reached before the Conference Panel, the president of the Conference Panel must serve the Accord on the persons specified above; and if the Accord was reached between the Bishop Diocesan and the Respondent under Canon IV.9, the Bishop Diocesan must serve the Accord on the persons specified above as well as the president of the panel to which the matter is assigned.

b. For an Accord pertaining to a Bishop Diocesan, Bishop Suffragan serving under Article II.5, or Bishop serving under Canon III.13, the Presiding Bishop must also serve a copy of the Accord on the Standing Committee of the Bishop's Diocese. For an Accord pertaining to any other Bishop, the Presiding Bishop must also serve a copy of the Accord on the Bishop Diocesan and the Standing Committee of the Bishop's Diocese.

c. In his or her discretion and for good cause to protect any Injured Person or allegedly Injured Person, the person required by this Section to serve a copy of the Accord may redact information about the Injured Person, including the Injured Person's identity, but provisions required by Section 1 and Section 9 of this Canon may not be redacted.

Pronounce Sentence on Accords. **Sec. 5.** The Bishop Diocesan shall have twenty days from the date on which the Accord is entered in which to advise in writing the Respondent, the Respondent's Advisor, the Respondent's counsel, if any, the Complainant, the Complainant's Advisor, the Church Attorney and the Conciliator or the president of the Conference Panel whether the Bishop Diocesan will pronounce the Sentence or accept the other terms of the Accord as recommended. The Bishop Diocesan shall advise that he or she will (a) pronounce the Sentence as recommended, or (b) pronounce a lesser Sentence than that recommended and/or, (c) reduce the burden on the Respondent of any of the other terms of the Accord. If a Sentence of Admonition, Suspension or Deposition is imposed, the Bishop Diocesan shall pronounce Sentence not sooner than twenty days following the date on which the Accord is entered and not later than forty days following such date. The Bishop Diocesan's pronouncement of a lesser Sentence than that recommended or other modification shall not affect the validity or enforceability of the remainder of the Accord. In the case of an Accord under Canon IV.9, the Bishop Diocesan shall pronounce Sentence not sooner than the day after the date the Accord becomes effective and irrevocable.

Sec. 6. An Order issued by a Conference Panel or Hearing Panel may (a) provide any terms which promote healing, repentance, forgiveness, restitution, justice, amendment of life and reconciliation among the Complainant, Respondent, affected Community and other persons; (b) place restrictions on the Respondent's exercise of ministry; (c) recommend to the Bishop Diocesan that the Respondent be admonished, suspended or deposed from ministry; (d) limit the involvement, attendance or participation of the Respondent in the Community; or (e) any combination of the foregoing. An Order providing for suspension from Ministry shall specify on what terms or conditions and at what time the suspension shall cease. Any Order providing for limitation upon the involvement, attendance or participation of the Respondent in the Community shall also provide conditions for restoration.

Order issued by Panels.

Sec. 7. Prior to the issuance of an Order by a Conference Panel or a Hearing Panel, the issuing Panel shall afford the Bishop Diocesan, the Respondent and the Complainant each with an opportunity to be heard on the proposed terms of the Order.

Sec. 8

Pronounce Sentence on Orders.

a. Except for an Order from a Conference Panel to which the Respondent or Church Attorney has timely filed a notice of objection, the Bishop Diocesan shall have twenty days from the date of the issuance of the Order in which to advise in writing the Respondent, the

Respondent's Advisor, the Complainant, the Complainant's Advisor, the Church Attorney, and the president of the Conference Panel or Hearing Panel (whichever Panel issued the Order) whether the Bishop Diocesan will pronounce the Sentence or accept the other terms of the Order as recommended. The Bishop Diocesan shall advise that he or she will (a) pronounce the Sentence as recommended or (b) pronounce a lesser Sentence than that recommended and/or (c) reduce the burden on the Respondent of any of the other terms of the Order.

b. The Bishop Diocesan shall pronounce Sentence not sooner than twenty days following the issuance of the Order and not later than forty days following the issuance of the Order. Notwithstanding anything in this section to the contrary, no Sentence shall be pronounced while an appeal of the matter is pending. However, the Bishop Diocesan may, while an appeal is pending, place restrictions upon the exercise of the Respondent's ministry, or place the Respondent on Administrative Leave, or continue any such restriction or Administrative Leave as was in effect at the time of the issuance of the Order. The Bishop Diocesan's pronouncement of a lesser Sentence than that recommended or other modification shall not affect the validity or enforceability of the remainder of the Order.

Provisions of Accords and Orders. **Sec. 9.** An Accord or Order shall include, in addition to such terms and provisions as are consistent with Canons IV.14.1 and IV.14.6, (a) the name of the Respondent; (b) a reference to the Canon(s), section(s) and subsection(s) specifying the Offense; and (c) general information regarding the Offense sufficient to afford protection from proceedings which are barred under Canon IV.19.13.

Sec. 10. An Accord under Canon IV.9 shall be effective as provided in Canon IV.9.3. An Accord under Canon IV.10 or IV.12 shall be effective thirty days following the date on which the Accord is signed by the Conciliator or the president of the Panel. An Order is effective thirty days following the date on which the Order is issued.

Sec. 11. If the Order is issued by a Conference Panel, the Respondent or the Church Attorney may object to the Order as provided in Canon IV.12.12 and the matter shall be referred to a Hearing Panel for hearing as provided in Canon IV.13.

Objection to an Order.

Sec. 12. If there has been no objection by the Respondent or the Church Attorney to the Order(s), notice of Accords and Orders which have become effective shall be given without delay as follows:

Notice of Accords and Orders.

a. In the case of any Accord or Order pertaining to a Priest or Deacon, the Bishop Diocesan shall give notice of the Accord or Order to every Member of the Clergy in the Diocese, each Vestry in the Diocese, the Secretary of Convention, and the Standing Committee of the Diocese, which shall be added to the official records of the Diocese; to the Presiding Bishop, to all other Bishops of the Church, and where there is no Bishop, to the Ecclesiastical Authority of each Diocese of the Church; to the President of the House of Deputies; to the Recorder of Ordinations; to the Archives; to the Secretary of the House of Bishops and the Secretary of the House of Deputies; and to the Office of Transition Ministry, which shall insert a copy of the notice of Accord or Order, on the Respondent's OTM Portfolio.

b. In the case of any Accord or Order pertaining to a Bishop, the Presiding Bishop shall give notice of the Accord or Order to the Ecclesiastical Authority of every Diocese of the Church, to the Recorder of Ordinations, to the Secretary of the House of Bishops, to all Archbishops and Metropolitans, to all Presiding Bishops of Churches in full communion with this Church, and to the Office of Transition Ministry, which shall insert a copy of the notice of Order or Accord, on the Respondent's OTM Portfolio.

c. All notices given pursuant to this Canon shall reference the Canon(s), section(s) and subsection(s) specifying the Offense which is the subject of the Accord or Order.

d. Similar notice shall be given whenever there is any modification or remission of any Order for which notice has previously been given pursuant to this Canon.

Disclosure. **Sec. 13.** In every case, notwithstanding any other provision of this Title to the contrary, the Bishop Diocesan may disclose such information concerning any Offense or allegations thereof or concerning any Accord or Order as the Bishop Diocesan deems appropriate.

Canon 15: Of Review

Delay of proceedings. **Sec. 1.** If proceedings before the Hearing Panel are unreasonably delayed or suspended, and are not resumed within sixty days following a written request for resumption of proceedings from the Church Attorney or the Respondent, the Church Attorney or the Respondent may file a written request with the Court of Review for an order directing the Hearing Panel to resume the proceedings. Upon receipt of the request, the President of the Court of Review shall appoint a panel consisting of one bishop, one priest or deacon and one lay person from among the members of the Court of Review. The appointments shall be made within fifteen days of receipt of the request. No person appointed shall be from the Diocese in which the Hearing Panel is sitting. The Court of Review shall consider the request as follows:

a. The person filing the request shall provide copies of the request to the presidents of the Hearing Panel and of the Disciplinary Board. The request shall include a statement of the status of the proceedings and the reason, if known, for the delay or suspension of proceedings, and a description of all actions taken by the person filing the request or by any other person to resolve any impediment to the proceedings or other cause for the delay.

b. Within fifteen days of receipt of the copy of the request, the president of the Hearing Panel shall file a response to the request with the Court of Review, with a copy to the Church Attorney, the Respondent and the president of the Board.

Court of Review. c. The appointed panel of the Court of Review shall convene, either personally, by video conference, or telephonically, to consider the request and the response, if any, from the Hearing Panel. The Court shall then either issue an order directing resumption of the proceedings or an order declining to direct resumption with an explanation of the reasons therefor. The order issued by the Court of Review shall be binding upon the Hearing Panel.

d. In the event a Hearing Panel, having been ordered to resume proceedings, either refuses to do so or is unable to do so, the Church Attorney or the Respondent may request that the Court of Review order the transfer of the proceedings to a Hearing Panel of another Diocese within the same Province, including an order to the Board of the originating Diocese to transmit the complete record of the proceedings to the successor Hearing Panel.

Sec. 2. Within forty days after the Hearing Panel issues an Order, the Respondent or the Church Attorney may appeal to the Court of Review by serving written notice of the appeal upon the Bishop Diocesan with copies of the notice to the president of the Hearing Panel and the president of the Court of Review. The notice of appeal must be signed by the Respondent's counsel or the Church Attorney, must include a copy of the Order from which the appeal is taken, and must state the grounds of the appeal.

Appeal of Orders.

Sec. 3. Any Order from a Hearing Panel finding that the Respondent did not commit an Offense involving a question of the Doctrine, Faith, or Worship of the Church may be appealed by the Bishop Diocesan upon the written request of at least two Bishops Diocesan of other Dioceses within the Province who are not members of the Court of Review. Such an appeal may be taken only on the question of the Church's Doctrine, Faith, or Worship, and may not seek to reverse the finding of the Hearing Panel that the Respondent did not commit an Offense. The Bishop Diocesan may take an appeal under this section by serving a notice of appeal upon the Respondent, the Church Attorney, the President of the Hearing Panel, and the President of the Court of Review within forty days after the Hearing Panel issues the Order.

Bishop may appeal.

Sec. 4. An appeal shall be heard on the record of the Hearing Panel. The record on appeal may be corrected, if defective, but no new evidence shall be taken by the Court of Review.

Record an appeal.

Standards for appeal.

Sec. 5. The standards for and conditions of appeal to the Court of Review shall be as follows:

a. Where an Order is issued against a Respondent who fails to appear before the Hearing Panel or who otherwise fails to participate in proceedings before the Hearing Panel, such Order shall be upheld unless a review of the record on appeal shows the Hearing Panel made a clear error in issuing such Order. The Court of Review shall review the facts and record in the light most favorable to the Respondent.

b. In all other appeals, the Court of Review shall grant relief to the appealing party only if, on the basis of the record on appeal, it determines that the party seeking review has been substantially prejudiced by any of the following:

1. The action taken below violates the Constitution and Canons of the Church or the Diocese;

2. The Hearing Panel has exceeded the jurisdiction conferred by this Title;

3. The Hearing Panel has not decided all of the issues requiring resolution;

4. The Hearing Panel has erroneously interpreted or applied the Constitutions or Canons of the Church;

5. The Hearing Panel has committed a procedural error or engaged in a decision-making process contrary to this Title;

6. The factual determinations of the Hearing Panel are not supported by substantial evidence when viewed in the whole light of the record on appeal.

Appeal record.

Sec. 6. It shall be the duty of the Hearing Panel to produce the record on appeal, consisting of a transcript of the proceedings before the Hearing Panel together with documentary and tangible evidence received by the Hearing Panel. The record shall be printed or otherwise reproduced as authorized by the President of the Court of Review. Within thirty days after receiving the record on appeal from the Hearing Panel, the party appealing shall serve two copies of the record on appeal, the notice of appeal and the appealing party's brief, if any, upon the opposite party and shall deliver five copies to the President of the Court of Review. Within thirty days after receiving a copy of the record on appeal, the party opposing the appeal shall serve the brief in opposition, if any, upon the appealing party, with five copies to the President of the Court of Review. Any reply brief of the appealing party shall be served likewise within fifteen days following service of the brief in opposition.

Sec. 7. All members and alternates of the Court of Review serving for an appeal shall be present for any oral proceedings of the appeal.

Attendance.

Sec. 8. The Court of Review shall keep a record of all proceedings. The Court of Review shall appoint a reporter who shall provide for the recording of the proceedings and who shall serve at the pleasure of the Court of Review.

Proceedings.

Sec. 9. At the hearing of the appeal, the Court of Review shall afford the Respondent and the Church Attorney the opportunity to be heard. The Court of Review may regulate the number of counsel to be heard.

Sec. 10. No Order or determination of a Hearing Panel shall be overturned solely for technical or harmless error.

Sec. 11. If, after a notice of appeal has been filed, the appealing party fails to pursue the appeal as provided in this Canon, the Court of Review may dismiss the appeal.

Sec. 12. As soon as possible, the Court of Review shall make documents available to members of the Church and the Church media as set forth in this Section. The documents shall be disseminated in such a way as to make them broadly known to members of the Church and the Church media. For a matter in which a Priest or Deacon is the Respondent, dissemination shall include, at a minimum, posting the documents on the diocesan website of the diocese that conducted the Hearing Panel proceeding. For a matter in which a Bishop is the Respondent, dissemination shall include, at a minimum, posting the documents on the websites of The Episcopal Church and of the General Convention.

Document dissemination.

a. The documents covered by this Section are all documents filed with or issued by the Court of Review or by any party or person including but not limited to motions, briefs, affidavits, opinions, objections, decisions, notices, challenges, and Orders, including documents in a proceeding pursuant to Section 1 of this Canon.

b. The notice under Sec. 2 shall be made available no later than ten business days after the notice is received by the President of the Hearing Panel.

c. Notwithstanding the above, the Court of Review, at its discretion and for good cause to protect any Injured Person or allegedly Injured Person, may require the redaction of documents provided for in Sec. 12.a, after consultation with the Church Attorney, the Respondent's counsel, the Respondent's Advisor, the Complainant's Advisor or Complainant's counsel, if any, and, where appropriate, the Bishop Diocesan.

Sec. 13. If at any time after a matter has been appealed to a Court of Review or is before a Court of Review pursuant to Sec. 1, an Accord is reached that ends the proceedings before the Court of Review issues an Order or issues its decision, the Bishop Diocesan shall make the Notice of Accord available to the Church and Church media as provided in Sec. 12 as well as to the Court of Review and the Hearing Panel from which the appeal was taken or about whom a request was filed pursuant to Sec. 1.

Determination. Sec. 14. Following a hearing of the appeal and private deliberation, the Court of Review may (a) dismiss the appeal; (b) reverse or affirm in whole or in part the Order of the Hearing Panel; or (c) grant a new hearing before the Hearing Panel.

Decisions of the Court. Sec. 15. The concurrence of a majority of the Court of Review shall be required to decide an appeal. The Court of Review shall issue its decision in writing, signed by the members concurring therein, stating its decision and the reasons for the decision. The decision shall be attached to the record. If there is not a concurrence by a majority of the Court of Review, the Order of the Hearing Panel shall stand as affirmed except for any part of the Order for which there is concurrence.

Sec. 16. Upon determination of the appeal, the President of the Court of Review shall give notice of the determination in writing to the appealing party, the party in opposition and to the Bishop Diocesan and Church Attorney. The appeal record shall be certified by the clerk of the Court of Review and the president, and shall be delivered to the Bishop Diocesan along with a copy of the record on appeal from the Hearing Panel.

Canon 16: Of Abandonment of The Episcopal Church

A. By a Bishop

Sec. 1. If the Disciplinary Board for Bishops receives information suggesting that a Bishop may have abandoned The Episcopal Church (i) by an open renunciation of the Doctrine, Discipline or Worship of the Church; or (ii) by formal admission into any religious body not in full communion with this Church; or (iii) by exercising Episcopal acts in and for a religious body other than the Church or another church in full communion with the Church, so as to extend to such body Holy Orders as the Church holds them, or to administer on behalf of such religious body Confirmation without the express consent and commission of the proper authority in the Church, the Board shall promptly notify the Presiding Bishop and the Bishop in question that it is considering the matter. Upon receipt of such notification, the Presiding Bishop may, with the advice and consent of the Advisory Council to the Presiding Bishop, place restrictions on the ministry of the Bishop in question for the period while the matter is under consideration by the Board. If, after consideration of the matter, the Board concludes, by a majority vote of all of its members, that the Bishop in question has abandoned The Episcopal Church, the Board shall certify the fact to the Presiding Bishop and with the certificate send a statement of the acts or declarations which show such abandonment, which certificate and statement shall be recorded by the Presiding Bishop. The Presiding Bishop shall then place a restriction on the exercise of ministry of said Bishop until such time as the House of Bishops shall investigate the matter and act

Certification of abandonment.

thereon. During the period of such restriction, the Bishop shall not perform any Episcopal, ministerial or canonical acts.

Liable to
Deposition.

Sec. 2. The Presiding Bishop, or the Presiding Officer of the House of Bishops, shall forthwith give notice to the Bishop of the certification and restriction on ministry. Unless the restricted Bishop, within sixty days, makes declaration by a verified written statement to the Presiding Bishop, that the facts alleged in the certificate are false or utilizes the provisions of Canon III.12.7, the Bishop will be liable to Deposition or Release and Removal. If the Presiding Bishop is reasonably satisfied that the statement constitutes (i) a good faith retraction of the declarations or acts relied upon in the certification to the Presiding Bishop or (ii) a good faith denial that the Bishop made the declarations or committed the acts relied upon in the certificate, the Presiding Bishop, with the advice and consent of the Disciplinary Board for Bishops, shall terminate the restriction. Otherwise, it shall be the duty of the Presiding Bishop to present the matter to the House of Bishops at the next regular or special meeting of the House. The House may, by a majority of the whole number of Bishops entitled to vote, (1) consent to the deposition of the subject Bishop, in which case the Presiding Bishop shall depose the Bishop from the ordained ministry of The Episcopal Church, and pronounce and record in the presence of two or more Bishops that the Bishop has been so deposed, or (2) consent to the release and removal of the subject Bishop from the ordained ministry of The Episcopal Church, in which case the Presiding Bishop shall declare such release and removal in the presence of two or more Bishops.

B. By a Priest or Deacon

Determination
of Offense.

Sec. 3. If it is reported to the Standing Committee of the Diocese in which a Priest or Deacon is canonically resident that the Priest or Deacon, without using the provisions of Canon III.7.8-10 or III.9.8-11, may have abandoned The Episcopal Church, the Standing Committee shall promptly notify the Bishop Diocesan and the Priest or Deacon in question that it is considering the matter. Upon receipt of such notification, the Bishop Diocesan may, with the advice and consent of the Standing Committee, place restrictions on the ministry of the Priest or Deacon in question for the period while the matter is under consideration by the Standing Committee. The Standing Committee shall ascertain and consider the facts, and if it shall determine by a vote of three-fourths of all the members that the Priest or Deacon has abandoned The Episcopal Church by an open renunciation of the Doctrine, Discipline or worship of the Church, or by the formal admission into any religious body not in full communion with the Church, or in any other way, it shall be the duty of the Standing Committee of the Diocese to transmit in writing to the Bishop Diocesan its determination, together with a statement setting out in a reasonable detail the acts or declarations relied upon in making its determination. If the Bishop Diocesan affirms the determination, the Bishop Diocesan shall place a restriction on the exercise of ministry by that Priest or Deacon for sixty days and shall send to the Priest or Deacon a copy of the determination and statement, together with a notice that the Priest or Deacon has the rights specified in Section 4 of this Canon and at the end of the sixty day period the Bishop Diocesan will consider deposing the Priest or Deacon in accordance with the provisions of Section 4.

Sec. 4. Prior to the expiration of the sixty-day period of restriction, the Priest or Deacon may utilize the provisions of Canon III.7.8-10 or III.9.8-11, as applicable. If within such sixty day period the Priest or Deacon shall transmit to the Bishop Diocesan a statement in writing signed by the Priest or Deacon, which the Bishop Diocesan is reasonably satisfied constitutes a good faith retraction of such declarations or acts relied upon in the determination or good faith denial that the Priest or Deacon committed the acts or made the declarations relied upon in the determination, the Bishop Diocesan shall withdraw the notice and the restriction on ministry shall expire. If, however, within the sixty day period, the Bishop Diocesan does not declare the release and removal of the Priest or Deacon in accordance with Canon III.7.8-10 or III.9.8-11, as applicable, or the Priest or Deacon does not make retraction or denial as provided above, then it shall be the duty of the Bishop Diocesan either (i) to depose of the Priest or Deacon, or (ii) if the Bishop Diocesan is

Retraction or Deposition.

satisfied that no previous irregularity or misconduct is involved, with the advice and consent of the Standing Committee, to pronounce and record in the presence of two or more Priests that the Priest or Deacon is released and removed from the ordained Ministry of this Church and from the obligations attendant thereto, and (for causes which do not affect the person's moral character) is deprived of the right to exercise in The Episcopal Church the gifts and spiritual authority conferred in Ordination.

Role of Standing Committee. **Sec. 5.** For the purposes of Section 3 and 4 of this Canon, if there is no Bishop Diocesan, the Standing Committee shall submit the matter to the Bishop Diocesan of an adjacent Diocese, who shall have the authority of a Bishop Diocesan in the matter.

Canon 17: Of Proceedings for Bishops

Sec. 1. Except as otherwise provided in this Canon, the provisions of this Title shall apply to all matters in which a Member of the Clergy who is subject to proceedings is a Bishop.

Definition of terms. **Sec. 2.** In all matters in which the Member of the Clergy who is subject to proceedings is a Bishop, the following terms used in Canons IV.5 through IV.16 and Canons IV.18 and IV.19 shall have the following respective meanings:

a. Disciplinary Board shall mean the Disciplinary Board for Bishops as provided in Canon IV.17.3.

b. Intake Officer shall mean a person appointed by the Presiding Bishop.

c. Bishop Diocesan shall mean the Presiding Bishop, unless the Member of the Clergy who is subject to proceedings is the Presiding Bishop, in which case Bishop shall mean the Bishop authorized by Canon IV.19.24.

d. Church Attorney shall mean a person appointed by the Disciplinary Board for Bishops to serve as the Church Attorney.

e. Investigator shall mean any person who is qualified to serve as an Investigator under this Title, selected by the Disciplinary Board for Bishops.

f. Court of Review shall mean the Court of Review for Bishops as provided in Canon IV.17.8.

Sec. 3.

Disciplinary Board for Bishops.

a. The Disciplinary Board for Bishops is hereby established as a court of the Church to have original jurisdiction over matters of discipline of Bishops and to hear Bishops' appeals from imposition of restriction on ministry or placement on Administrative Leave.

b. The Disciplinary Board for Bishops consists of ten Bishops elected by the House of Bishops at a regular meeting of the General Convention, and four Priests or Deacons and four Lay Persons elected by the House of Deputies at a regular meeting of the General Convention. All Lay Persons elected or appointed to serve must be confirmed adult communicants in good standing.

Board Membership.

c. Members of the Board will serve staggered terms, with the terms of one-half of the Bishops and one-half of the Lay Persons, Priests, and Deacons collectively expiring upon the adjournment of every regular meeting of the General Convention.

d. Unless elected or appointed to fill the remainder of an unexpired term, each member will serve from the adjournment of the General Convention at which the member was elected until the adjournment of the second regular meeting of the General Convention after election and until the member's successor is elected and qualifies.

e. A vacancy among the member Bishops must be filled by the Presiding Bishop with the advice and consent of the Bishop members of the Executive Council. A vacancy among the other members must be filled by the President of the House of Deputies with the advice and consent of the lay, Priest, and Deacon members of the Executive Council.

Vacancy.

f. Notwithstanding any expiration of a member's term of office, there will be no change in the composition of any Conference Panel or Hearing Panel while a matter remains pending before the Panel; and a member of the

Board sitting on such a Panel and whose term of office otherwise would expire will nevertheless continue in office until the matter is resolved and solely for that purpose.

Elect president. **Sec. 4.** Within sixty days following each General Convention, the Board must convene to elect a president for the following interval between regular meetings of the General Convention. The president must be a Bishop. If there is no president, the Bishop who is senior by consecration must perform the duties of the president.

Conference and Hearing Panel Membership. **Sec. 5.** The Conference Panel shall consist of three Bishops, one Priest or Deacon and one lay person. The Hearing Panel shall consist of three Bishops, one Priest or Deacon and one lay person, except that the Hearing Panel for the Offense specified in Canon IV.14.1.h.2 pertaining to Doctrine Offenses shall consist of five Bishops only.

Sentencing of a Bishop. **Sec. 6.** The provisions of Canons IV.14.1.d and IV.14.6.c pertaining to recommendations that a Respondent be suspended or deposed from ministry shall not apply where the Respondent is a Bishop. Where the Respondent is a Bishop, an Accord or Order may provide for the suspension or deposition of the Respondent. In such event, the Sentence of suspension or deposition shall be pronounced by the president of the Disciplinary Board for Bishops. The president shall have no discretion to decline to pronounce the Sentence or to pronounce a lesser Sentence. Where an Accord provides for the suspension or deposition of a Respondent who is a Bishop, the president shall pronounce Sentence within thirty days after the date on which the Conciliator or the president signs the Accord. Where an Order provides for the suspension or deposition of a Respondent who is a Bishop, the president shall pronounce Sentence not sooner than forty days following the issuance of the Order and not later than sixty days following the issuance of the Order. Notwithstanding anything in this section to the contrary, no Sentence shall be pronounced while an appeal of the matter is pending. However, the president may, while an appeal is pending, place restrictions upon the exercise of the Respondent's ministry, or place the Respondent on Administrative Leave, or continue any such restriction or

Administrative Leave as was in effect at the time of the issuance of the Order.

Sec. 7. Notwithstanding any provision of this Title to the contrary, no proceeding shall be brought under this Title against a Bishop in which the Offense alleged is violation of Canon IV.4.1.h.2 for holding and teaching, or having held and taught, publicly or privately, and advisedly, any Doctrine contrary to that held by the Church unless a statement of disassociation shall have first been issued by the House of Bishops as provided in Canon IV.17.7.a and thereafter the consent of one-third of the Bishops qualified to vote in the House of Bishops has been received to initiate proceedings under this Title as provided in Canon IV.17.7.b.

Statement of disassociation.

a. Any ten Bishops Diocesan in the Church may file with the Presiding Bishop a written request, signed by such Bishops, that the House of Bishops issue a statement of disassociation. Such request shall include a statement of the Doctrine alleged to be contrary to that held by the Church, the name or names of the Bishop or Bishops alleged to have held and taught publicly or privately, and advisedly, such Doctrine, and a concise statement of the facts upon which the requestfor the statement of disassociation is based. Contemporaneously with the filing of the request, there shall be filed with the Presiding Bishop a proposed statement of disassociation and a brief in support thereof. The Presiding Bishop shall thereupon serve a copy of the request for a statement of disassociation upon each Bishop who is the subject thereof, together with the proposed statement of disassociation and a copy of the supporting brief. The Presiding Bishop shall fix a date for the filing of a response and brief in support thereof, which date shall be not less than ninety days from the date of service, and may extend the time for responding for not more than sixty additional days. Upon the filing of a response and supporting brief, if any, or upon the expiration of the time fixed for a response, if none be filed, the Presiding Bishop shall forthwith transmit copies of the request for a statement of disassociation, proposed statement of disassociation, response, and briefs to each member of

the House of Bishops. The request for a statement of
disassociation shall be considered by the House of
Bishops at its first regularly scheduled meeting held at
least one month after copies of the request for a
statement of disassociation, proposed statement of
disassociation, response, and briefs are transmitted to
each member of the House of Bishops. The House of
Bishops may amend the proposed statement of
disassociation. If a statement of disassociation is not
issued by the conclusion of the meeting, there shall be
no further proceedings under this Title against any
Bishop who is the subject thereof for holding and
teaching the Doctrine alleged in the request for a
statement of disassociation.

Offenses of
Doctrine by a
Bishop.

b. Not later than ninety days following the issuance of a
statement of disassociation by the House of Bishops as
provided in Canon IV.17.7.a, any ten Bishops Diocesan
may file with the Presiding Bishop a written request,
signed by such Bishops, that the House of Bishops
initiate proceedings under this Title against any Bishop
who is the subject of such statement of disassociation for
violation of Canon IV.4.1.h.2 with regard to the same
Doctrine as was alleged in the request for the statement
of disassociation. Such request for initiation of
proceedings under this Title shall include an explanation
why the issuance of the statement of disassociation was
not a sufficient response to the matters alleged in the
request for statement of disassociation and shall be
accompanied by a brief in support of the request for
initiation of proceedings. The Presiding Bishop shall fix a
date for the filing of a response, which shall include an
explanation why the issuance of the statement of
disassociation was a sufficient response to the matters
alleged in the request for statement of disassociation,
and brief in support thereof, which date shall be not less
than ninety days from the date of service, and may
extend the time for responding for not more than sixty
additional days. Upon the filing of a response and
supporting brief, if any, or upon the expiration of the
time fixed for a response, if none be filed, the Presiding
Bishop shall forthwith transmit copies of the request for

initiation of proceedings under this Title, response, and briefs to each member of the House of Bishops. No proceeding under this Title for violation of Canon IV.4.1.h.2 shall be initiated unless the written consent of one-third of the Bishops qualified to vote in the House of Bishops shall be received by the Presiding Bishop within sixty days of the date on which the copies of the request for initiation of proceedings under this Title, response, and briefs were sent to them. In case the Presiding Bishop does not receive the written consent of one-third of all the Bishops eligible to vote within sixty days of such date, the Presiding Bishop shall declare the matter dismissed and no further proceedings may be had thereon. If the Presiding Bishop receives the necessary written consents within sixty days as specified above, the Presiding Bishop shall forthwith notify the president of the Disciplinary Board for Bishops. The president shall promptly select from the Disciplinary Board for Bishops, by lot or by other random means, a Hearing Panel consisting of nine Bishops and shall designate a president of the Hearing Panel. The president of the Disciplinary Board for Bishops shall promptly forward to the president of the Hearing Panel and to the Church Attorney copies of the request for initiation of proceedings under this Title, response, and briefs, and the matter shall proceed under this Title as a matter which has been referred to a Hearing Panel.

Sec. 8. The Court of Review for Bishops is hereby established as a court of the Church to have jurisdiction over appeals from Hearing Panels of the Disciplinary Board for Bishops.

Court of Review for Bishops.

a. The Court of Review for Bishops consists of nine members, all of whom must be Bishops. Three Bishops will be elected by the House of Bishops at any regularly scheduled meeting of the House of Bishops, to serve until the adjournment of the third succeeding regular meeting of General Convention and until their successors are elected and qualify; but there shall be no change in the composition of the Court with respect to a particular Respondent following any hearing in the matter and while it is pending unresolved before the Court.

Vacancies.   **b.** The Presiding Bishop must fill any vacancies on the Court of Review for Bishops.

President.   **c.** From among their number, the members of the Court of Review for Bishops must elect a president.

Expenses.   **d.** The reasonable and necessary expenses of the Court of Review for Bishops, including fees, costs, disbursements, and expenses of the members, clerks, reporters, and Church Attorneys, will be charged upon the General Convention and paid by the Treasurer of the General Convention upon Order of the president of the Court of Review. The Court of Review for Bishops has the authority to contract for and bind the General Convention to pay these expenses.

Agreement for discipline by a Bishop.   **Sec. 9.** An Accord between the Presiding Bishop and a Bishop resulting from an agreement for discipline pursuant to Canon IV.9 shall be (a) subject to the right of withdrawal provided in Canon IV.9.3 and (b) submitted by the Presiding Bishop to the Disciplinary Board for Bishops for approval promptly after it is signed by the Presiding Bishop and the respondent. Unless withdrawn under Canon IV.9.3, it shall be effective upon approval of the Disciplinary Board for Bishops and not subject to appeal.

Canon 18: Of Modification and Remission of Orders

Application.   **Sec. 1.** Any Member of the Clergy who is the subject of an Order which has become effective may apply to the Bishop Diocesan of the Diocese from which the Order issued, or the Presiding Bishop in the case of a Bishop, for modification or remission of the Order. If the Bishop is satisfied that sufficient reasons exist for granting the modification or remission sought, in whole or in part, the procedures provided in this Canon for modification or remission shall apply.

Consent of Board.   **Sec. 2.** In the case of an Order pertaining to a Priest or Deacon, any provision of any Order other than a provision recommending deposition of the Priest or Deacon may be modified or remitted by the Bishop Diocesan of the Diocese from which the Order issued with the advice and consent of two-thirds of the members of the Disciplinary Board.

Sec. 3. In the case of a deposition of a Priest or Deacon pursuant to an Order, such deposition may be remitted and terminated by the Bishop Diocesan of the Diocese from which the Order issued only upon the following conditions: (a) the remission shall be done with the advice and consent of two-thirds of the members of the Disciplinary Board of the Diocese from which the Order issued; (b) the proposed remission, with the reasons therefor, shall be submitted to the judgment of five of the Bishops Diocesan whose Dioceses are nearest to the Diocese from which the Order issued, and the Bishop Diocesan shall receive in writing from at least four of those Bishops their approval of the remission and their consent thereto; (c) if the person deposed maintains legal residence or canonical residence in a Diocese other than the Diocese from which the Order issued, the proposed remission, with the reasons therefor, shall be submitted to the judgment of the Bishop(s) Diocesan of the Diocese(s) of legal and canonical residence and such Bishop(s) shall give his or her (or their) written approval of the remission and consent thereto; and (d) before such remission, the Bishop Diocesan shall require the person deposed, who desires to be restored to the ordained ministry, to subscribe to the declaration required in Article VIII of the Constitution.

Conditions.

Sec. 4. In the case of an Order pertaining to a Bishop, any provision of the Order may be modified or remitted by the president of the Disciplinary Board for Bishops with the advice and consent of a majority of the members of the Board and the Bishops who are then serving on the Court of Review.

In case of a Bishop.

Sec. 5. In the case of any Order deposing a Member of the Clergy for abandoning the Church, no application for remission shall be received by the Bishop Diocesan until the deposed person has lived in lay communion with the Church for not less than one year next preceding application for the remission.

In case of abandonment.

Sec. 6. No Order may be modified or remitted unless the Member of the Clergy, the Church Attorney and each

Opportunity to be heard.

Complainant have been afforded sufficient opportunity to be heard by the Disciplinary Board, or the Disciplinary Board together with the Bishops who are then serving on the Court of Review, as the case may be, as to why the proposed modification or remission should or should not be permitted.

Canon 19: Of General Provisions

Discipline of the Church.

Sec. 1. Proceedings under this Title are neither civil nor criminal but ecclesiastical in nature. These proceedings represent the responsibility of the Church to determine who shall serve as Members of the Clergy of the Church, reflecting the polity and order of this hierarchical church. Members of the Clergy have voluntarily sought and accepted positions in the Church and have thereby given their consent to subject themselves to the Discipline of the Church. They may not claim in proceedings under this Title constitutional guarantees otherwise associated with secular court proceedings.

Secular courts.

Sec. 2. No member of the Church, whether lay or ordained, may seek to have the Constitution and Canons of the Church interpreted by a secular court, or resort to a secular court to address a dispute arising under the Constitution and Canons, or for any purpose of delay, hindrance, review or otherwise affecting any proceeding under this Title.

Sec. 3. No secular court shall have authority to review, annul, reverse, restrain or otherwise delay any proceeding under this Title. No action shall be brought in any secular court to enforce the terms or provisions of any Accord or Order unless otherwise expressly provided therein.

Limitation on proceedings.

Sec. 4

a. A Member of the Clergy shall not be subject to proceedings under this Title for acts committed more than ten years before the initiation of proceedings except:

  1. if a Member of the Clergy is convicted in a criminal Court of Record or a judgment in a civil Court of Record in a cause involving immorality, proceedings

may be initiated at any time within three years after the conviction or judgment becomes final;

2. if an alleged Injured Person was under the age of twenty-one years at the time of the alleged acts, proceedings may be initiated at any time prior to the alleged Injured Person's attaining the age of twenty-five years; or

3. if an alleged Injured Person is otherwise under disability at the time of the alleged acts, or if the acts alleged were not discovered, or the effects thereof were not realized, during the ten years immediately following the date of the acts alleged, the time within which proceedings may be initiated shall be extended to two years after the disability ceases or the alleged Injured Person discovers or realizes the effects of the acts alleged; *provided, however*, the time within which proceedings may be initiated shall not be extended beyond fifteen years from the date the acts are alleged to have been committed.

b. The time limits of Subsection a above shall not apply with respect to persons whose acts include physical violence, sexual abuse or sexual exploitation, if the acts occurred when the alleged Injured Person was under the age of twenty-one years; in any such case, proceedings under this Title may be initiated at any time.

c. The time limits of Subsection a above shall not apply with respect to persons whose acts include sexual misconduct, provided proceedings are initiated under this Title between January 1, 2019 and December 31, 2021.

d. Except as provided in Subsection .b above, the time limitations for initiation of proceedings in this Section shall be retroactive only to January 1, 1996.

e. No proceedings under this Title shall be initiated for acts which are alleged to violate Canon IV.3.1.a or to constitute a breach of Canon IV.4.1.b, .c, .e or .h.2 unless the acts were committed within or continued up to two years immediately preceding the time the proceedings are initiated.

f. For purposes of this Section 4, proceedings are initiated under this Title with respect to a particular Offense when specific allegations of the commission of that Offense are made to the Intake Officer.

Jurisdiction and venue.

Sec. 5. Jurisdiction and venue for proceedings under this Title shall be as follows:

a. A Member of the Clergy shall be subject to proceedings under this Title for the alleged commission of an Offense in the Diocese in which the Member of the Clergy is canonically resident or in any Diocese in which an Offense is alleged to have occurred.

b. Whenever a referral of a matter is to be made by an Intake Officer regarding a Member of the Clergy who is not canonically resident in the Intake Officer's Diocese, the Bishop Diocesan of the Intake Officer's Diocese shall promptly notify the Bishop Diocesan of the Diocese where the Member of the Clergy is canonically resident that the Intake Officer's Diocese intends to conduct proceedings under this Title regarding the matter. The Bishop Diocesan of the Diocese of canonical residence shall have thirty days following the receipt of such notice within which to object to assumption of jurisdiction over the matter by the Intake Officer's Diocese. Such objection shall be made in writing to the Bishop Diocesan of the Intake Officer's Diocese. If the Bishop Diocesan of the Diocese of canonical residence fails to so object within the time provided, it shall be deemed that the Bishop Diocesan of the Diocese of canonical residence has agreed to assumption of jurisdiction over the matter by the Intake Officer's Diocese.

c. If objection is made by the Bishop Diocesan of the Diocese of canonical residence as provided in Canon IV.19.5.b, the Bishop Diocesan of the Diocese of canonical residence and the Bishop Diocesan of the Intake Officer's Diocese shall promptly agree as to which Diocese will assume jurisdiction over the matter and conduct proceedings. If the two Bishops cannot promptly agree, the disagreement will be resolved as follows:

1. Either may promptly request the President of the Court of Review to decide which Diocese shall conduct the proceedings.

2. The requesting Bishop shall provide a copy of the request to the other Bishop. A reply to the request may be made by the non-requesting Bishop within fourteen days of service of the request.

3. The President shall have the discretion to hear from the Bishops Diocesan or the Church Attorneys for the respective Dioceses, either personally or telephonically, concerning the request and any reply. The President shall have the discretion to request additional submissions from the Bishops Diocesan or the Church Attorneys.

4. The President shall decide which Diocese shall conduct the proceedings within fourteen days of service of the request.

5. It is a goal of these processes to not delay unduly the progress of any proceeding under this Title. Therefore, the parties shall not use the full extent of these deadlines for the purpose of prolonging the proceedings.

Sec. 6. In any proceeding under this Title in which the Respondent fails to appear before the Conference Panel as required by Canon IV.12.4, or to appear before the Hearing Panel as required by Canon IV.13.2.a, or to file in a timely manner with the Hearing Panel the written response required by Canon IV.13.2.c, such Panel may, in its discretion, proceed in the absence of the Respondent. In proceedings under this section, such panels may consider the materials described in Canon IV.12.1, and any other types of evidence whose use is permitted in proceedings conducted before such Panels. The failure of a Respondent to appear, or to fail to file a written response, as described in this Section shall not, in itself, provide the basis for a finding that any Offense has been committed, other than any Offense specifically arising from such failure to appear, or failure to file.

Failure to appear.

Sentence of suspension or restriction on Ministry.

Sec. 7. Unless otherwise expressly provided in writing in the restriction on ministry or Sentence of suspension, a Member of the Clergy under a restriction on Ministry or Sentence of suspension shall not exercise any authority of his or her office over the real or personal property or temporal affairs of the Church except such matters as may not be exercised by a person other than the holder of the office, and may exercise authority in those matters only with the advice and consent of the Vestry or Bishops Committee, in the case of congregational property or affairs, or the Standing Committee, in the case of Diocesan property or affairs. The Sentence of suspension of a Rector shall terminate the pastoral relation between the Rector and the Vestry or Congregation unless (i) the Vestry by two-thirds vote requests of the Ecclesiastical Authority within thirty days that the relation continue and (ii) the Ecclesiastical Authority approves such request. If the pastoral relation has not been terminated, religious services and sacramental ministrations shall be provided for that Parish as though a vacancy exists in the office of the Rector. This Section shall not prohibit the application of Canon III.9.13.

Sec. 8. In computing any period of time for proceedings described in this Title, the day of the act or event from which the designated time period begins to run shall not be included. The last day of the time period shall be included, unless it is a Saturday, Sunday or legal holiday in that jurisdiction, in which event the period runs until the end of the next day which is not a Saturday, Sunday or legal holiday in that jurisdiction. Whenever a party has the right or is required to do an act within a prescribed period after the service of notice or other paper, if the service is by mail, five days shall be added to the prescribed period. Whenever it is provided in this Title that an act be done promptly or without delay, such act shall be done as quickly as is reasonably possible under the circumstances.

Quorum.

Sec. 9. In all cases in this Title where an action is performed or power exercised by a canonical body consisting of several members, including Reference Panels, Conference Panels, Hearing Panels and Courts of Review, and the full membership has been notified to convene, a majority of the members of the body shall be a quorum; and a majority of the members present when a quorum exists shall be competent to act.

Sec. 10. Each Diocese shall make provision for Advisors to be available to Respondents and Complainants as provided in this Canon for the purposes of support, assistance, consultation and advice regarding the process provided in this Title and the rights, responsibilities, consequences and alternatives pertaining thereto.

Advisors.

a. The Bishop Diocesan shall make an Advisor available to the Respondent not later than the earliest of (1) reference for conciliation, to the Conference Panel or to the Hearing Panel, (2) the imposition of restriction on ministry or placement on Administrative Leave, (3) the Respondent or Bishop Diocesan proposing terms of discipline to the other under Canon IV.9, or (4) any interrogation or request for a statement or other information from the Respondent.

b. The Bishop Diocesan shall make an Advisor available to the Complainant not later than the earliest of (1) the forwarding of the intake report to the Reference Panel, (2) 15 days after the Complainant receiving word of a dismissal under Canon IV.6.5, (3) the Respondent or Bishop Diocesan proposing terms of discipline to the other under Canon IV.9, or (4) the Bishop's designation of an Injured Person as a Complainant.

c. The following shall be disqualified from serving as an Advisor: the Bishop Diocesan, the Church Attorney, any member of the Disciplinary Board, the Intake Officer, any Investigator, any person who is likely to be a witness in any pertinent proceeding and the Chancellor or any Vice Chancellor of the Diocese.

d. No Respondent or Complainant shall be required to accept the services of any Advisor made available by the Bishop Diocesan. Any Respondent or Complainant may use the services of any Advisor of his or her choice after designating that person as Advisor in writing to the Intake Officer.

e. All communications between the Respondent and his or her Advisor or attorney and between the Complainant and his or her Advisor or attorney shall be privileged.

f. The reasonable costs and expenses of providing Advisors made available by the Bishop Diocesan shall be the obligation of the Diocese in which the matter of Discipline is proceeding unless otherwise provided in an Accord or Order. The reasonable costs and expenses of providing Advisors chosen by the Respondent or Complainant and not made available by the Bishop Diocesan shall be the obligation of such Respondent or Complainant unless otherwise provided in an Accord or Order.

g. In all proceedings under this Title at which the Respondent or the Complainant has the right to be present, their Advisors shall also have the right to be present.

Improper influence.

Sec. 11. No person subject to the authority of the Church may attempt to coerce or improperly influence, directly or indirectly, the actions of any body performing functions under this Title, or any member of such body or any other person involved in such proceedings.

Right to counsel.

Sec. 12. In all proceedings under this Title whenever a Respondent or a Complainant is required or permitted to appear or to participate or to be heard or to be present, they each shall have the right to be accompanied by and to be represented by counsel of their choice. Whenever any notice or other document is provided to or served upon a Respondent or a Complainant under this Title, such shall also simultaneously be provided to or served upon their respective counsel, if Respondent or Complainant, as the case may be, has notified the Bishop of the identity and contact information for such counsel. Nothing in this Title shall be construed as requiring any Respondent to be represented by counsel. Anything in this Title required or permitted to be done by the Respondent's counsel may be done by the Respondent personally.

Liability for retrial barred.

Sec. 13. Proceedings under this Title, other than pastoral responses, shall be barred to the extent that the specific

Offense has been the subject of any prior proceeding under this Title against the same Member of the Clergy which resulted in an Order or Accord. Additionally, in the case of a Member of the Clergy who has been the subject of proceedings under any predecessor to this Title, proceedings under this Title, other than pastoral responses, shall be barred to the extent that the specific Offense was previously included in a presentment against the Member of the Clergy or was expressly set forth in the Member of the Clergy's waiver and voluntary submission to discipline upon which a Sentence has been pronounced or in the report of a conciliator.

Sec. 14. Impartiality of officials and bodies described in this Title shall be addressed as follows:

Concerning impartiality.

a. Any Bishop Diocesan exercising authority under this Title shall disqualify herself or himself in any proceeding in which the Bishop's impartiality may reasonably be questioned. The Bishop shall also disqualify himself or herself when the Bishop, the Bishop's spouse, or a person within the third degree of relationship to either of them, or the spouse of such person, is the Respondent, Complainant or an Injured Person.

b. The Church Attorney or any member of any Panel provided for in this Title shall disqualify himself or herself in any proceeding in which such person's impartiality may reasonably be questioned. The person shall also disqualify himself or herself when the person, the person's spouse, any person within the third degree of relationship to either of them, or the spouse of such person, (1) is the Respondent, Complainant or an Injured Person, (2) is likely to be a witness in the proceeding, (3) has a personal bias or prejudice concerning the Respondent, Complainant or any Injured Person, (4) has personal knowledge of disputed evidentiary facts concerning the proceeding, (5) has a personal financial interest in the outcome of the proceeding or in the Respondent, Complainant, any Injured Person or any other interest that could be substantially affected by the outcome or (6) is a member of the same congregation or otherwise has a close personal or professional relationship with the Respondent, the Complainant, any Injured Person or any witness in the matter.

c. The Church Attorney or any member of any Panel provided for in this Title who has not disqualified himself or herself as provided in this section may be subject to challenge by the Church Attorney or the Respondent on grounds described in this section. The Complainant or the Complainant's Advisor may inform the Church Attorney of any such grounds. The challenge shall be investigated by the remaining members of the Panel who shall determine whether the challenged person should be disqualified and replaced according to the procedures of this Title for filling vacancies.

d. No Bishop Diocesan or Panel shall accept from the Church Attorney or from the Respondent any waiver of any ground for disqualification enumerated in this section unless preceded by full disclosure of the basis for the disqualification, on the record.

Integrity of Board.

Sec. 15. In addition to any challenge permitted under Canon IV.19.14, the integrity of the Disciplinary Board shall be preserved by a system of challenge as to the membership of any Panel of the Board appointed for a proceeding. Each Diocese shall provide by Canon for a system of challenge. If the Canons of the Diocese make no provision for challenging a member of the Board, any member of a Panel appointed for a proceeding may be challenged by the Church Attorney or the Respondent on grounds of conflict of interest or undue bias. The remaining members of the Board shall determine whether the challenge is relevant and factually supported and shall determine whether the challenged member shall be excused from that proceeding. If the member is excused, another member of the Board shall be appointed to the Panel to fill the vacancy created by the challenge, maintaining the appropriate balance of lay and ordained members.

Presumption of innocence.

Sec. 16. There shall be a presumption that the Respondent did not commit the Offense. The standard of proof required for a Hearing Panel to find an Offense by a Respondent shall be that of clear and convincing evidence.

Sec. 17. In all matters under this Title, it shall be the burden of the Church through the Church Attorney to establish an Offense by any Respondent.

Burden of proof.

Sec. 18. Except as otherwise provided in this Title, or except for good cause shown as determined by the Hearing Panel, it shall be the duty of all members of the Church to appear and testify or respond when duly served with a notice to do so from any Panel in any matter arising under this Title.

Duty of Church members.

Sec. 19. No Chancellor or Vice Chancellor of a Diocese shall serve as Church Attorney in that Diocese. No Chancellor or Vice Chancellor of any Province shall serve as Church Attorney in any Diocese of that Province or any provincial proceeding. Neither the Presiding Bishop's Chancellor nor the Chancellor to the President of the House of Deputies shall serve as Church Attorney in any proceeding. The Church Attorney in any proceeding shall not be from the same law firm as any Chancellor or Vice Chancellor otherwise disqualified under this section.

Church Attorney.

Sec. 20. Notices or other papers to be served according to procedures of this Title shall be deemed to have been duly served if a copy is delivered to the person to be served, is left with an adult resident of the abode of the person to be served, is mailed by certified mail to the person's usual place of abode, or is sent by electronic means with receipt confirmed in writing. Notice by publication shall be made in a newspaper of general circulation in the jurisdiction of the person's usual place of abode. Acceptance of service renders unnecessary any further process.

Notices duly served.

Sec. 21. A reference in this Title to a Bishop Diocesan shall include a Bishop Coadjutor if specific jurisdiction for matters contemplated by this Title has been assigned to the Bishop Coadjutor pursuant to Canon III.11.9.a.2, and a Bishop Suffragan or Assistant Bishop if specific responsibilities for matters contemplated by this Title have been expressly assigned to the Bishop Suffragan or Assistant Bishop by the Bishop Diocesan.

Bishop with jurisdiction.

Sec. 22. A Disciplinary Board or Court of Review may in its discretion obtain legal counsel to give it or the president of the Board or one of its Panels opinions on any questions of

Legal counsel.

law, procedure or evidence. Such legal counsel, if any, shall have no vote in any proceeding before the Disciplinary Board, one of its Panels, or Court of Review.

Expenses. **Sec. 23.** Except as expressly provided in this Title, applicable Diocesan Canon, or in any Accord or Order, all costs, expenses and fees, if any, shall be the obligation of the party, person or entity incurring them.

    a. The necessary costs, expenses and fees of the Investigator, the Church Attorney, the Conference Panel, the Hearing Panel and any pastoral response shall be the expense of the Diocese.

    b. The necessary costs and expenses of the Court of Review shall be the expense of the General Convention.

    c. The necessary costs and expenses of the Disciplinary Board for Bishops and the Court of Review for Bishops shall be the expense of the General Convention.

    d. Nothing in this Title precludes the voluntary payment of a Respondent's costs, expenses and fees by any other party or person, including a Diocese.

If Presiding Bishop is unavailable. **Sec. 24.** If the Presiding Bishop is unavailable to act by virtue of absence, disability or other disqualification, actions to be performed by the Presiding Bishop in this Title shall be performed by that Bishop who would be the Presiding Officer of the House of Bishops as provided by Article I, Section 3, of the Constitution in the event of the resignation, infirmity, disability or death of the Presiding Bishop.

Diocese to arrange for a Bishop. **Sec. 25.** If there is neither a Bishop Diocesan nor a Bishop Coadjutor nor a Bishop Suffragan nor an Assistant Bishop expressly assigned the administration of clergy discipline in a Diocese and not under a restriction on ministry or Sentence of suspension, the Diocese shall, by agreement pursuant to Canon III.13.2, arrange for a Bishop to perform the duties of the Bishop Diocesan under this Title before commencing or continuing with any proceedings under this Title. A Bishop performing the duties of the Bishop Diocesan under this Section has all the authority and powers of the Bishop Diocesan under this Title.

Sec. 26. Wherever in this Title it is provided that any communication, deliberation, investigation or proceeding shall be confidential, no person having knowledge or possession of confidential information derived from any such communication, deliberation, investigation or proceeding shall disclose the same except as provided in this Title, in any Accord or Order, or as required by any applicable law.

Confidential communication.

Sec. 27. Privileged Communication shall not be disclosed, nor shall any negative inference be drawn respecting the claim of the privilege, unless the privilege is waived by the person to whom the privilege belongs. Waiver of a privilege may occur by (a) voluntary disclosure; (b) failure to timely object to use of a Privileged Communication; or (c) placing the Privileged Communication at issue. Notwithstanding any provision of this section to the contrary, no waiver by a penitent of the privilege which attaches to communications or disclosures made within the Rite of Reconciliation of a Penitent shall work to require any confessor to divulge anything pertaining to any such communications or disclosures, the secrecy of the confession being morally absolute as provided in the Book of Common Prayer.

Privileged communication.

Sec. 28. Noncompliance with any procedural requirements set forth in this Title shall not be grounds for the dismissal of any proceeding unless the non-compliance shall cause material and substantial injustice to be done or seriously prejudice the rights of a Respondent as determined by the Panel or Court before which the proceeding is pending on motion and hearing.

Sec. 29. Solely for the purposes of the application of these Canons to persons who have received the pronouncement of the former Sentence of removal, the former Sentence of removal shall be deemed to have been a Sentence of deposition.

Removal.

Sec. 30

Preserve records.

a. Records of proceedings shall be preserved as follows:

1. Each Hearing Panel, Court of Review and Court of Review for Bishops shall keep a complete and accurate record of its proceedings by any means from which a written transcript can be produced.

When all proceedings have been concluded, the president of the Panel or Court shall certify the record. If the president did not participate in the proceeding for any reason, the Panel or Court shall elect another member of the Panel or Court to certify the record.

2. The Panel or Court shall make provision for the preservation and storage of a copy of the record of each proceeding in the Diocese in which the proceeding originated.

Deliver to the Archives.

3. The Panel or Court shall promptly deliver the original certified record of its proceedings to The Archives of The Episcopal Church.

b. The Bishop Diocesan shall:

1. promptly deliver to The Archives of The Episcopal Church a copy of any Accord or Order which has become effective and a record of any action of remission or modification of any Order, and

2. provide for the permanent preservation of copies of all Accords and Orders by means which permit the identification and location of each such copy by the name of the Member of the Clergy who is the subject thereof.

c. When printed records are submitted under this Canon, there shall be delivered to The Archives of The Episcopal Church an electronic copy or version of the records required to be preserved under this Section in such format as The Archives of The Episcopal Church may specify.

Database.

d. The Archives of The Episcopal Church (the "Administrator") shall create, administer and maintain a limited access secure central database registry to track data pertinent to proceedings under this Title (the "Database") for the purpose of providing data and statistical information to assist in the furtherance of policymaking, education, ministry, and other governance objectives of the Church (collectively the "Database Purposes").

1. The Database shall only include disciplinary matters under this Title that are referred to the Reference Panel pursuant to Canon IV.6.6 or IV.6.7.

2. The Diocese, Disciplinary Board, Church Attorney and Respondent (or Respondent's Advisor) as applicable shall complete and submit forms to the best of their knowledge, including questionnaires as prescribed and created by the Standing Commission on Structure Governance Constitution and Canons or its successor standing commission in consultation with the Administrator, Chief Legal Officer, and Office of Pastoral Development.

3. The Database shall not contain: (i) the personal identifying information of the Respondents, Complainants, Injured Persons, or witnesses; (ii) Privileged Communications; or (iii) other information that would be otherwise prohibited from disclosure under this Title or other applicable law.

4. The Administrator shall make reports from the Database accessible to the Standing Commission on Structure, Governance, Constitution and Canons, Chief Legal Officer, Office of Pastoral Development, and Executive Council. The Administrator will also make reports from the Database accessible to other Church governance bodies or other Church officials provided that such bodies and officials are seeking to use reports from the Database in furtherance of the Database Purposes and have received the approval of the Executive Council and the Chief Legal Officer of the Church. From time to time the Executive Council or the Standing Commission on Structure, Governance, Constitution and Canons may publish statistical information and other reports derived in from the Database provided that such publication is consistent with this canon.

Sec. 31. Any Member of the Clergy canonically resident in the Diocese who deems himself or herself to be under imputation, by rumor or otherwise, of any Offense for which proceedings could be had under this Title, may on his or her   *Imputation.*

own behalf request the Intake Officer to conduct an inquiry with regard to such imputation. Upon receipt of such request by a Member of the Clergy, it shall be the duty of the Intake Officer to undertake an initial inquiry pursuant to Canon IV.6 and to report the result to the Member of the Clergy.

Sec. 32. No Member of the Clergy shall be accountable for any Offense if the act or omission constituting the Offense shall have occurred only prior to the effective date of this Title, unless such act or omission would have constituted an offense under the predecessor to this Title.

Canon 20: Of Transitional Provisions and Conforming Amendments to Other Canons

Transition to Title IV revision. **Sec. 1.** Capitalized terms used in this Canon and which are not otherwise defined in this Title shall have the meanings provided in the predecessor to this Title.

Sec. 2. The effective date of this Title shall be July 1, 2011. Except as otherwise provided in this Canon, the predecessor to this Title shall stand repealed on the effective date of this Title.

Sec. 3. Matters which are pending under the predecessor to this Title on the effective date of this Title shall proceed as follows:

a. A Temporary Inhibition shall continue in accordance with its terms until it expires in accordance with Canon 1.2(f) of the predecessor to this Title. A Temporary Inhibition which is effective prior to the effective date of this Title and which expires by reason of the lapse of time as provided in Canon 1.2(f)(vi) of the predecessor to this Title may be extended and reviewed (1) as provided in the predecessor to this Title in the case of any matter proceeding in accordance with the predecessor to this Title as provided in this section or (2) in the case of any other matter, through the issuance of a restriction on ministry or the placement of the subject Member of the Clergy on Administrative Leave or both in accordance with the provisions of this Title.

b. A Charge against a Priest or Deacon which is pending on the effective date of this Title, and upon which the Diocesan Review Committee has neither issued a Presentment nor voted not to issue a Presentment, shall be referred to the Reference Panel and the matter shall proceed in accordance with the provisions of this Title.

c. A Charge against a Bishop, which is pending on the effective date of this Title, and upon which the Review Committee has neither issued a Presentment nor voted not to issue a Presentment, shall be referred to the Reference Panel and the matter shall proceed in accordance with the provisions of this Title.

d. A request for a statement of disassociation which is pending on the effective date of this Title shall proceed in accordance with Canon IV.17.7.a, and the matter shall thereafter further proceed, if at all, in accordance with the provisions of this Title.

e. A Presentment against a Bishop under Canon 3.21(c) of the predecessor to this Title which is pending on the effective date of this Title shall proceed in accordance with Canon IV.17.7, and the matter shall there after further proceed, if at all, inaccordance with the provisions of this Title.

f. A case in which a Presentment against any Member of the Clergy is issued prior to the effective date of this Title, and in which the Respondent's answer or other response is not made or does not become due until after the effective date of this Title, shall be referred to the Conference Panel and the matter shall proceed in accordance with the provisions of this Title.

g. A case which is pending before any Ecclesiastical Trial Court of any Diocese, and in which the Respondent's answer or other response is made or becomes due prior to the effective date of this Title, and in which no Trial has been had, shall proceed in accordance with the provisions of the predecessor to this Title unless the Church Attorney, the Respondent and the president of the Disciplinary Board shall agree in writing that the case shall proceed under the provisions of this Title, in which event the matter shall be referred to the Hearing Panel and the matter shall proceed in accordance with the provisions of this Title.

h. An appeal from any Judgment rendered by any Ecclesiastical Trial Court of any Diocese after the effective date of this Title shall proceed in accordance with the provisions of this Title.

i. A case which is pending before any Court of Review of the Trial of a Priest or Deacon shall proceed in accordance with the predecessor to this Title unless the Church Attorney, the Respondent and the president of the Provincial Court of Review shall agree in writing that the case shall proceed under the provisions of this Title, in which event the matter shall be referred to the Provincial Court of Review and the matter, including any grant of a new hearing, shall proceed in accordance with the provisions of this Title

j. A case which is pending before the Court for the Trial of a Bishop, and in which the Respondent's answer or other response is made or becomes due prior to the effective date of this Title, and in which no Trial has been had, shall proceed in accordance with the provisions of the predecessor to this Title unless the Church Attorney, the Respondent and the president of the Disciplinary Board for Bishops shall agree in writing that the case shall proceed under the provisions of this Title, in which event the matter shall be referred to the Hearing Panel and the matter shall proceed in accordance with the provisions of this Title.

k. A case which is pending before the Court of Review of the Trial of a Bishop shall proceed in accordance with the predecessor to this Title unless the Church Attorney, the Respondent and the president of the Court of Review for Bishops shall agree in writing that the case shall proceed under the provisions of this Title, in which event the matter shall be referred to the Court of Review for Bishops and the matter, including any grant of a new hearing, shall proceed in accordance with the provisions of this Title.

Title V: General Provisions

Canon 1: Of Enactment, Amendment, and Repeal

Sec. 1. No new Canon shall be enacted, or existing Canon be amended or repealed, except by concurrent Resolution of the two Houses of the General Convention. Such Resolution may be introduced first in either House, and shall be referred in each House to the Committee on Constitution and Canons thereof, for consideration, report, and recommendation, before adoption by the House; *provided* that in either House the foregoing requirement of reference may be dispensed with by a three-fourths vote of the members present.

Procedure required.

Sec. 2. Whenever a Canon is amended, enacted, or repealed in different respects by two or more independent enactments at the same General Convention, including the enactment of an entire Title, the separate enactments shall be considered as one enactment containing all of the amendments or enactments, whether or not repealed, to the extent that the change made in separate amendments or enactments, are not in conflict with each other. The two members of the Committee on Constitution and Canons from each House of General Convention appointed pursuant to Canon V.1.5 shall make the determination whether or not there is a conflict and certify the text of the single enactment to the Secretary of the General Convention.

Separate enactments affecting the same Canon.

Sec. 3. Whenever a Canon which repealed another Canon, or part thereof, shall itself be repealed, such previous Canon or part thereof shall not thereby be revived or reenacted, without express words to that effect.

Sec. 4. If a Canon or Section of a Canon or Clause of a Section of a Canon is to be amended or added, the enactment shall be in substantially one of the following forms: "That Canon . . .(Canon, Section or Clause designated as provided in Canon V.2.2) . . . be hereby amended to read as follows: (here insert the new reading)"; or "That Canon . . . (Canon or Section designated as provided in Canon V.2.2) . . . be hereby

Form of amendment.

amended by adding a Section (or Clause) reading as follows: (here insert the text of the new Section or Clause)." If amendments are to be made at one meeting of the General Convention to more than one-half of the Canons in a single Title of the Canons, the enactment may be in the following form: "That Title . . . of the Canons be hereby amended to read as follows: (here insert the new reading of all Canons in the Title whether or not the individual Canon is amended)." In the event of insertion of a new Canon, or a new Section or Clause in a Canon, or of the repeal of an existing Canon, or of a Section or Clause, the numbering of the Canons, or of a division of a Canon, which follow shall be changed accordingly without the necessity of enacting an amendment or amendments to that effect.

Certification of changes.

Sec. 5. The Committee on Constitution and Canons of each House of the General Convention shall, at the close of each regular meeting of the General Convention, appoint two of its members (a) to certify the changes, if any, made in the Canons, including a correction of the references made in any Canon to another, and to report the same, with the proper arrangement thereof, to the Secretary of the General Convention; and (b) to certify in like manner the changes, if any, made in the Constitution, or proposed to be made therein under the provisions of Article XII of the Constitution, and to report the same to the Secretary of the General Convention, who shall publish them in the Journal. The committee shall also have and exercise the power of renumbering of, and correction of references to, Articles, Sections and Clauses of the Constitution required by the adoption of amendments to the Constitution at a meeting of the General Convention in the same manner as provided with respect to the Canons.

When Canons take effect.

Sec. 6. All Canons enacted during the General Convention of 1943, and thereafter, and all amendments and repeals of Canons then or thereafter made, unless otherwise expressly ordered, shall take effect on the first day of January following the adjournment of the General Convention at which they were enacted or made.

Canon 2: Of Terminology Used in These Canons

Use of the term Diocese.

Sec. 1. Whenever the term "Diocese" is used without qualification in these Canons, it shall be understood to refer both to "Dioceses" and to "Missionary Dioceses," as these terms are used in the Constitution, and also, whenever applicable, to the "Convocation of Episcopal Churches in Europe."

Use of the term Canon.

Sec. 2. Whenever in these Canons a reference is made to a Canon or a Section of a Canon or a Clause of a Section of a Canon, the word "Canon" shall be set out, followed in order by the numerical or alphabetical designation of the Title, the Canon, the Section and the Clause, in each case separated by a period.

Canon 3: Of Bodies of General Convention; Quorum

Report membership.

Sec. 1. The membership of all committees, subcommittees, task forces, panels, or other bodies elected or appointed by any church-wide body or leader throughout The Episcopal Church including, but not limited to, the House of Deputies; the House of Bishops; the Executive Council; and Standing Commissions, Committees, Agencies, and Boards of The Episcopal Church; and their respective Presiding Officers and Chairs shall report their membership to the Office of General Convention, which shall publish the information within 30 days after election or appointment.

Quorum.

Sec. 2. Except where the Constitution or Canons of the General Convention provide to the contrary, a quorum of any body of the General Convention consisting of several members, the whole having been duly cited to meet, shall be a majority of said members; and a majority of the quorum so convened shall be competent to act.

Canon 4: Of Vacancies on Canonical Bodies

Causes for removal.

Sec. 1

a. Except where the Constitution or Canons of the General Convention provide to the contrary, the term of a member in any body of the General Convention consisting of several members shall become vacant as follows:

   1. upon absence from two regularly scheduled meetings of the body between successive regular meetings of the General Convention unless excused by the body;

   2. upon any restriction on exercise of ministry; placement on Administrative Leave; entry of an Order or Accord, which Order or Accord includes a Sentence of Admonition, Suspension, or Deposition of a Member of the Clergy then serving on the body;

   3. upon the pronouncement of the release and removal from the ordained ministry of this Church of a Member of the Clergy;

   4. upon the certification to the Presiding Bishop by the Disciplinary Board for Bishops as to the abandonment of this Church by a Bishop pursuant to Canon IV.16.A;

   5. upon the certification by the Standing Committee as to the abandonment of this Church by a Priest or Deacon pursuant to Canon IV.16.B; or

   6. for cause deemed sufficient by a two-thirds vote of all the members of the body.

Vacancies due to change in status.

b. The term of any member specified to be filled by a Priest or Deacon shall become vacant upon that member's ordination to the episcopacy.

c. The term of any Member of the Clergy specified to be filled by virtue of a provincial or diocesan canonical residence shall become vacant upon the change of canonical residence to another diocese or to a diocese in a different province, as the case may be.

d. The term of any Lay Person specified to be filled by virtue of a provincial or diocesan residence shall become vacant upon the change of residence to another diocese or to a diocese in a different province, as the case may be.

Sec. 2

a. The position of a lay member becomes vacant upon loss of status as a communicant in good standing.

b. The position of any member specified to be filled by a Lay Person shall become vacant upon that member's ordination.

RULES OF ORDER

House of Bishops

I. Services and Devotions

Placement of Holy Scriptures.

A. As an indication of our humble dependence upon the Word and Spirit of God, and following the example of primitive Councils, a copy of the Holy Scriptures shall always be reverently placed in view at all meetings of this House.

Opening devotions.

B. On each day of the Session of the House, the meeting shall be opened with prayer and the reading of the Holy Scriptures.

Noonday prayers.

C. At the hour of noon on each day of the Session, there shall be a devotional service, including prayers for the Church in its mission, as provided for in the Book of Common Prayer.

Close of session.

D. The last session of the House shall be closed with the Benediction pronounced by the Bishop presiding.

Holy Eucharist.

E. At every session of the House of Bishops there shall be daily worship at such time and place as the Presiding Bishop or Vice-President of the House shall appoint.

F. Preceding the balloting for the election of a Presiding Bishop, of a Missionary Bishop, or on the proposed transfer of a Missionary Bishop from one Diocese to another, there shall be a celebration of the Holy Eucharist, with a special prayer for the guidance of the Holy Spirit.

Opening Service of General Convention.

G. The opening service of the General Convention and selection of the Preacher shall be in charge of the Presiding Bishop, the Vice-President of the House of Bishops, and the Bishop of the Diocese wherein the Convention is to be held. The sermon shall be delivered by the Presiding Bishop, unless the Presiding Bishop shall elect to appoint some other Bishop as Preacher.

II. First Day of Session

A. The House of Bishops shall meet for business at such *Call to order.*
    time and place as shall have been duly notified by the
    Presiding Bishop, or the Vice-President of the House, to
    the members of this House, and shall be called to order
    by the Presiding Bishop or the Vice--President, or, in
    their absence, by the Senior Bishop, with jurisdiction,
    present.

B. The House shall then proceed to elect a Secretary if the *Secretary and*
    office is vacant; and the person elected shall serve until *Assistant*
    the end of that meeting of the Convention. At the end of *Secretaries.*
    each meeting of the Convention, the House shall proceed
    to elect a Secretary who shall continue in office until the
    conclusion of the next regular meeting of the Convention
    following that election. With the approval of the bishop
    presiding, the Secretary may then, or later, appoint
    Assistant Secretaries.

C. The roll of members shall be called by the Secretary. On *Roll.*
    the second and third days the Secretary shall make a
    note of the late arrivals who shall inform the Secretary of
    their presence.

D. The minutes of the last meeting shall then be read by the *Minutes.*
    Secretary and acted on by the House. Such reading may
    be dispensed with by a majority vote of the House.

E. Bishops appearing in the House for the first time after *Presentation of*
    their Consecration shall then, or at such other time at *new Bishops.*
    that meeting appointed by the Presiding Bishop, be
    presented to the House in a manner prescribed by the
    Presiding Bishop.

F. At a time deemed suitable, the Presiding Bishop shall *Memorials.*
    then announce, without comment, the fact and the date
    of the death of any members who have died since the last
    preceding meeting; after which the House shall be led in
    prayer.

G. The House shall then proceed to elect a Vice-President, if *Vice-Chair.*
    the office is then vacant, after hearing the report of the
    nominating committee of the House and after receiving

any other nominations from the floor; and the person elected shall serve until the conclusion of the next regular meeting of the Convention. At the conclusion of each meeting of the Convention, the House, using the same procedure, shall proceed to elect a Vice-President who shall continue in office until the conclusion of the next regular meeting of the Convention following that election. The Vice-President, in the absence of the Presiding Bishop, or at the request of the Presiding Bishop, shall be the Presiding Officer of the House. In the absence of the Vice-President, the Presiding Bishop may ask another member of the House to preside.

III. Daily Orders

Regular order of business.

A. The regular order of business of the House shall be as follows:

1. Devotions.

2. Roll call or late registrations.

3. Minutes of the previous meeting.

4. Presentation of new members.

5. Communications from the Presiding Bishop.

6. Report of the Committee on Dispatch of Business.

7. Petitions and Memorials.

8. Messages from the House of Deputies not yet disposed of.

9. Motions of Reference.

10. Reports of Legislative Committees in the order in which the Committees are named in section IV

11. Reports of Commissions.

12. Reports of Special Committees.

13. Miscellaneous business.

Special order of business.

B. At any Special Meeting of the House, the Secretary shall present the Official Call for such meeting and incorporate such Call in the Minutes. The order of business at any Special Session shall be as follows:

1. Call to order.

2. Devotions.

3. Roll call.

4. Presentation of new members.

5. Communications from the Presiding Bishop.

6. The special Business of the Meeting.

7. Reports of Special Committees.

8. Reading of the Minutes.

9. Adjournment.

C. On the second day of the Session, after Devotions, the Presiding Bishop shall lay before the House a statement of official acts during the recess of the General Convention.

Official acts of Presiding Bishop.

D. On the days when the House of Bishops is expected to meet with the House of Deputies and others in Joint Session, the first order of business shall be the consideration of such matters as the Committee on Dispatch of Business shall report as urgently demanding attention. Then shall follow consideration of Messages from the House of Deputies not disposed of, Reports from Standing Committees, and other business for which time shall remain. If the Joint Session shall adjourn before the customary hour for adjournment of the House of Bishops, the House may resume its sitting. Any part of this rule may be suspended by a majority vote.

Order of business on days of Joint Sessions.

E. The Secretary shall keep a Calendar of Business, on which shall be placed, in the order in which they are presented, Reports of Committees, Resolutions which lie over, and other matters undisposed of, indicating the subject of each item.

Calendar of Business.

F. The secretary shall keep a Consent Calendar, which shall be published daily and distributed to the members before the convening of the House on each legislative day, and

Consent Calendar.

designate it as a separate calendar. Matters shall be listed on the Consent Calendar in separate groupings according to the date that they have been placed thereon. All matters to which amendments have been proposed by a Committee shall be so designated.

No debate is in order regarding any matter appearing on the Consent Calendar. However, the President shall allow a reasonable time for questions from the floor and answers to those questions.

Prior to a vote on final passage of any matter appearing on the Consent Calendar, it shall be removed from the Consent Calendar if (1) any three Bishops, or (2) the sponsor of the matter, or (3) the Committee on Dispatch of Business requests, in writing, that the Secretary remove the matter from the consent calendar. Any matter so removed may not be placed thereafter on the Consent Calendar but shall be restored to the Daily Calendar.

No amendment other than an amendment contained in a Committee report is in order regarding any matter on the Consent Calendar. Any amendments contained in Committee reports on such matters shall be deemed adopted unless the matter is objected to and removed from the Consent Calendar.

Matters appearing on the Consent Calendar shall be taken up immediately following the noon recess of the next legislative day following their placement on the Consent Calendar, or otherwise by unanimous consent or by adoption of a special order of business.

A matter may be placed on the Consent Calendar by vote of a Legislative Committee, if the Committee's vote to report the matter with a recommendation for adoption (with or without amendments), or for discharge, or for rejection was by three quarters (3/4) of the members present.

Order of Day. G. The Order of the Day shall be taken up at the hour appointed, unless postponed by a two-thirds vote of those present and voting.

H. Bishops invited to honorary seats may be introduced by   *Visiting Bishops.*
the Bishop presiding whenever no other business
occupies the House.

IV. Appointment of Committees

A. Committees of this House shall be appointed by the   *Legislative*
Presiding Bishop unless otherwise ordered. The   *Committees.*
Presiding Bishop, not later than the third day of the
session, shall name the members of all the Committees
to serve on an annual basis, and shall designate the Chair
ofeach Committee. The following shall be the
Committees of the House:

   1. Standing Committees:

      a. Dispatch of Business.

      b. Certification of Minutes.

      c. Rules of Order.

      d. Privilege and Courtesy.

      e. Resignation of Bishops.

      f. Pastoral Letter.

   2. Legislative Committees as needed, that may include:

      a. Constitution and Canons.

      b. Structure.

      c. World Mission.

      d. National and International Concerns.

      e. Social and Urban Affairs.

      f. Small Congregations.

      g. Evangelism.

      h. Prayer Book, Liturgy and Church Music.

      i. Ministry.

      j. Education.

      k. Church Pension Fund.

    l. Stewardship and Development.

    m. Ecumenical Relations.

    n. Resignation and Deployment of Bishops.

   3. Other Committees as needed, that may include:

    a. Communications.

    b. Miscellaneous Resolutions.

    c. Religious Communities.

    d. On Nominations and Elections.

    e. Admission of New Dioceses.

B. The Chair of each Committee shall appoint a Vice-Chair and a Secretary.

C. The Presiding Bishop may at any time refer to any Committee of the House, for its consideration, matters which arise and which should receive consideration at the next meeting of the House.

V. General Rules for Meetings of This House

A. No Memorial, Petition, or Address shall come before this House unless presented by a Bishop who is a member of this House, or some other Bishop present.

Distribution of printed matter.

B. Nothing other than Reports and other documents printed for the use and by the order of the House, except the private correspondence of its members, shall be distributed in the House without having first been entrusted to the Secretary, and submitted to the approval of the Bishop presiding.

Resolutions and motions.

C. All Resolutions shall be reduced to writing, and no motion shall be considered as before the House until seconded. In all cases where a Resolution seeks to amend a Canon or an entire Title of Canons, the form of Resolution submitted shall set out the enactment in the form prescribed by Canon V.1.4, shall include with a dash overstrike on each letter any words which are deleted by the amendment and shall underline any words which are added by the amendment; Provided that if the amendment of an entire Title is to be covered by one enactment under Canon V.1.4, the deleted text and the underlining of the next text need not be included but the proponent shall make adequate written explanation of the changes. All resolutions of Bishops shall be proposed by one Bishop and be endorsed by not less than two additional Bishops, all three being from different dioceses. Individual Bishops shall be limited to proposing not more than three resolutions. *Limitations.*

D. a. Reports of Committees shall be in writing, and shall be received in due course. Reports recommending or requiring any action or expression of opinion by the House shall be accompanied by specific Resolutions. *Reports of Committees.*

b. Legislative Committee Reports *Committee Recommendation.*

1. Each Legislative Committee must take final action on every Resolution and othermatter referred to it for action to recommend that the House takes one of thefollowing actions:

i. adopt as proposed; *Adopt.*

ii. adopt as amended by the Committee; all amendments made by a Committee will apply automatically to the Resolution and the matter before the House when the Resolution is considered will be the Resolution as amended by the Committee;

iii. adopt a substitute Resolution: *Adopt Substitute.*

a. A substitute Resolution must be on the same subject as the Resolution referred to the Legislative Committee for action.

b. A substitute Resolution may only cover one Resolution referred to the Legislative Committee for action.

c. If the House declines to adopt a substitute, the original Resolution will be automatically referred back to the Committee for additional consideration.

*Adopt
Consolidated
Substitute.*

iv. adopt a consolidated substitute Resolution:

    a. A consolidated substitute Resolution must be on the same subject as the Resolutions referred to the Legislative Committee for action.

    b. Its report on the final action on that Resolution must identify all the other Resolutions the substitute is intended to cover.

    c. A vote by the Legislative Committee to recommend adoption of a consolidated substitute Resolution will be an automatic recommendation to take no further action on all other Resolutions the consolidated substitute Resolution is intended to cover.

    d. If the House declines to adopt a consolidated substitute Resolution, the original Resolutions will be automatically referred back to the Committee for additional consideration.

v. reject;

*Referral to an
Interim Body.*

vi. refer to a specified Standing Commission, General Convention Task Force, Executive Council or other body of the Church for study, action, or to make recommendations on the subject to the next General Convention;

*Take No Further
Action.*

vii. take no further action because:

    a. the matter has already been dealt with by action of the House of Bishops at this meeting of General Convention;

    b. the matter is covered by a Resolution of a prior General Convention;

    c. for other reasons.

viii.   If the Resolution or matter has been acted on by the House of Deputies:

If Acted on by the House of Deputies.

   a.   concur with the action of the House of Deputies;

   b.   concur as proposed to be amended by the House of Bishops Legislative Committee;

   c.   concur with substitute as proposed by the House of Bishops Legislative Committee;

   d.   not concur and take a different action;

   e.   not concur.

2.   Minority Report

Minority Report.

   i.   If there is a minority position on a final action on a Resolution or other matter and the minority requests to make a minority report to the House, the Chair will include the minority report in the Legislative Committee's report on the final action on the Resolution or other matter.

   ii.   A minority position consists of at least one-quarter (1/4) of the members of the Legislative Committee present and voting on the Resolution, Memorial, or other matter.

c.   Each report shall be dated, signed by the Chair or Secretary of the Committee, and transmitted to the office of the Secretary of the House, who shall endorse thereon the date of receipt thereof. If there is a minority position in the Committee and a minority spokesperson requests a minority position report, the Chair shall include the same in the report.

Report to be signed.

Any resolution which involves an amendment to the Constitution or Canons shall be referred to the appropriate Legislative or Special Committee for action and simultaneously to the Committee on Constitution or the Committee on Canons, as the case may be, and such Committee shall make certain that the Resolution is in proper constitutional or

Amendments to Constitution or Canons to be in proper form.

canonical form, achieves consistency and clarity in the Constitution or Canons, and includes all amendments necessary to effect the proposed change, and shall promptly communicate its recommendations to the Legislative or Special Committee. In such case the Committee shall neither concern itself with, nor report on, the substance of the matter referred to it, but whenever requested to do so by the Presiding Officer of the House, the Committee shall in its report to the House make recommendations as to substance.

Reports of Interim Committees.

E. Reports of Committees appointed to sit during the recess, if not acted upon at once, shall, when presented, be made the Order of the Day for a time fixed. Printed Committee Reports which have been delivered to, and circulated among, the members of the House of Bishops, in advance of the making of such Reports upon the floor of the House, shall be presented by title and the Chair or Committee member presenting said Report shall be allowed five minutes for summarizing the same, which time may be extended only by a two-thirds vote of those present and voting.

Messages to the House of Deputies.

F. All Resolutions which are to be communicated to the House of Deputies, unless they contain information of action incomplete in this House, or be temporarily withheld by order of this House at the time of their passage, shall be transmitted to the House of Deputies as soon as conveniently may be, under the direction of the Bishop presiding.

Messages from the House of Deputies.

G. Committees from the House of Deputies shall be admitted immediately. Messages from the House of Deputies shall be handed by the Secretary of this House to the Bishop Presiding, to be laid before the House as early as may be convenient. However, consideration of such Message shall be subject to a motion for the appointment of a Committee of Conference as hereinafter provided in these Rules. All such Messages communicating any legislative action on the part of the House of Deputies shall, without debate, be referred to the proper Committee, unless, without debate, the House shall decide to consider such Messages without such reference. When the consideration of such Message shall have been begun, it shall continue to be the Order of the Day until final action thereon.

The final action of this House upon any Message from the House of Deputies shall be by vote upon the question "Shall this House concur in the action of the House of Deputies as communicated in their Message No._____?" Messages requiring no action by the House may be received by Title.

H. If, during the consideration by this House of any action taken by the House of Deputies, a motion is made stating the position of this House and requesting a Committee of Conference, such motion shall have precedence and be put to a vote without debate, and if passed by a majority of the members of this House then present, a Committee of Conference shall be appointed. A Committee of Conference shall also be in order, with or without motion, (1) in cases where the House of Deputies has concurred, with amendments, in action taken by this House, or (2) in cases where this House has concurred, with amendments, in action taken by the House of Deputies. When a Committee of Conference has been appointed, final action upon the matter under consideration shall be deferred until the Committee of Conference shall have reported to this House; Provided, such report shall be made no later than the next business day or within one hour after the convening of the last meeting of this House in Convention assembled, whichever event shall first occur. Further, the Chair of any Standing or other Committee shall have full authority, either alone or with members of the Committee, to confer with the Chair of the cognate Committee of the House of Deputies.

Committee of Conference.

I. Two Bishops may be appointed by the Bishop Presiding to act with the Secretary in preparing daily reports of the action of this House, and furnishing them, at their discretion, to the public press.

Daily reports.

Guests with seat and voice.

J. The Committee on Privilege and Courtesy may recommend the courtesy of seat and voice to (1) any Bishop of a Church in the Anglican Communion who has been nominated by a Bishop of this House whose jurisdiction has entered into a formal companion diocese relationship approved by the Executive Council of this Church or (2) any Bishop who is a guest of the Presiding Bishop upon the nomination of the Presiding Bishop. The Committee on Privilege and Courtesy must receive nominations for the courtesy of seat and voice thirty days prior to the stated or called meeting of the House at which such courtesy is to be granted. The nominations for the courtesy of seat and voice shall be circulated in writing to the members of the House before the nominations shall be presented to the House. Bishops granted the courtesy of seat and voice shall be assigned a seat and shall have such seat and voice only for meeting of the House at which such courtesy was granted. Bishops granted courtesy of seat and voice shall at all times be entitled to be present except when the House is in Executive Session. At such a call, the Secretary shall ask the guests to leave the House.

Advisory Committee.

K. There shall be a Council of Advice, composed of Bishops who are the Presidents or Vice-Presidents of each Province, which will act as advisory council to the Presiding Bishop between meetings of the House of Bishops. The Committee shall elect its own officers.

Committee on Pastoral.

L. The Committee on the Bishop's Pastoral shall be composed of persons eminently qualified for the task, and empowered to enlist additional assistance, with the consent of the Presiding Bishop, as may seem wise. The Committee shall make a Report at each Session of the House.

Ballot.

M. **Elections of Bishops and Membership in the House**

1. When it is proposed to give consent to the consecration or confirmation of a Bishop-elect, or of a Bishop adjutor-elect, or of a Bishop-elect Suffragan, it shall be competent for any six voting members of the House to call for a vote by ballot.

2. The Secretary shall prepare a ballot for each election listing alphabetically the names of all persons nominated. On each ballot, each voting member shall vote for the number of nominees to be or remaining to be elected, and any ballot with votes less than or in excess thereof shall be void. The nominees receiving the largest number of votes shall be deemed elected, provided that votes equal to or in excess of a majority of the ballots cast on any ballot shall be required for election.

3. Any Bishop of a Church in the Anglican Communion who is in exile from a Diocese, or is without membership in a House of Bishops because the Diocese is temporarily in an extra- provincial status, and who is resident in any jurisdiction in this Church, or any other Bishop of a Church in the Anglican Communion who has resigned his or her position in that Church, who has made his or her primary residence in any jurisdiction in this Church may be admitted to this House as a collegial member. Such membership may be extended to such a Bishop by a two- thirds vote of those present and voting on each Bishop, taken by secret ballot if requested by at least six members of the House, considered by the members of the House present at any regularly called meeting, and shall continue until such time as the collegial member removes from the jurisdiction of this Church, or until such time as it is withdrawn by a like vote. Such collegial member shall be assigned a seat, and have a voice, in this House. No vote shall be accorded such collegial member, in keeping with the Constitution of this Church.

    Collegial Members.

    The Committee on Privilege and Courtesy must receive, one month in advance of any meeting of this House, nominations for collegial membership in this House, said nomination to be made only by the Bishop in whose jurisdiction the proposed collegial member resides. The nominations for collegial membership shall be circulated in writing to the members of the House before the nominations shall be presented to the House.

    Nominations for Collegial Membership.

Honorary Members.

Any Bishop of an extra-provincial Diocese which originated in the Church or any Bishop of this Church who removed from the jurisdiction of this Church to the jurisdiction of a Church in the Anglican Communion may be continued in relationship to this House as an honorary member. Thirty days prior to each stated or called meeting of the House such honorary members shall give written notice of their intention to be present to the Presiding Bishop. Seat and voice shall then be accorded such honorary members, upon the nomination to the House by the Bishop presiding. No vote shall be accorded the honorary member.

Bishops admitted to honorary and collegial seats in the House shall at all times be entitled to be present except when the House is in Executive Session. At such a call, the Secretary shall ask the guests to leave the House.

Nonvoting membership.

4. Any Bishop of this Church who resigns a position for reasons other than those specified in Article I.2 of the Constitution, but whose resignation is not for reasons related to the Bishop's moral character, may, on motion and by a majority vote, be accorded non-voting membership in the House. Until further contrary action by the House, any such non-voting member shall have the right to seat and voice at all meetings, the right to serve on committees, and all other rights of membership except that of voting on any matter.

Debate and Decorum.

N. **Debate and Decorum**

1. Members in discussion shall address the Chair, and shall confine themselves to the Question in debate. No member shall speak more than twice in the same debate without leave of the House. At the conclusion of any speech, the Bishop presiding, alone, or any member of the House, may call for a vote, without debate, on a proposal for a recess of conference to define and clarify the issues of the debate and the way in which the House is working. If the proposal of a member is supported by at least four other

members, it is to be put to a vote. If passed by a two-thirds vote of those present and voting, members of the House will form small groups for a ten-minute conference, at the end of which debate will resume with any speakers who had already been recognized at the time of the motion for conference.

2. Officers of the House of Bishops, when addressing the House in debate, shall in all cases do so from the floor of the House.

3. When a division is called for, every voting member present shall be counted. When, in such procedure, the vote of the Bishop presiding produces a tie, the motion shall be considered as lost.

   Division.

4. On any question before the House the ayes and nays may be required by any six voting members, and shall in such cases be entered on the Journal.

5. When a Question is under consideration, the following motions shall have precedence in the order listed: to lay upon the table, to postpone to a time certain, to commit or to refer, to substitute another motion dealing with the same Question, to amend, or to postpone indefinitely; Provided, that, in consideration of a message from the House of Deputies, the provisions of Rules V. G and H shall apply, and a motion made thereunder for a Committee of Conference shall have precedence; and Provided, further, that a proposal for a Recess of Conference shall always be in order, under the conditions set forth in Rule V.N.1.

   Precedence of motions.

6. On motion duly put and carried, the House may resolve itself into a Committee of the Whole, at which no records shall be made of its action. On separate motion duly put and carried, those present at such sessions may be limited to members of the House.

   Committee of the Whole.

7. On motion duly put and carried, the House may go into Executive Session, at which only members of the House shall be present. The Chair of the Committee

   Executive Session.

on Dispatch of Business shall act as clerk and make a record of all motions adopted.

Questions of order.

8. All questions of order shall be decided by the Chair without debate, but appeal may be taken from such decision. The decision of the Chair shall stand unless overruled by a two-thirds vote of those present and voting. On such appeal, no member shall speak more than once without express leave of the House.

Amendments.

9. Amendments shall be considered in the order in which they are moved. When a proposed amendment is under consideration, a motion to amend the same may be made. No after-amendment to such second amendment shall be in order, but a substitute for the whole matter may be received. No proposition on a subject differing from the one under consideration shall be received under color of a substitute.

Reconsideration.

10. A Question being once determined shall stand as the judgment of the House, and shall not be again drawn into debate during the same session of the House, except with the consent of a two-thirds vote of those present and voting. A motion to reconsider can be made only on the day the vote was taken, or on the next succeeding legislative day, and must be made and seconded by those who voted with the majority.

Time limit on new business.

11. a. Except by a two-thirds vote of those present and voting, no new business shall be introduced for the consideration of the House after the second day of the Session. All matters originating in this House requiring concurrent action by both houses shall be considered before the last legislative day except for Resolutions of Privilege and Courtesy.

   b. No resolution proposing amendments to the Constitution or Canons of this Church may be presented in the House of Bishops for an initial vote on the last legislative day of General Convention; Provided, however, that any such resolution previously considered and voted upon by this House may be considered on the last legislative day in order to consider changes to the resolution approved by the House of Deputies.

12. Except by a two-thirds vote of those present and voting, no member of the House may introduce a Resolution at a special meeting unless the Resolution has been circulated thirty days in advance to the members. This rule shall not be construed in any way to prevent a Committee of the House from introducing Resolutions at special meetings.

Circulate Resolutions in advance.

O. **Rules of Order**

Rules of Order.

1. These rules shall be in force in subsequent Sessions of this House unless otherwise ordered.

2. Additions and amendments to, or suspension or repeal of these rules shall require a two-thirds vote of those present and voting.

Amendment of Rules.

3. Except when in conflict with the Constitution or Canons, or any Rule herein contained, the latest edition of Robert's Rules of Order shall govern the interpretation of these rules, and the parliamentary procedures to be followed in this House.

Robert's Rules apply.

VI. The Presiding Bishop

A. On the day following the Joint Session to which the Joint Nominating Committee has reported pursuant to Canon I.2.1.d, the House of Bishops shall meet in executive session in a church to discuss the nominees presented at the Joint Session, and to elect a Presiding Bishop from among those nominees.

Election.

B. All members of the House of Bishops present shall remain within the confines of the church where the election has been held, until word has been received of the action of the House of Deputies.

Awaiting confirmation from Deputies.

VII. Missionary Bishops

Vacant episcopate.

A. When a vacancy occurs or is about to occur in the Missionary Episcopate, it shall be the duty of the Presiding Bishop to investigate the situation existing in the Diocese, to consult with those persons in the field and at home best fitted to advise as to the conditions in the Diocese, and to submit to the members of the House such information as the Presiding Bishop may secure.

Notice of election in call for Meeting.

B. Before any vacancy in the Missionary Episcopate is to be considered or filled at any Meeting of the House, notice to this effect shall be given in the call of such Meeting. The ballot for the election to any such vacancy shall not, without unanimous consent, be taken at a Special Meeting until at least the first day, nor at a Meeting of the General Convention until at least the second day, after nominations have been made to the House. In the event of the occurrence of a vacancy in a Missionary Diocese, or the resignation of a Missionary Bishop, between the issuance of the call for a Special Meeting of the House of Bishops and the meeting thereof, the House, by a two-thirds vote of those present and voting, shall be competent to fill such vacancy, or to act upon such resignation.

C. Further proceedings for the election of a Missionary Bishop shall be as follows:

Joint Nominating Committee.

1. In the case of each vacancy to be filled, a special Joint Nominating Committee shall be appointed. The Committee shall be composed of three persons from the jurisdiction concerned, chosen by its Council of Advice or in some other manner as ordered by the Presiding Bishop, and three members of this House appointed by the Presiding Bishop. The Joint Nominating Committee shall elect its own officers and shall nominate three persons for the vacancy. Three weeks before the Meeting of the House these names shall be sent in confidence to each Bishop.

Presiding Bishop may nominate.

2. The Presiding Bishop may, in the exercise of discretion, make nominations for such vacancies.

3. At the Meeting of the House, the names of the persons proposed by the Joint Nominating Committee shall be formally placed in nomination, and opportunity shall also be given for nominations from the floor.

Nominations from floor.

4. The Joint Nominating Committees and the Bishops making nominations, and other having knowledge of the persons nominated, shall give to appropriate committees full information regarding the nominees, and any such committees, having secured further information as may be possible, shall report to the House in Executive Session such further information concerning the intellectual, moral, and physical qualifications of the persons nominated, with dates of birth, graduation, and specific statements as to theological attainment, proficiency in languages, and any specialty in sacred duties to which such persons may have devoted themselves. Questions may be asked and other information given by the Bishops.

Information about nominees.

5. All nominations for vacant Missionary Dioceses shall be made in Executive Session. The names of the nominees shall be made known to the public only after the election.

Executive Session.

6. In the case of a declination, another election can be held from the same names without further formality than renomination; but if new names are introduced, the order prescribed above shall be repeated.

Declination.

7. In the case of the proposed transfer of a Bishop in charge of a Missionary Diocese to another Diocese, action shall be as in the case of the election of Missionary Bishops.

Transfer to another Diocese.

8. All proceedings in Executive Session shall be held strictly confidential. In the case of elections held in Executive Session the names of those elected shall not be made known until they are ordered to be sent to the Standing Committees.

Confidentiality.

VIII. Standing Orders

Ordination and consecration of Bishops.

A. Whereas, by provisions of Canon III.11.5, and Canon III.11.9.c.3.iii, the Presiding Bishop is empowered to take order for the ordination and consecration of Diocesan and Missionary Bishops, either in the Presiding Bishop's own person or by commission issued to three Bishops; It is hereby ordered, that, in all cases where the Presiding Bishop takes order for the ordination of a Bishop in a Diocese or Missionary Diocese, the place for the same shall be designated with the consent of the Ecclesiastical Authority in whose Diocese or Jurisdiction such proposed place is; the Bishop-elect shall have the right to designate the preacher and the two Bishops by whom the Bishop-elect is to be presented; and, in the absence of the Presiding Bishop, the Senior Bishop with jurisdiction by consecration who is present shall preside, unless some other Bishop shall have been designated by the Presiding Bishop.

B. Seniority among the Bishops is according to the date of the consecration of each Bishop.

Daily sessions at General Convention.

C. The House of Bishops shall assemble on every morning during the period of the General Convention, except the Lord's Day, for business, unless adjournment beyond that morning has been ordered by the vote of the House.

Committee on Journal.

D. Two or more of the Bishops shall be appointed at each General Convention to take charge, together with the Secretary of the House of Bishops, of the Journal of its proceedings, and to see that the whole, or such parts of it as the House may direct, be entered in its proper place in the Journal of the General Convention.

Official Register.

E. The Secretary of the House of Bishops shall keep a permanent record of the members and officers of the House from the beginning, and shall record therein the names of the Bishops who are or have been members of this House, the date and place of their consecration, the names of their consecrators, together with the date of the termination, by death, resignation, or otherwise, of the membership of such Bishops as have ceased to have seats in this House, all of which facts shall be recorded only upon official notification, for which it shall be the duty of the Secretary to call upon such persons as may be competent to furnish the same. The said record shall be the official Register of this House, and the roll of the House communicate the same to the House, as its official roll, as soon as the Presiding Officer shall have taken the chair. Such roll shall be subject to change only by vote of the House.

F. In making up the list of the Bishops who have retained their constituted rights to seats in this House, the Secretary is instructed to leave the name of any Bishop resigned in the place which the Bishop occupies in the order of consecration, with the addition of the word "Bishop," which shall be considered as the sufficient title of such resigned Bishop.

Resigned Bishop.

G. At every meeting of the House of Bishops a seat for the Chair of the Committee on Dispatch of Business shall be assigned near the front of the House.

Chair of Dispatch.

H. At every meeting of the House of Bishops seats on the platform shall be assigned to such Bishops present as have formerly held the office of Presiding Bishop, and at every service of the General Convention such Bishops have formerly held the office of Presiding Bishop shall be assigned places immediately in front of the Chaplain of the Presiding Bishop.

Former Presiding Bishops.

I. Whenever the House shall make a determination under Article I.2 of the Constitution that a resigned Bishop shall or shall not retain a seat and vote in the House, the following understanding of the intent of the pertinent terms of that provision of the Constitution shall apply:

Definitions.

1. "advanced age" shall mean at least 62 years of age;

2. "bodily infirmity" shall mean either a condition for which one is eligible for disability retirement benefits from the Church Pension Fund or Social Security Administration, or a physical or mental impairment that a physician or psychiatrist (approved by the Presiding Bishop) certifies would likely result in eligibility for such disability

retirement benefits should the Bishop continue in active episcopal ministry;

3. "office created by the General Convention" shall mean a ministry funded by the The Episcopal Church budget and approved by the Presiding Bishop; and

4. "mission strategy" shall mean a strategy that would allow the election of an indigenous member of the clergy of a non-domestic diocese as Bishop, or that would allow a diocese to implement a new mission strategy as determined by the Presiding Bishop, or that would allow a transition in episcopal leadership after a Diocesan Bishop or Bishop Suffragan has served 10 or more years in either or both of those offices.

IX. Standing Resolutions

Resolutions for resigning Bishops.

A. Resolved, That the Standing Committee on the Resignation of Bishops be requested to prepare a Resolution taking note of the service of each Bishop whose resignation is being accepted, such Resolution to be presented to the House of Bishops along with the recommendation on the resignation. Where a resignation is accepted between Meetings of the House, such Resolution shall be presented at the next Meeting.

Memorial messages.

B. Resolved, That the Presiding Bishop be requested to appoint, on each occasion, a Committee of three or more Bishops to prepare, on behalf of the House of Bishops, and send to the family of each Bishop who dies, a Memorial Message, such Committee to represent the House of Bishops at the funeral, where it is practical for them to attend.

Conveners of Commissions.

C. Resolved, That, within six months after the appointment of any Committee or Commission, the Secretary of the House of Bishops shall communicate with the Bishop Convener of each Commission and Committee, and inquire whether the Commission or Committee has convened and organized, keeping a record of the replies received.

House of Deputies

I: The Holy Scriptures

A. Placement of Holy Scriptures

1. The President and Secretary will ensure that a copy of the Holy Scriptures is reverently displayed at all meetings of the House of Deputies.

B. Daily Prayers

1. The daily session of the House will begin with prayers.   *Call to Prayer.*

2. The President may call for prayers at other times.

3. Any Deputy may ask the President to call for prayer at other times.

II: General Rules

A. Duty of Deputies

1. Deputies will prepare for and give their attention to the business of the House.

2. Deputies will attend all sessions of the House unless excused by the President.

B. Communications Devices

1. The President may allow Deputies to bring cell phones, computers, and other communication devices to the House, except as provided in these rules during closed sessions.   *Communication.*

2. No talking on communications devices is allowed while the House is in session.

3. All communications devices will be set to the silent mode.

4. Deputies will respect those around them as they use such devices.

C. Distribution of Printed, Digital, and Other Materials

Official documents only.

1. Only official reports, papers, and documents necessary for the business of the House may be distributed to the House, except with the approval of: (i) the President; or (ii) the House by a majority vote.

2. These rules apply to physical materials on the floor and digital materials distributed through official legislative software or devices.

D. Quorum

Quorum.

1. To transact business the Constitution, Article I Sec. 4, requires:

   i. a majority of the Dioceses entitled to representation in this House must have at least one clerical Deputy present; and

   ii. a majority of the Dioceses entitled to representation in this House must have at least one lay Deputy present.

E. Minutes

Certified minutes.

1. The Minutes of the House will be kept by the Secretary or Assistant Secretaries and reviewed by the Committee on the Certification of Minutes.

2. The Committee on the Certification of Minutes will review, approve, and publish the final Minutes for each day before the start of the next day's session.

3. The Committee on the Certification of Minutes will report its action at the next scheduled session.

4. The House may require that the Minutes for any session be approved by the House.

Memorial Roll.

F. Memorial Roll

1. The Secretary will prepare a Memorial Roll of all previous Deputies who have died since the last meeting of the House or who have not otherwise been remembered at a meeting of the House.

2. At each General Convention, time will be set aside to read aloud the names on the Memorial Roll and for prayers by the Chaplain.

III: Deputations

A. Chair of Deputation

   1. At least one year before the first legislative session of the General Convention, each Deputation will:

      i. designate a Chair; and

      ii. notify the Secretary of the House of Deputies of the name of the Chair.

Duties of Chair.

   2. The Deputation Chair will:

      i. serve as the primary contact for House of Deputies communications;

      ii. certify the Deputation's votes by orders;

      iii. certify changes in the Deputation during General Convention;

      iv. perform other duties as directed by the President.

B. Certification of Alternate Deputies as Deputies

   1. Alternate Deputies may not sit or vote with their Deputations, unless and until certified by the Committee on Credentials as a substitute for a Deputy.

Alternate Deputies.

   2. The Committee on Credentials will certify Alternate Deputies as Deputies before each session.

   3. The procedures for certification will be those determined by the Secretary of the House of Deputies.

   4. An Alternate Deputy will serve for one or more legislative sessions as Deputy but only until the Deputy for whom he or she substituted is able to resume their seats.

   5. The Committee on Credentials will hear and decide any disputes on certification of Deputies and will report their decision to the House.

IV: Floor Privileges and Arrangements

Floor admittance.

A. Floor Privileges. No one will be admitted to the floor except Deputies, officers of the House, and:

1. the Treasurer of the General Convention;

2. other persons authorized by the President or Secretary, to assist in the conduct of the business of the House;

3. other persons invited or authorized by the President.

4. infants under one year of age with a parent or guardian who is a deputy;

5. children over one-year-old who require nursing or bottle-feeding only while feeding;

6. caregivers of children, to bring a child to a feeding parent when the child needs to be fed, escorted in and out as directed by the President.

Seat and Voice.

B. Seat and Voice. The following will have seat and voice on the floor of the House:

1. two ordained persons and two lay persons who are duly authorized representatives of The Episcopal Church in Liberia;

2. members of the Official Youth Presence;

3. other persons authorized by the Joint Rules, the Constitution, or Canons.

Platform.

C. Platform. Only officers of the House of Deputies, designated members of the Committee on Dispatch of Business, and other persons authorized or invited by the President may be on the platform of the House.

Deputation placement.

D. Placement of Deputations and Others. Deputations will be seated together on the floor of the House in random order, except that:

1. Deputations with members serving on the platform may be seated near the platform;

2. Deputations requiring language interpretation or with other needs may be seated in proximity to one another; and

3. the President may seat deputations and others as necessary to assist in the business of the House.

E. Seating Adjacent to the Floor

1. The President and the Secretary will designate a visitor's gallery.   *Visitors.*

2. The President and Secretary may designate areas adjacent to the floor of the House of Deputies as seating for Alternate Deputies, members of Executive Council, and others.

F. Revocation of Floor Privileges   *Revocation of*
                                                          Floor Privileges.
1. Any person, including Deputies and officers, may be excluded for good cause from the floor of the House by a two-thirds vote.

2. Any motion to exclude must specify the length of time, up to the final adjournment, that the person is excluded from the floor.

3. The motion may provide that the person discontinues serving as a member of a committee during the person's exclusion from the floor.

G. Child Care Accommodations. Space will be provided to permit nursing or bottle-feeding while on the floor and access to voting while in the area. A nursing parent will not be asked to wear a cover or move to the designated feeding area.   *Child Care*
                                                          Accomodations.

V: Officers

A. President. The President of the House of Deputies will be elected in accordance with the Canons.

1. The President will preside over all meetings of the House, unless the President relinquishes the Chair for a temporary period.   *Presiding Officer*
                                                          and Chair.

2. If the President relinquishes the Chair:

    i. the Vice-President will preside; or

    ii. if the Vice-President is unable or unwilling to Preside, the President may appoint any Deputy to preside.

3. If the President has relinquished the Chair, the President may resume the Chair at any time.

Other officers.

B. Vice-President. The Vice-President of the House of Deputies will be elected in accordance with the Canons.

1. The Vice-President will preside over all meetings of the House in the absence of the President.

2. If the Vice-President is presiding and wishes to relinquish the Chair, the Vice-President may appoint any Deputy to preside.

3. If the Vice-President has relinquished the chair to a Deputy, the Vice-President may resume the chair at any time.

C. Secretary and Assistant Secretaries

1. The Secretary of the House of Deputies will be elected in accordance with the Canons.

2. The Secretary may appoint Assistant Secretaries with the confirmation of the House.

D. Parliamentarian

1. The President may appoint one or more Parliamentarians and Vice-Parliamentarians to advise the President or presiding officer on parliamentary procedure.

2. A Parliamentarian may be a member of the House or another person at the discretion of the President.

3. The Parliamentarian may address the House or any committee of the House at the direction of the President or presiding officer to facilitate the business of the House.

E. Chaplain

  1. The President may appoint one or more Chaplains to the House, who may, but need not be, members of the House. The President will specify the duties of the Chaplain.

F. Sergeant-at-Arms

  1. The President may appoint a Sergeant-at-Arms and necessary assistants.

  2. The Sergeant-at-Arms and assistants may be members of the House or other persons at the discretion of the President.

  3. The President will specify the duties of the Sergeant-at-Arms. Duties may include:

      i. locating Chairs of legislative committees and escorting them to the platform;

      ii. escorting distinguished visitors and performing ceremonial duties;

      iii. maintaining order and decorum in the House;

      iv. ensuring only authorized persons are seated on the floor during sessions of the House except when there is a Joint Session of both Houses; and

      v. ensuring that only authorized persons are present during Closed Sessions.

VI: Regular Session Schedule

A. Regular Order of Business

  1. The regular Order of Business of each session of the House will be as follows, unless modified by the House in the schedule adopted by the House.

      Regular schedule.

      i. Opening Prayer

      ii. Report of the Certification of the Minutes

      iii. Report from the Committee on Credentials

      iv. Communications from the President

     v. Messages from the House of Bishops

     vi. Report of the Committee on the Dispatch of Business

     vii. Report on Elections

     viii. Committee Reports and Legislation

Daily calendar
of business.

2. Order of Committee Reports. The order of legislation and Committee Reports will be determined as follows:

     i. The Committee on Dispatch will adopt and publish a daily legislative calendar the day before each legislative session.

     ii. During the time allotted for daily Committee Reports and legislation, Resolutions will be considered in the order on the published calendar.

     iii. Following the adjournment for the day, the Committee on Dispatch will update the calendar for the subsequent day and modify the order of Committee Reports and legislation as necessary to consider high priority legislation.

     iv. Once legislation is added to the Calendar, the legislation will remain on the Calendar unless removed or acted upon by the House.

B. Special Order of Business

1. Priority over regular business. If the House adopts a Special Order of Business, it will have priority over any other item of business, including any pending motions, reports, or Resolutions.

2. Vote. A Special Order of Business requires a two-thirds vote to be adopted or amended.

Special business.

3. Special Consideration of Business. The President at any time no other Matter is being considered, may present any Matter to the House for its immediate consideration and action.

C. Consent Calendar

1. Business placed upon the Consent Calendar. A Consent Calendar will be maintained by the Secretary and voted upon once a day as the first legislative order of the day.

2. Publishing the Consent Calendar.

   Publication of Consent Calendar.

   i. The Consent Calendar must be published at least twenty-four hours before the beginning of the session at which the Consent Calendar is to be voted upon.

   ii. The Consent Calendar must be posted by the Secretary either:

      a. online, to the General Convention web site; or

      b. in hard copy, at a preannounced place and distributed to the Deputies.

3. Placing items on the Consent Calendar. Every Committee Reports on Resolutions or other matters will be placed on the Consent Calendar automatically unless:

   All items are on Consent Calendar.

   i. the committee votes to exclude it from the Consent Calendar;

   ii. it is removed in accordance with these Rules;

   Exceptions.

   iii. the Rules of Order, the Joint Rules of Order, the Canons, or the Constitution require a different procedure for considering the item;

   iv. the item has been set by a Special Order of Business; or

   v. the item is one of the following:

      a. an election;

      b. a Resolution of privilege or courtesy;

      c. the confirmation of the election of the Presiding Bishop.

Who may remove.

4. Who may remove items from the Consent Calendar. An item may be removed from the Consent Calendar any time before the final vote on the Calendar by:

   i. the Legislative Committee proposing the action;

   ii. the Chair of the Committee on Dispatch of Business;

   iii. the proposer of the Resolution or Memorial;

   iv. any three Deputies;

   v. the President of the House.

Procedure to remove.

5. Procedure to remove items from the Consent Calendar. An item may be removed by:

   i. providing notice to the Secretary; or

   ii. announcement on the floor of the House.

Voting on Consent Calendar.

6. Voting on the Consent Calendar. When voting on the Consent Calendar, the House will vote on all items at once. A majority vote is required to adopt the calendar.

   i. Affirmative Vote. A vote to adopt the Consent Calendar is a vote to take the action recommended by the respective Legislative Committees for all items on the Consent Calendar.

   ii. A Negative Vote. If the House rejects the Consent Calendar, all items on the Consent Calendar will be placed on the Calendar by the Committee on Dispatch.

VII: Resolutions and Memorials

Legislation.

A. Resolutions. Resolutions are matters by which the House or the General Convention speaks to a particular subject or concern, amends the Constitution or Canons, or expresses the mind of the House.

B. Memorials

   1. Memorials are statements about matters of great importance that urge General Convention to take action on a particular topic.

   2. Memorials are referred to a legislative committee to inform the committee's work and deliberation.

   3. A committee may propose a Resolution in response to a Memorial.   *Response to a Memorial.*

C. Form. A Resolution or Memorial will take the form prescribed by the Secretary.

D. Proposing. A Resolution or Memorial may be proposed by: *Who may propose.*

   1. a Deputy, if:

      i. two other Deputies endorse the Resolution or Memorial; and

      ii. the Deputy proposes no more than a total of three Resolutions and three Memorials.

   2. the President of the House of Deputies;

   3. a House of Deputies Legislative Committee;

   4. a Message from the House of Bishops;

   5. a Diocese;

   6. a Province;

   7. a Standing Commission, Task Force, or body required to report to the General Convention; or

   8. the Executive Council.

E. Submission Deadline. No Resolution or Memorial may be first submitted to the House after the end of the second legislative day, unless it is: *Deadline.*

   1. a Resolution of privilege or courtesy;

   2. proposed by a House of Deputies Legislative Committee;

   3. proposed by the President of the House of Deputies;

   4. a Message from the House of Bishops; or

   5. voted on by the House to consider it.

VIII: Legislative Committees

A. General Rules on Legislative Committees

   1. Appointment and Creation

President may appoint Committees.

     i. No later than 90 days before the first legislative day of General Convention, the President will appoint Legislative Committees for the work of the House of Deputies at General Convention.

     ii. The Legislative Committees may include the following and any others that the President designates:

Rules of Order.

     a. Rules of Order. Reviews and proposes Resolutions to revise the rules that govern the House.

C & C.

     b. Constitution & Canons. Receives and proposes Resolutions that propose amendments to the Constitution or Canons.

Governance & Structure.

     c. Governance & Structure. Receives and proposes Resolutions that address the governance and structure of the Church including General Convention, Executive Council, and the Anglican Communion.

World Mission.

     d. World Mission. Receives and proposes Resolutions on mission personnel, world mission strategy, and covenant relationships with other Anglican Provinces or bodies.

Social Justice & International Policy.

     e. Social Justice & International Policy. Receives and proposes Resolutions on social justice issues in the Church's extra-US dioceses and the international peace and justice work of the Church, including engagement with the Anglican Communion.

Social Justice & U.S. Policy.

     f. Social Justice & United States Policy. Receives and proposes Resolutions on social justice issues facing the United States, including its international engagement.

g. Congregational Vitality. Receives and proposes Resolutions on the health, development, and redevelopment of congregations and faith communities including church planting, college and university communities, and new and non-traditional contexts.

Congregational Vitality.

h. Evangelism & Communications. Receives and proposes Resolutions on evangelism within the Church's jurisdictions; receives and proposes Resolutions on communication strategies and technologies to strengthen the Church's communication of the Gospel and opportunities for information management and exchange within the Church.

Evangelism & Communications.

i. Prayer Book, Liturgy & Music. Receives and proposes Resolutions on the Book of Common Prayer, liturgy, and music of this Church.

BCP, Liturgy & Music.

j. Formation & Education for Ministry. Receives and proposes Resolutions on Christian formation and education for all the baptized, and all matters related to ordained ministry.

Formation & Education.

k. Church Pension Fund. Receives and proposes Resolutions on the purpose, scope, structure, and work of the Church Pension Fund including, but not limited to, pensions, disability, health insurance, other insurance and products for lay and ordained employees of the Church, insurance for Church institutions, and publishing.

Church Pension Fund.

l. Stewardship & Development. Receives and proposes Resolutions on stewardship, stewardship education, development, and planned giving.

Stewardship & Development.

m. Ecumenical & Interreligious Relations. Receives and proposes Resolutions on relations between the Church and other

Ecumenical & Interreligious.

Churches, the Church and other religions, interchurch cooperation and unity, and interreligious dialogue and action.

Environmental Stewardship.

n. Environmental Stewardship & Care of Creation. Receives and proposes Resolutions on environmental stewardship and the care of creation.

Confirmation of Election.

o. Confirmation of the Presiding Bishop. Receives the Report from the House of Bishops regarding the election of a Presiding Bishop, and recommends action regarding confirmation.

Committees requiring appointment.

iii. Special Legislative Committees. The President will appoint the following Special Legislative Committees for the work of the House of Deputies at General Convention no later than 90 days before the first legislative day of General Convention. These committees are not required to hold hearings under these Rules before taking any action.

a. Dispatch of Business. Proposes the agenda for the House, determines the Calendar of the Day, proposes Special Orders of Business, and schedules elections.

b. Certification of Minutes. Reviews the Minutes of the previous legislative day, corrects the Minutes and reports on their completion to the House.

c. Privilege & Courtesy. Receives and proposes Resolutions that commend individuals or organizations and proposes Resolutions that express the House's appreciation for groups or persons.

d. Credentials. Registers Deputies and reports on the number of voting members in the House of Deputies at each session and acts as tellers for elections.

2. Membership and Composition

   i. The President will determine the size of each *Committee size.*
   Legislative Committee and appoint the members.

   ii. All members of Legislative Committees must be
   Deputies.

   iii. The President is a member of all Legislative
   Committees, *ex officio.*

   iv. The President will seek to balance the committee *Balance.*
   members across the provinces of the Church,
   where feasible.

3. Committee Officers and Assistants

   i. The President will appoint the Chair, Vice-Chair,
   Secretary, and any other officers deemed
   necessary, of each Legislative Committee.

   ii. The President must appoint the officers of *Officers*
   Legislative Committees no later than 90 days *appointed 90*
   before the first legislative day of General *days before.*
   Convention.

   iii. The President may appoint Legislative Aides to
   assist Legislative Committees in the conduct of
   business prior to and during General Convention.

4. Publication of Committee Appointments

   i. The Secretary of the House of Deputies will make
   the information about Legislative Committees
   known to the Church.

5. Role and Authority of Legislative Committees. Each *Role and*
   Legislative Committee will have the following roles *authority.*
   and responsibilities:

   i. Consider Resolutions, Memorials, and other
   matters referred to it for action or information.

   ii. Propose Resolutions on subjects that have not
   been referred to it for action but which are
   within the scope of the description of their
   responsibilities in Rule VIII.A.1.ii or as assigned
   by the President.

    iii. Hold hearings.

    iv. Prepare reports and recommend actions on Resolutions, Memorials, and other matters referred to it.

6. Committee Meetings

    i. Meetings may be held in person or electronically in a way that all members can participate with all other members.

        a. All electronic meetings shall be livestreamed and recorded, except for those noted in Rule VIII.A.6.x.

    ii. The Secretary of the House of Deputies will arrange logistics for each Legislative Committee meeting, whether conducted in person or electronically.

Notice of meetings.

    iii. Information about how to attend meetings for each Legislative Committee will be made available to the House and the public by the Secretary of the House.

    iv. Legislative Committees may convene and consider matters referred to them prior to the time set for legislative committee meetings at the General Convention site by the Joint Standing Committee on Planning and Arrangements. Such meetings may be held electronically in a way that all members can participate with all other members.

    v. A meeting may be called by the Chair or by a majority of the members.

Quorum.

    vi. In accordance with Canon V.3.2 a quorum will be a majority of all the members.

Voting in Committee.

    vii. Legislative Committees may, but are not required to, meet with a parallel House of Bishops Legislative Committee assigned to consider the same matter or matters. The House of Deputies Legislative Committee must always vote separately on the final action on any matter referred to it.

viii. Only members of the Legislative Committee may speak during meetings, unless the Chair invites other persons to speak.

ix. All meetings of Legislative Committees will be open to the public unless the Committee votes to hold a closed meeting. *Public meetings.*

x. A Legislative Committee may hold a closed meeting upon a two-thirds vote of the members present. Any motion to enter a closed session must specify the topic to be discussed. No final action on a matter referred to the Committee may be taken during a closed meeting. *Closed meetings.*

xi. Before entering a closed session to discuss a Resolution, the Committee must first hold a public hearing on the Resolution. *Public hearing.*

7. The Secretary of the Legislative Committee will keep (or cause to be kept) a record of: *Minutes to be kept.*

    i. time and place of each meeting;

    ii. attendance of Committee members at each meeting;

    iii. Resolutions and other matters considered at each meeting and all actions taken on them; and

    iv. all other motions and actions of the Committee.

8. The Secretary of the Legislative Committee will file the record of each Legislative Committee meeting with the Secretary of the House. The record will be delivered by the deadline set by the Secretary of the House. *Secretary to file minutes.*

B. Legislative Committee Hearings

   1. Hearings Required

       i. Legislative Committees must hold a hearing on every Resolution, Memorial, and other matter referred to them for action or proposed by them before taking final action. Such hearings may be *Hearings must be held.*

held in person or electronically in a way that enables all participants to participate with all speakers.

ii. Legislative Committees should try to schedule all Resolutions, Memorials, or other matters on the same subject for hearing at the same time.

iii. Hearings may be held by Legislative Committees as early as 90 days before the first legislative day of General Convention.

2. Notice of Hearings

Seven-days notice.

i. For hearings to be held between 90 and 14 days prior to the first legislative day of General Convention, a Legislative Committee will deliver a Notice of Hearing to the Secretary of the House of Deputies at least seven days before the hearing. Upon receipt the Notice of Hearing will be posted by the Secretary on the General Convention website.

Eight-hours notice.

ii. For hearings to be held during or not more than one day before the first legislative day of General Convention, a Legislative Committee will deliver the Notice of Hearing to the Secretary of the House of Deputies so that it can be posted by the Secretary on the General Convention website at least eight hours before the hearing. For hearings scheduled before 10:00 a.m., the Notice of Hearing must be posted by the Secretary by 6:00 p.m. of the day before the hearing.

iii. The Secretary of the House of Deputies will specify the form for the Notice of Hearing.

3. Testimony at Hearings

i. Any person may testify at a hearing before a Legislative Committee.

Witness registration.

ii. All persons who wish to testify at a hearing before a Legislative Committee must register in a manner provided for by the Committee.

iii. At electronic meetings, those wishing to testify must be provided the opportunity to declare their intent to testify up to and including the day of the hearing.

iv. Persons testifying must identify themselves by name, status (Deputy, Bishop, Alternate, or Visitor), Diocese, organization represented, if any, and the Resolution or matter on which they wish to testify.

v. The committee shall provide for means of taking day of testimony, noting restrictions the chair may impose pursuant to Rule VIII.B.3.vi.

vi. The Chair may limit the number of persons who may testify, set time limits, alternate pro and con, give preference to Deputies or other groups of persons and otherwise regulate the hearing.

4. Record of Hearings

    i. The Secretary of the Legislative Committee will keep (or cause to be kept) a record of the:

Record of Hearings.

      a. time and place of each hearing;

      b. attendance of Committee members at each hearing;

      c. resolutions and other matters considered at each hearing;

      d. name and identifying information of each person testifying before the Legislative Committee and the Resolution or matter upon which each spoke; and

      e. digital recording of public portions of each electronic hearing.

Secretary to file hearing records.

    ii. The Secretary of the Legislative Committee will file the record of each Legislative Committee hearing with the Secretary of the House at the conclusion of each hearing.

C.   Legislative Committee Reports

Committee reports.

1.   Each Legislative Committee must take final action on every Resolution and other matter referred to it for action to recommend that the House takes one of the following actions:

Adopt.

i.   adopt as proposed;

Adopt as amended.

ii.   adopt as amended by the Committee; all amendments made by a Committee will apply automatically to the Resolution and the matter before the House when the Resolution is considered will be the Resolution as amended by the Committee;

Substitute.

iii.   adopt a substitute Resolution:

    a.   A substitute Resolution must be on the same subject as the Resolution referred to the Legislative Committee for action.

    b.   A substitute Resolution may only cover one Resolution referred to the Legislative Committee for action.

    c.   If the House declines to adopt a substitute, the original Resolution will be automatically referred back to the Committee for additional consideration.

Consolidated substitute.

iv.   adopt a consolidated substitute Resolution:

    a.   A consolidated substitute Resolution must be on the same subject as the Resolutions referred to the Legislative Committee for action.

    b.   Its report on the final action on that Resolution must identify all the other Resolutions the substitute is intended to cover.

    c.   A vote by the Legislative Committee to recommend adoption of a consolidated substitute Resolution will be an automatic recommendation to take no further action on all other Resolutions the consolidated substitute Resolution is intended to cover.

  d. If the House declines to adopt a consolidated substitute Resolution, the original Resolutions will be automatically referred back to the Committee for additional consideration.

v. reject;   *Reject.*

vi. refer to a specified Standing Commission, General Convention Task Force, Executive Council or other body of the Church for study, action, or to make recommendations on the subject to the next General Convention;   *Refer.*

vii. take no further action because: *No action.*

  a. the matter has already been dealt with by action of the House of Deputies at this meeting of General Convention;

  b. the matter is covered by a Resolution of a prior General Convention;

  c. for other reasons.

viii. If the Resolution or matter has been acted on by the House of Bishops: *Concur.*

  a. concur with the action of the House of Bishops;

  b. concur as proposed to be amended by the House of Deputies Legislative Committee;

  c. concur with substitute as proposed by the House of Deputies Legislative Committee;

  d. not concur and take a different action;

  e. not concur.   *Committee*

ix. A House of Bishops Message to discharge will be treated as take no further action.   *discharge.*

2. Minority Report

Minority position.

    i. If there is a minority position on a final action on a Resolution or other matter and the minority requests to make a minority report to the House, the Chair will include the minority report in the Legislative Committee's report on the final action on the Resolution or other matter.

    ii. A minority position consists of at least one-quarter (1/4) of the members of the Legislative Committee present and voting on the Resolution, Memorial, or other matter.

IX: Other Committees

A. General Rules on Other Committees

  1. Appointment and Creation

    i. The President may designate other Committees for the work of the House of Deputies at General Convention no later than 90 days before the first legislative day of General Convention except that Conference Committees will be appointed during General Convention as needed.

    ii. The Committees may include the following and any others that the President designates:

      a. Resolution Review

Polity, form, and funding review.

        1. The Resolution Review Committee will review all Resolutions submitted prior to General Convention to review that they are consistent with the polity of this Church, that they are in the form required by the Canons.

        2. The Committee will prepare an advisory report on each Resolution and provide it to the chair of the Legislative Committee to which the Resolution is referred for action. The Committee will continue the review process while General Convention is in session.

3. The Committee may draft or redraft any matter in the proper language upon request by the President, a Legislative Committee, a Deputy, or the House.

Power to redraft.

2. Membership and Composition

i. The President will determine the size of each other Committee and appoint the members.

ii. Members of other Committees need not be Deputies.

iii. The President is a member of all other Committees, *ex officio.*

3. Committee Officers

i. The President will appoint the Chair, Vice-Chair, Secretary, and any other officers deemed necessary, of each other Committee.

ii. The Secretary of the House of Deputies will make the information about other Committees known to the Church.

B. Committee Meetings

1. The Secretary of the House of Deputies will arrange a meeting space for each Committee.

C. Conference Committees

1. Creation. A Conference Committee will be created:

a. by a vote by the House to refer legislation passed by the House of Bishops to a Conference Committee; or

Legislative Conference.

b. when the House of Bishops has concurred, with amendment, on the legislation already acted on by the House, and the House does not concur with the House of Bishops' amendment.

2. Appointment. The President will appoint a Chair and all members of a Conference Committee from the House of Deputies.

3. Final Action. When a Committee of Conference has been formed, the final action upon the matter under

consideration will be deferred until the Conference Committee has reported to this House.

X: Special Committees

A. The President may designate Special Committees for the work of the House of Deputies at or between sessions of the General Convention.

B. Membership and Composition

1. The President will determine the size of each Special Committee and appoint the members.

2. Members of Special Committees need not be Deputies.

3. The President will be a member of all Special Committees, *ex officio*.

C. Committee Officers

1. The President will appoint the Chair, Vice-Chair, Secretary, and any other officers deemed necessary, of each Special Committee.

2. The Secretary of the House of Deputies will make the information about Special Committees known to the Church.

XI: Sessions of the House

A. Legislative Sessions

1. Purpose. A Legislative Session is a regular session of the House of Deputies where the House considers Resolutions, hears reports from committees, and provides Deputies an opportunity to debate.

B. Special Order Sessions

1. Purpose. A Special Order Session is a session set by the House to consider a particular Resolution or other matter under special rules for deliberation and debate. Sessions can be used to consider important or strategic matters in an informal manner for conversation and connection.

2. How brought. A Special Order Session may be scheduled by a two-thirds vote of the House.

C. Closed Sessions

1. Purpose. A closed session of the House has limited attendance and is used to discuss sensitive or pastoral matters. No action may be taken by the House in a closed session.

Closed Sessions.

2. How brought. The Deputies may vote to enter a closed session by a majority vote.

3. Who may attend. Only the following may attend a closed session:

   i. Deputies;

   ii. Officers of the House of Deputies;

   iii. persons given seat on the floor of the House;

   iv. other persons authorized by the House;

   v. other persons authorized by the President.

4. Special Rules regarding Closed Sessions

   i. Minutes will be kept by the Secretary for all Closed Sessions. Minutes taken during an closed session may only be reviewed and revealed in a closed session.

   ii. Personal electronic devices may not be used to communicate or record during a closed session.

   iii. Members are honor bound to keep the proceedings of a closed session confidential.

XII: Debate

A. Deputies may debate.

1. Any Deputy or person given seat and voice on the floor of the House may participate in debate, unless a Rule of the House specifies otherwise.

Eligibility for debate.

2. Any Deputy or person participating in debate will provide their name and the Diocese they represent.

3. Any Deputy may speak only after being recognized by the Presiding Officer.

B. Definitions

1. Debate. Debates are an opportunity for Deputies to engage in discussion on any matter.

Matters before the House.

2. Matter. A matter includes any Resolution, Memorial, motion, message from the House of Bishops, or Committee report, that is presented to the House to consider and act upon.

C. Deputies may engage in debate on any matter except when:

1. debate has been ended by a vote of the House;

2. debate is not allowed due to a Rule of the House, a Joint Rule, a Canon, or the Constitution.

D. Time Limits

1. A total of 30 minutes is the maximum time allowed to debate on:

    i.   any matter; and

    ii. all motions related to that matter.

2. If a person rises to speak during the first six minutes of debate on a matter, no member may move the following unless no person seeks to debate on the matter:

    i.   amend the motion or Resolution;

    ii. move a substitute;

    iii. end debate.

3. During a debate on any motion or other matter, a member may:

Time limit on speaking.

    i.   speak up to two minutes; and

    ii. speak twice.

Translation.

4. For each speech that requires translation or interpretation, all time limits on debate in these rules, or adopted by a special rule of order, will be extended by two minutes.

5. Debate will end following: *End of debate.*

    i.   a successful vote to end debate;

    ii. the end of the time allowed for debate by a Rule or Special Order; or

    iii. by ruling of the Presiding Officer if:

        a. at least three Deputies have spoken in favor of the matter and no one rises to speak against it; or

        b. at least three Deputies have spoken against the matter and no one rises to speak in favor of it; or

        c. no one rises to speak on the matter.

XIII: Motions

A. How Made

1. Motions may be made by any Deputy or other person authorized to make a motion by the Rules of the House.

2. A Deputy wishing to make a motion must:

    i.   provide their name and the Diocese they represent;

    ii. acknowledge his or her intent to make a motion in any queuing system; and

    iii. be recognized by the President or presiding officer.

B. Types of Motion. Any Deputy may make one of the following motions and no other motions may be made on the floor of the House, except as otherwise provided by these Rules.   *Motions allowed on House floor.*

1. Motions that affect the general business of the House.

    i.   Adjourn or Recess: *Adjourn.*

        a. is used to end (adjourn) a session or take a short recess;

b. has the following characteristics:

1. no debate is allowed;

2. no amendments may be made;

3. a majority vote is required.

ii. Adjourn and reconvene at a specific time:

a. is used to end a session and set a time to reconvene;

b. has the following characteristics:

1. debate is only allowed on the time;

2. amendments are only allowed on the time.

Appeal ruling.

iii. Appeal the ruling of the President or presiding officer:

a. is used to appeal any decision of the President or presiding officer on any question of procedure;

b. has the following characteristics:

1. debate is allowed;

2. amendments are not allowed;

3. a majority vote is required;

4. must be made immediately after the Presiding Officer's ruling.

Special Orders.

iv. To Create a Special Order of Business or Change the Order of Business:

a. is used to create a Special Order of Business that is not included in the Convention schedule or change an existing Order of Business. It may also include special rules to govern how the order is to be carried out.

b. Has the following characteristics:

1. amendments are allowed;

2. debate is allowed;

3. a two-thirds vote is required.

v. To Suspend the Rules: *Suspend Rules.*

   a. is used to suspend or modify the Rules of the House that interfere with a particular goal of the House;

   b. has the following characteristics:

     1. amendments are allowed;

     2. debate is allowed;

     3. a two-thirds vote is required.

2. Motions that affect debate on a Resolution or other matter.

  i. End Debate and Vote Immediately: *End debate.*

   a. is used to end the debate on a motion, Resolution, report, or other action item and force a vote. It is also sometimes known as "moving the previous question."

   b. has the following characteristics:

     1. affects only the matter being debated;

     2. no debate is allowed;

     3. a two-thirds majority vote is required.

  ii. Postpone Debating a Motion or Resolution until a Specific Time: *Postpone.*

   a. is used to postpone debating and considering a motion or Resolution until a certain time, after a certain time has elapsed, or after an event has occurred. It cannot be used to postpone action until after General Convention has adjourned.

   b. has the following characteristics:

     1. debate is allowed;

     2. amendments are allowed;

     3. a majority vote is required.

Recall.   iii. To Recall from a Committee:

      a. is used to bring something out of a legislative committee and immediately to the floor of the House;

      b. has the following characteristics:

         1. may not be brought until the fourth legislative day;

         2. debate is allowed;

         3. no amendments are allowed;

         4. a two-thirds vote is required.

Refer back.   3. Motions that affect what is done with a matter.

    i. To Refer Back to the Originating Committee, a Different Committee, a Standing Commission, or Other Body:

      a. is used to refer a matter to a legislative committee or group to study the matter and report back suggested amendments or actions;

      b. has the following characteristics:

         1. may be debated;

         2. may be amended as to the body referred;

         3. a majority vote is required.

No action.   ii. Take No Further Action:

      a. is used to stop considering a particular Resolution or Memorial and remove it from further consideration at the current meeting of the House;

      b. has the following characteristics:

         1. debate is allowed;

         2. no amendments are allowed;

         3. a majority vote is required.

iii. To Amend or Substitute:

Amend or
substitute.

   a. is used to modify or change a Resolution or motion. This would include a technical change or a substantive change that would alter the meaning or the intent of a Resolution or motion. Amendments must be related to the item in the Resolution or motion that they are trying to change.

   b. Secondary Amendments are:

      1. proposed changes to an amendment. Secondary Amendments must relate to the specific subject of an amendment and may not be used to alter other parts of a Resolution or parts not affected by an amendment.

   c. has the following characteristics:

      1. debate is allowed;

      2. only Secondary Amendments are allowed;

      3. a majority vote is required.

iv. To Divide the Matter:

Division.

   a. is used to divide a Matter or Resolution into separate parts and vote separately. If the Matter is easily divisible into separate subjects, it may be divided by the Chair at a request of a member.

   b. process to use this matter:

      1. first make the request to divide the question and explain where the question should be divided;

      2. the President then rules on whether the question is divisible or not;

      3. if the question is divisible, the House proceeds to debate and act on the divided parts of the question;

4. If the President rules the question is not divisible, any Deputy may appeal the ruling.

Reconsideration.

v. To Reconsider Something Previously Acted Upon:

a. is used to reconsider a Matter which was previously voted upon by the House at the current meeting of the General Convention;

b. has the following characteristics:

1. any Deputy may move to reconsider a Matter;

2. no amendments are allowed;

3. debate is allowed if the Matter being reconsidered is debatable;

4. a majority vote is required;

5. a Matter may only be reconsidered once;

6. if the motion for reconsideration is adopted, the Resolution is restored to where it was immediately before the previous action being reconsidered was taken by the House.

XIV: Voting

Voting required.

A. Every Deputy must vote when a matter is put to a vote, except the Presiding Officer. If the Presiding Officer is a Deputy, the Presiding Officer should not ordinarily vote on any matter unless the Presiding Officer's vote will affect the outcome of the matter, the vote is a vote by orders, or the vote is being conducted by a secret ballot.

B. The President may excuse a Deputy from voting on a matter, if:

1. the Deputy has a conflict of interest; or

2. for other good cause.

Votes to pass a Resolution.

C. Vote necessary to adopt a matter. The amount of votes necessary to pass a Resolution or other matter is:

1. a majority vote consists of more than half of the votes;

2. a two-thirds vote consists of at least two-thirds of the votes;

3. a majority Vote by Orders consists of a more than half of the lay deputations and more than half of the clergy deputations.

D. Counting the votes. The amount necessary to pass a matter will be determined by those present and voting.

E. Vote by Orders under Art. 1 Sec. 5 of the Constitution. *Vote by Orders.*

1. Procedure:

   i. Vote by Orders will be taken on any matter at the request of the clerical or lay deputations of at least three separate dioceses or as required by the Constitution or Canons;

   ii. the vote of each order, Clerical and Lay, will be counted separately and each order in each Diocese will have one vote;

   iii. to carry in the affirmative any question being voted on by orders requires concurrence in the affirmative by both orders;

   iv. concurrence in the affirmative by an order requires the affirmative vote in that order by a majority of the Dioceses present in that order unless a greater vote is required by the Constitution or by the Canons;

   v. an affirmative vote of a Clerical or Lay order requires a majority of the Deputies present in that order in that Diocese.

2. No vote. A no vote (i.e., not in the affirmative) occurs when the majority of a Clerical or a Lay deputation's vote is against a matter or is tied.

3. Two-thirds vote. If a motion under the Rules requires a two-thirds vote, and a Vote by Orders is duly called, the motion will pass if there is an affirmative vote in each order of two-thirds of the Dioceses.

4. Counting. The count on a Vote by Orders will be by either electronic and/or written means as required by the President or presiding officer.

5. Publishing the results. The results of all Votes by Orders will be posted promptly in a manner that is readily accessible to the House and the public and includes how each order in each diocese voted.

6. Polling. The vote of the individual Deputies of a Diocese must be stated and recorded when requested by a member of the Deputation.

XV: Elections

Nominations.   A. Nominations

1. The submission of the Report of the Joint Standing Committee on Nominations to the General Convention of its nominees will automatically nominate those persons for any election to be conducted by the House.

2. Any two Deputies may nominate additional eligible persons to be conducted by the House.

3. Each nomination must be submitted to the Secretary, in a form adopted by the Joint Standing Committee on Nominations. The Secretary will publish all nominations by the end of the third legislative day.

4. All Nominations must be submitted by the adjournment of the third legislative day, except that:

    i. Nominations for the office of Vice President of the House must be submitted by the adjournment of the next legislative day after the election of the President of the House of Deputies has been completed.

5. No nominating speeches will be held for any office or position. In a contested election for President or Vice President of the House, a candidate forum may be organized by the Secretary to allow the nominees to give a brief speech and Deputies the opportunity to ask questions of the nominees.

B. Voting Requirements

1. All elections will be by individual secret ballot, paper   *Secret ballot for*
    or electronic, except where there are no more   *elections.*
    nominees than open seats, in which case a voice vote
    may be held at the discretion of the President.

2. A majority vote is required to elect unless the
    Constitution, Canons, or Rules of Order requires a
    different vote. In any election in which more than
    one position will be filled from the same pool of
    nominees, a majority is calculated based upon the
    number of voters who cast a ballot in that election.

3. On any ballot prepared by the Secretary, the
    candidates will be listed in alphabetical order by last
    name.

C. Balloting Procedures

1. In all elections in which there are eight or fewer   *Balloting.*
    nominees, the following voting procedure will be
    used if the election has not been completed:

    i.   After the third ballot, the nominees will be
         reduced to two more than the number of
         vacancies to be filled in the election; and

    ii. After the fifth ballot, the nominees will be
         reduced to one more than the number of
         vacancies to be filled in the election.

2. In all elections in which there are more than eight
    nominees, the following procedure will be used if the
    election has not been completed:

    i.   After the third ballot, the nominees will be
         reduced to four more nominees than the number
         of vacancies to be filled in the election; and

    ii. After the fifth ballot, the nominees will be
         reduced to one more nominee than the number
         of vacancies to be filled in the election.

3. In all cases where nominees are to be reduced under
    these rules, the nominees with the lowest number of
    votes will be eliminated.

4. If more nominees receive a majority vote than the number of positions to be elected, those nominees receiving the highest number of votes will be elected.

5. If there is a tie to either eliminate or elect a nominee, a runoff ballot will be held between the nominees tied.

Election of a Deacon for Joint Nominating Committee for the Election of the Presiding Bishop.

D. Special Rule for the Election of the Required Deacon to the Joint Nominating Committee for the Election of the Presiding Bishop

1. In the selection of the Clergy and Lay members of the Joint Nominating Committee for the Election of the Presiding Bishop under Canon I.2.1.a, the House shall first elect a Deacon to the Committee. The nominees for this election shall include all the Deacons nominated.

2. After a Deacon has been elected under subsection 1, the House shall proceed to elect the remaining Clergy and Lay members of the Committee. The first ballot of the election for the remaining Clergy members shall include all Priest and Deacon nominees other than the Deacon elected under subsection 1 above.

XVI: Confirmation of the Election of a Presiding Bishop

A. When the President receives the name of the bishop elected by the House of Bishops to serve as Presiding Bishop, the President will refer the name to the Legislative Committee on the Confirmation of the Presiding Bishop.

Committee recommends.

B. The Legislative Committee on the Confirmation of the Presiding Bishop will make a recommendation to the House on whether to confirm or not to confirm the choice of the House of Bishops.

C. The House may choose to receive the Committee's report to the House in a closed session.

D. If the House chooses to receive the report in a closed session, the House may continue in a closed session for the purpose of debate.

E. Following the end of debate, the House will move out of a closed session. The Committee will repeat its recommendation and the House will immediately vote on the recommendation.

F. The House will vote by individual secret ballot, paper or electronic, unless a Vote by Orders is requested.

G. A majority vote is required to confirm.

XVII: Parliamentary Authority

A. The latest edition of Robert's Rules of Order, Newly Revised will govern the interpretation of these Rules and Procedures to the extent that Roberts is not inconsistent with these Rules.

Robert's Rules of Order.

B. The Constitution, Canons, Joint Rules, and Rules of this House take precedence when there is a conflict with Robert's Rules of Order.

XVIII: Supremacy and In Force Clause

A. These Rules are subordinate to the Constitution, Canons, and Joint Rules of Order of the General Convention.

Subordination.

B. These Rules remain in force at each meeting until amended, revoked, or replaced by the House.

XIX: Amendments to the Rules of Order

A. The House may amend these Rules at any time by a two-thirds vote of the members present.

Two-thirds vote to amend.

B. The Legislative Committee on Rules of Order will consider all proposed amendments to the Rules and make recommendations to the House.

C. All amendments to these Rules take effect immediately unless expressly provided otherwise.

Immediate effect.

Joint Rules – House of Bishops and House of Deputies

I: Composition of Joint Standing Committees and Joint Legislative Committees

May authorize by Joint Rule.

1. By Joint Rule or Joint Resolution the House of Bishops and the House of Deputies may authorize or direct the appointment of Joint Legislative Committees and Joint Committees.

Membership.

2. a. The Joint Rule may specify the size and composition and shall specify the duties of each Committee. The membership of such Committees shall be limited to Bishops having vote in the House of Bishops, members of the House of Deputies, and such *ex officiis* members as may be provided in the Joint Rule creating such a Committee.

Terms.

b. The terms of all members of Joint Standing Committees shall be equal to the interval between the regular meeting of the General Convention preceding their appointment and the adjournment of the succeeding regular meeting of the General Convention and until their successors are appointed;

Replacing any member not re-elected a Deputy.

except, that unless otherwise specified in these Joint Rules, if any Clerical or Lay member has not been elected as a Deputy to the succeeding General Convention by the 31st day of January in the year of the said Convention, then the President of the House of Deputies will appoint a replacement for the unexpired term of such member. Any other vacancy, by death, change of status, resignation, or any other cause, shall be filled by appointment by the Presiding Officer of the appropriate House, and such appointments, likewise, shall be for the unexpired terms. The terms of all members of Joint Legislative Committees shall be only from the time of appointment until the adjournment of the first regular meeting of the General Convention following their appointment.

c. The Presiding Bishop shall appoint the Episcopal members and the President of the House of Deputies the Lay and Clerical members of Joint Standing Committees as soon as practicable after the adjournment of the General Convention, and of Joint Legislative Committees not later than sixty days in advance of each General Convention. Vacancies shall be filled in similar manner.

Appointments.

d. The Presiding Bishop, in respect of Bishops, and the President of the House of Deputies, in respect of Clergy and Lay Persons, may appoint members and staff of the Executive Council, or other experts, as consultants to any such Committee, to assist in the performance of its function. Notice of such appointment shall be given to the Secretaries of both Houses. Each such Committee shall have power to constitute subcommittees and engage the services of consultants and coordinators necessary to the carrying on of its work.

Consultants and subcommittees.

e. The Presiding Bishop and the President of the House of Deputies shall be members *ex officiis* of every such Committee, with the right, but no obligation, to attend meetings, and with seat and vote in the deliberations thereof, and shall receive their minutes and an annual report of their activities; *provided* that the said presiding officers may appoint personal representatives to attend meetings in their stead, but without vote.

Ex officiis members.

f. The Executive Officer of the General Convention, shall, not later than the month of January following the meeting of the General Convention, notify the members of the respective Houses of their appointments upon Joint Committees and their duty to present Reports to the next Convention. One year prior to opening day of the Convention, the Executive Officer of the General Convention shall remind the Chairs and the Secretaries of all Joint Committees of this duty.

Notification of appointments.

Officers appointed.

g. Except as otherwise provided, the Presiding Bishop and the President of the House of Deputies shall designate a Chair and Vice-Chair, or Co-Chairs, of such Committees. Each such Committee shall elect its own Secretary.

Referrals.

h. It shall be the privilege of either House to refer to such a Committee any matter relating to the subject for which it was appointed; but neither House shall have the power, without the consent of the other, to instruct such Committees as to any particular line of action.

Duties.

i. All such Committees shall perform all of the duties with respect to their work that are imposed on Standing Commissions by Canon I.1.2.i through m.

Electronic meetings.

j. Any Joint Standing Committee and any of its committees, sections and subcommittees may meet in person or by electronic means whereby all participants can hear each other.

II: Proposals for Legislative Consideration

Resolutions to be referred.

1. Each proposal for legislative consideration, however addressed to the General Convention or to either House thereof, received prior to a date in advance of the Convention agreed upon by the Presiding Bishop and the President of the House of Deputies, shall be referred to the proper Standing Committee or Special Committee of the appropriate House by its presiding officer.

Resolutions to be in proper form.

2. Each proposal for legislative consideration which includes the language of a proposed addition to or amendment of an existing Constitutional, Canonical, or Rule of Order provision shall be shown as follows:

Text as it will appear if approved.

a. Begin the text of the resolution with the following text in bold, with an extra return before and after this text:
<Amended text as it would appear if adopted and concurred. Scroll below the line of asterisks (******) to see the version showing all deleted and added text:>

b. Place the text of the final resolution, inclusive of all proposed changes, as it would appear if adopted and concurred. This means that there should be no strikethrough text or italics text in this version of the text.

c. Then add the following text in bold, with an extra return before and after this text:
   ******

   <Proposed amended resolution text showing exact changes being made:>

d. Insert the text of the resolution showing the exact changes being made by marking any text being removed using a ~~strikethrough~~ and any new text being added using *italics*. Where practicable, proposers should strikethrough entire words and phrases, while still showing exactly what is being modified. Do not strikethrough a portion of a word. Bold text may not be used in the text of the legislative proposal.

   Text showing all changes with markup.

e. Each such proposal calling for action shall designate the individual or body for communication and implementation, but if no such designation is included in the resolution as adopted, it shall be referred to the Office of the Secretary of General Convention for communication and implementation.

   Implementation of actions.

f. No proposal for legislative consideration which approves, endorses, adopts, or rejects a report, study, or other document that is not generally known by the members of the House or readily available may be considered by the General Convention unless such material is first distributed to both Houses. It is the responsibility of the proposer to provide the necessary copies to the Secretary of each House.

   Reports or studies must be readily available.

3. a. By joint action, the Presiding Bishop and the President of the House of Deputies may determine that one House shall be assigned responsibility for initiating legislation in respect of any such proposals

   House of initial action.

(and any other proposals germane thereto introduced in either House prior to the close of the third legislative day), in which event, reference in that House shall be *for action* and reference in the other House shall be *for information.* No legislative action with regard to any proposal referred for information shall be initiated on the floor of the House to which it has been so referred until the close of the third legislative day.

Exception.

All restrictions hereby imposed with regard to any proposal referred for information shall expire at the close of the third legislative day.

Nothing herein shall affect the right of any Committee of either House to deliberate with regard to any proposal referred for information.

b. Resolutions not reported by a legislative committee or not acted upon by both Houses shall have no further force or effect following the adjournment of the General Convention at which they are introduced.

III: Summary of General Convention Action

Secretary to prepare a summary within 30 days of Convention.

The Secretary of the House of Deputies shall, with the cooperation of the Secretary of the House of Bishops, and of such Bishops as may be appointed by the Presiding Officer of the House of Bishops, prepare a summary of the actions of the General Convention of particular interest to the Congregations of the Church, and make the same available to the Congregations, through the Ministers-in-charge thereof, and to the Lay Deputies; such summary to be sent to the Clergy along with the Pastoral Letter put forth by the House of Bishops, and to be made available to all Deputies on the last day of the Convention, along with such Pastoral Letter, if

Pastoral Letter.

feasible to do so, or within thirty days thereafter.

IV: Joint Standing Committee on Planning and Arrangements

1. a. There shall be a Joint Standing Committee on
        Planning and Arrangements for the General
        Convention, which shall have responsibility between
        Conventions for the matters indicated by its title.
        The Committee shall be composed, *ex officio*, of the
        Executive Officer of the General Convention, the
        Vice-Presidents, Secretaries, and Chairs of the
        Committee on the Dispatch of Business of the two
        Houses, the Treasurer of the General Convention, the
        President and First Vice-President of the Episcopal
        Church Women, the General Convention Manager
        and one Presbyter or Deacon and one Lay Person
        appointed by the President of the House of Deputies.
        In the case of a General Convention for which a
        meeting site has been selected, the Committee shall
        also include the Bishop and the General Chairman of
        Arrangements of the local Committee of the Dioceses
        in which that General Convention shall be held.

    Membership.

    b. It shall be the duty of the Committee to consult with
        the Presidents of the two Houses, the Chairs of the
        Joint and Standing Committees and Commissions,
        Boards and Agencies of the General Convention, the
        Executive Council, and such other representative
        bodies as it may deem necessary, in the study and
        determination, prior to any meeting of the General
        Convention, of the arrangements for, and the nature
        of, the Agenda thereof, to be recommended by it to
        the General Convention for such meeting.

    Prepare agenda for Convention.

    c. It shall be the further duty of the Committee to take
        such action as may be provided by Canon for the
        selection of sites for meetings of the General
        Convention.

    Select sites.

    d. The Committee shall have an Executive Committee
        composed of the Presidents of the two Houses, the

    Executive Committee.

Chair of the Committee, the Executive Officer of the General Convention, the Treasurer of the General Convention, and the General Convention Manager.

V: Joint Standing Committee on Nominations

Charge.

1. There shall be a Joint Standing Committee on Nominations, which shall submit nominations for the election of:

   a. Trustees of The Church Pension Fund, serving as the Joint Committee referred to in Canon I.8.2.

   b. Members of the Executive Council under Canon I.4.1.d.

   c. The Secretary of the House of Deputies and the Treasurer of the General Convention under Canons I.1.1.j and I.1.7.a.

   d. Trustees of the General Theological Seminary.

   e. General Board of Examining Chaplains.

   f. Disciplinary Board for Bishops.

   g. Court of Review.

   h. The Joint Nominating Committee for the election of the Presiding Bishop.

Membership.

2. The Joint Standing Committee on Nominations is composed of three Bishops, two Priests, one Deacon, and six Lay Persons. Members who are Priests, Deacons or Lay Persons must have served as Deputies to the most recent General Convention; once appointed, they will continue to serve as members of the Joint Standing Committee on Nominations through the next succeeding General Convention, regardless of whether they are elected as a Deputy to such General Convention, and until their successors are appointed.

Solicit recommendations.

3. The said Committee is instructed to solicit recommendations from interested organizations and individuals, to be considered by them for inclusion among their nominees.

4. a. For the elections of the Secretary of the General
        Convention, the Treasurer of the General
        Convention, and the members of the Court of
        Review, the Joint Standing Committee on
        Nominations will nominate a minimum of one
        nominee for each vacancy.

    b. For the election of the members of Executive Council
        and the Trustees of The Church Pension Fund, the
        Joint Standing Committee on Nominations will
        nominate a minimum of two persons for each
        vacancy.

    c. For all other elections other than those described in
        parts a. and b. of this Joint Rule, for which the Joint
        Standing Committee on Nominations will present
        nominees, it will nominate a minimum number of
        nominees equal to one and one-half times the
        number of vacancies.

    d. In all elections for which it will present nominees,
        the Joint Standing Committee on Nominations is
        charged with: (i) ensuring that the nominees for
        each position, and as a group, as nearly as possible,
        represent the diverse constituencies of The Episcopal
        Church; (ii) obtaining biographical sketches with a
        facial image of all nominees, and (iii) reporting such
        nominations and sketches in the Reports to the next
        General Convention, otherwise known as the Blue
        Book.

    e. This Joint Rule does not preclude further
        nominations from the floor made pursuant to
        separate rules adopted by either House of the
        General Convention.

Nomination procedures.

5. a. The Joint Standing Committee on Nominations,
        through the Office of the Secretary of General
        Convention, will secure background checks on its
        and any other nominees for Secretary of the General
        Convention, Treasurer of the General Convention,
        President of the House of Deputies, Vice President of
        the House of Deputies, Executive Council, and

Background checks.

Trustee of The Church Pension Fund. These background checks will cover criminal records checks and sexual offender registry checks in any state where a proposed nominee has resided during the prior seven years, any appropriate professional licensing bodies with jurisdiction over a nominee's professional status and any violations of state or federal securities or banking laws. The records checks of proposed nominees from outside the United States will cover the same information from comparable authorities in the place of principal residence of the proposed nominee.

b. The required background check will be done prior to accepting a proposed nomination.

c. Background check results will be reviewed by the Office of the Secretary of General Convention. If that Office, after consultation with the Chief Legal Officer, determines that the results should preclude a person from holding the office sought, the Office shall share the determination with the proposed nominee and remit that determination, but not the background check results, to the nominating authority. Background check information shall not be shared beyond the Office of the Secretary of General Convention, the Chief Legal Officer, and proposed nominees who request their own information. The cost of background checks under this rule shall be covered by The Episcopal Church budget.

Floor Nominees **6.** Any person desiring to be nominated from the floor of
background   either House for any of the offices listed in Joint Rule
checks.   V.5.a shall, at a time determined by the Office of the
Secretary of General Convention, but no later than sixty days prior to the first legislative day of General Convention, submit the person's name and other necessary information to the Office of the Secretary of General Convention for the purpose of submitting to a background check in accordance with Joint Rule V.5.

VI Joint Legislative Committee on Committees and Commissions

There shall be a Legislative Committee to be designated the Joint Committee on Committees and Commissions to which shall be referred all Resolutions relating to the creation, continuation, merger or other changes in Standing Committees and Commissions, Boards and other Agencies of the Church.

VII: Task Forces of the General Convention

By concurrent action, the General Convention may from time to time establish Task Forces of the General Convention to consider and make recommendations to the General Convention on specific subjects of major importance to the Church and its ministry and mission requiring special attention and competence not otherwise provided for in the Canons and/or Joint Rules, or as shall be otherwise determined by the General Convention to require the appointment of such a Task Force. The Resolution shall specify the size and composition, the clear and express duties assigned, the time for completion of the work assigned and the amount and source of the funding of each such Task Force. No Task Force shall be continued beyond the time for completion of the work assigned except by a concurrent vote of two-thirds of the members present and voting in each of the Houses. Unless otherwise specifically provided in the establishing Resolution, the Presiding Bishop shall appoint the Episcopal members and the President of the House of Deputies shall appoint the Priests and Deacons and the Lay Persons. Such Resolution may, but need not, provide for the service of Executive Council staff and other experts as consultants and coordinators for the Task Force.

May be established by Convention.

Membership, duties, and funding.

Appointments.

Consultants.

VIII: Rules in Force

At the meetings of the House of Bishops and the House of Deputies, the Joint Rules of the previous Convention shall be in force, until they be amended or repealed by concurrent action of the two Houses and after their reports thereon.

Resolutions Amending the Constitution, Canons, and Rules of Order

The General Convention, Baltimore, Maryland, July 8–11, 2022

Number	Title	Article/Canon/Rule
A032	Amend Canon III.11.9.b to Correct an Oversight in a 2018 Canonical Amendment	Canon III.11.9.b
A033	Amend Canon I.1.2.n.1.iii to Revise the Title of Executive Council's By-laws	Canon I.1.2.n.1.iii
A037	Establish a New Standing Commission on Formation and Ministry Development	Canon I.1.2.n.4
A040	Specify Electronic Transmission of Certain Documents and Records	Canons I.1.1.e; I.6.5.a
A041	Amend Certain Joint Rules of Order to Permit Meeting by Electronic Means	JR I.2.j; JR II.10; JR III.11
A042	Permitting Sending Required Notices and Other Papers by Electronic Means	Canon IV.19.20
A044	Amend Canon IV.14.4 Provisions for Notices of Accords	Canon IV.14.4
A045	Amend Canon I.19.2.b to Update a Word	Canon I.19.2.b
A048	Amend Canons and Rules of Order to Implement the Recommendations of the Task Force on the Budget Process	Canons I.1.2.m; I.1.2.o; I.1.8; I.1.9; I.1.11; I.1.13; I.2.6; I.2.8; I.4.3; I.4.4; I.4.6; I.5.5; I.9.10; RHB V.D.d; RHB VIII.I.3; RHD VI.C.3.v.a; RHD IX.A.1.ii.a.1; JR II.10; JR IV.14; JR VII.21
A058	Resolution on Official Liturgical Website for The Episcopal Church	Canon I.1.2.n.2
A075	Resolution Amending Canon IV.5.4 Provision for the Court of Review	Canon IV.5.4.j

C021	Amend Canon I.9.1 to change the Diocese of Puerto Rico to Province II	Canon I.9.1
C070	Amend Canon III.9.5.d	Canon III.9.5.d
D052	Amending Canon III.11.8 regarding Objections to Episcopal Elections	Canon III.11.8
D055	Amend Canon I.9.1 to add the Diocese of Cuba	Canon I.9.1
D056	Amend Canon III.11.9.a to correct cross-reference	Canon III.11.9.a.4

Joint Rules renumbering

Due to two full section deletions the Joint Rules were renumbered in 2022. Reference the below table to find the corresponding new Joint Rule section number.

2018 subsection number	2022 subsection number
JR I.1	JR 1.1
JR 1.2.a–j	JR 1.2.a–j
JR II.10.a–d	Removed
JR III.11	JR II.1
JR III.12	JR II.2.a–f
JR III.13.a–b	JR II.3.a–b
JR IV.14	Removed
JR V.5	JR III
JR VI.16.a–d	JR IV.1.a–d
JR VII.17.a–f	JR V.1.a–h
JR VII.18	JR V.2
JR VII.19	JR V.3
JR VII.20	JR V.4.a–e
JR VII.21.a–c	JR V.5.a–c
JR VII.22	JR V.6
JR VIII.23	JR VI
JR IX.24	JR VII
JR X.25	JR VIII

Index to the Constitution, Canons, and Rules of Order

References to the Constitution are made to the article (Art.) number (e.g. Art I.1). The Canons are referenced by title, canon, and section number(s) (e.g. III.12.4.b). The Rules of Order are referenced by section number. Send corrections to gcoffice@episcopalchurch.org

– A –

– E –

– F –

– G –

– H –

Hymnal

– I –

– J –

– M –

- N -

- O -

– P –

– Q –

– R –

Recorder of ordinations. *See* General Convention

Records. *See also* Archives of The Episcopal Church, Ecclesiastical Discipline

Rectors. *See* Parishes, Missions, and Congregations: Rectors, Clergy in Charge

Reference Panels. *See* Ecclesiastical Discipline: Disciplinary Boards and Courts

Registrar of General Convention. *See* General Convention

Release and removal from the ordained Ministry

Religious Orders and other Christian Communities

Remission or modification or Sentences, ... IV.18

Removal from the Ministry. *See* Release and removal from ordained Ministry

Renunciation of the Ministry. *See* Release and removal from the ordained Ministry, Resignations and retirements

- S -